THE NATIONAL SECURITY BUREAU

WHITE BOOK

ON NATIONAL SECURITY
OF THE REPUBLIC OF POLAND

WARSAW 2013

Table of contents

FOREWORD BY PRESIDENT BRONISŁAW KOMOROWSKI 5
SYNTHESIS 7
INTRODUCTION 17

CHAPTER 1. DIAGNOSIS OF THE STATE OF NATIONAL SECURITY 25
1.1. Historical evolution of Poland's security 28
1.2. Poland's security potential 36
1.3. National interests and strategic objectives in the field of security 102

CHAPTER 2. THE SECURITY ENVIRONMENT OUTLOOK 107
2.1. The global dimension 109
2.2. The regional dimension 122
2.3. The national dimension 128
2.4. Strategic scenarios of the development of security conditions 145

CHAPTER 3. CONCEPT OF STRATEGIC ACTIVITIES
(OPERATIONAL STRATEGY) 153
3.1. Foundations and guiding principle of the operational strategy 155
3.2. Strategic tasks of national security operational subsystems 166
3.3. Strategic tasks of national security support subsystems 179

CHAPTER 4. CONCEPT OF PREPARING THE NATIONAL SECURITY
SYSTEM (PREPARATORY STRATEGY) 191
4.1. The foundations and the leading theme of the preparatory strategy 193
4.2. Preparation of the national security control subsystem 194
4.3. Preparation of the national security operational subsystems 203
4.4. Preparation of the national security support subsystems 224

CONCLUSION 235

LIST OF TABLES AND FIGURES 239

APPENDICES 243
1. Summary of the main recommendations of the National Security Strategic Review 245
2. List of the main conceptual categories 246
3. List of the basic legal acts pertaining to national security 250
4. List of the persons involved in the National Security Strategic Review 255
5. List of abbreviations 261

FOREWORD BY THE PRESIDENT OF THE REPUBLIC OF POLAND BRONISŁAW KOMOROWSKI

The past two decades brought about numerous dynamic changes in Poland's security strategic environment. Globalization and information revolution have contributed to the world's becoming more interconnected through increasingly tighter networks of interdependence. Along with the opportunities, new challenges, risks and threats to security have appeared. Uncertainties have grown, while the level of trust has gone down. Although the threat of mass-scale armed conflicts among states has become less imminent and the number of internal conflicts (after the initial increase in the 1990s) has dwindled, equally dangerous transnational and asymmetric threats have occured as well as new challenges have emerged, particularly for the societal and economic (financial, energy) security sectors. In addition, we are facing an eruption of threats in cyberspace. All this will require a new approach to national security.

Poland has grasped the opportunity provided by the peace dividend of the past twenty years. The Polish national security potential has grown, we have become a part of NATO and the European Union, and we develop strategic cooperation with the United States. This allows us to get engaged in stabilization operations in the world – we no longer "consume" security; now we also "produce" it. It does not mean, however, that we can rest on our laurels. We must continuously bear in mind the security of our country; we must constantly strive for it.

Today, at the onset of the second decade of the 21st century, we need to view national security in a comprehensive perspective. We must define our interests and strategic objectives as well as the manner of achieving them pursuant to the new circumstances. Simultaneously, we need to transform the entire system of national security, striving especially for its integration. These issues were the subject of analyses carried out by the National Security Strategic Review Commission which I called into being in November 2010. The Commission approached the issues of security in a complex manner, focusing not only on defence, which to me as the Supreme Commander of the Armed Forces of the Republic of Poland is of particular importance, but also on the protective, societal and economic aspects.

The review constituted an innovative, analytical and organizational project. Many of the issues have never been covered so extensively before. This concerned the multi-faceted approach to security issues, specification of national interests and strategic objectives, preparation of alternative scenarios of the development of the security environment as well as of corresponding concepts of strategic activities in the field of security and options regarding the preparation of the national security system for the implementation of these activities.

The key conclusions from the Review were set forth in a classified Report, which served as the basis for the present White Book on National Security. This Book is addressed to all fellow citizens, since the issues of national security are and should be important to us all. I also regard the publication of this Book as the fulfilment of my obligation to provide reliable information on issues relating to security.

I am deeply convinced that this Book will contribute to a widespread public debate about Poland's security.

I invite everyone to read it.

Bronisław Komorowski

SYNTHESIS

The purpose of the present White Book on National Security of the Republic of Poland, which is addressed to all state structures, public and non-public organizations and citizens, is to help deepen the knowledge and public awareness of the security of Poland and Polish citizens.

The Book has been elaborated on the basis of the National Security Strategic Review (NSSR), including, in particular, the Report of the NSSR Commission, containing key conclusions and recommendations concerning Poland's security policy, including the streamlining of the national security system.

Diagnosis of the state of national security

The basis for strategic planning in the area of security is to determine the national interests and resulting strategic objectives. The starting point for defining these objectives and interests was the diagnosis of Poland as a strategic security entity, made in the context of both the historical formation of Polish national identity and statehood, the present constitutional and political conditions, and the current defence, protection, societal and economic potential.

Historical experience proves that the geopolitical location of Poland between the West and the East was the most critical strategic factor which influenced the formation of Polish national identity and statehood as well as determined the fundamental nature and character of national interests and strategic objectives in the field of security. Due to numerous conflicts (external wars and internal crises), the security issues were in the centre of attention of the authorities and the people for a long time in Polish history. Ignoring these issues led either to the state's marginalization on the international scene (the period of division into several duchies) or a total collapse of the state (the partition period). The history also shows the importance of harmony (the right proportions) between particular interests (of an individual) and collective interests (of the state) as well as between material and intangible (spiritual) interests. The prevalence of individual or particular interests (dynastic interests, the gentry's "golden freedom", etc.) over the national ones and ignoring the constant need for the material development of the state have resulted in two major collapses of the Polish state. On the other hand, the cultivation of intangible values, culture and national identity during the partition period allowed the Polish nation to survive 123 years of enslavement.

In modern states, the individual liberty to interpret and implement national interests is limited primarily by the **system founding rules** for functioning of states, which are codified in constitutions. Such rules were also set forth in the Constitution of the Republic of Poland. The national interests formulated within such frameworks may be of various scale and strength; they may be more or less ambitious. This depends on the strategic potential of the state, which determines (i.e. limits or strengthens) these ambitions.

Poland's national interests and strategic objectives in the field of security are largely influenced by the **state of the national security system**. At present, the system is a sum of separate, variously interrelated operational and support subsystems and of a weakly coherent subsystem of national security control. This hampers the synergy effect. Responsibilities of specific entities are dispersed or duplicated; there are too many planning authorities, and coordination is limited. Consistent laws are lacking, especially with regard to the subsystem of national security control. On the one hand, such situation causes the risk of gaps in responsibilities; on the other hand, it leads to unnecessary duplication of efforts, therefore certain powers and resources are wasted and the system is uneconomical and ineffective.

National interests and strategic objectives are reinforced by international relations in the field of security. Poland is a credible member of NATO, the strongest defence alliance in the world, and an important and active member of the European Union. Moreover, Poland develops strategic relations with the United States and is actively involved in regional cooperation, including with its neighbours. This enables defining more ambitious national interests and strategic objectives.

Another factor having substantial influence on national interests and strategic objectives in the field of security is the **defence potential**. The foreign service (diplomacy), whose activities are focused on security, and the Polish defence industry both play an important role in this context. Its main element, however, is the Armed Forces of the Republic of Poland that maintain readiness to perform their three main missions: guaranteeing defence of the state and counteracting aggression in accordance with allied commitments; participating in the process of stabilization of the international situation and in crisis response and humanitarian operations; and supporting the internal security and assisting the population. The strategic potential of the Polish Armed Forces, including their combat capabilities, is systematically improved. The professionalization and transformation of the Armed Forces are oriented towards increasing their defence operational capabilities, which also provide an opportunity to participate in allied operations outside the territory of the country. The improvement of operational capabilities of the Polish Armed Forces in recent years has had a positive impact on the level of Polish strategic ambitions and at the same time on the scale and nature of national interests and strategic objectives in the field of security.

The **protection potential** (services and guards) plays a major role in defining interests and strategic objectives. It faces now a number of challenges resulting, *inter alia*, from the escalation of the broadly understood organized crime, the threat of terrorism (including cyber-terrorism), and an increase in illegal migration. It is also important to note the significant deficiencies, e.g. in the rescue system and, in particular, insufficient coordination of activities performed by the central and self-government administration, the lack of resources for preventive activities, and weaknesses of the warning system. Excessive number of services and dispersed supervision complicate coordination and weaken the effectiveness of the protection potential. Consequently, the possible level of ambitions in defining national interests and strategic objectives in the field of security is limited.

Analysis of Poland's **societal and economic potential** reveals its diverse impact on the definition of national interests and strategic objectives in the field of security. The strategic potential as well as the scale and nature of the state's national interests and strategic objectives are adversely influenced by difficulties in such areas as demography, science, and technology. Other significant challenges include: the high unemployment rate which has a direct impact on the state of economy, barriers to entrepreneurship, and difficulties in creating appropriate conditions for the development of the societal potential.

The development of economy is a favourable factor. Despite the current crisis, Poland has managed to maintain the growth of its gross domestic product (GDP). Moderation in defining interests, however, is imposed by the state of public finances, which is a consequence of general imbalance in the financial sector. The state of infrastructure in terms of security is also unsatisfactory.

Ensuring the energy security is another challenge for Poland. The expected shale gas resources offer an opportunity in this regard. Maintaining the necessary level of food self-sufficiency of the country, bio-safety of food products as well as drinking and industrial water resources – pose other challenges which must be considered when defining national interests and strategic objectives in the field of security.

The diagnosis of Poland's societal and economic potential shows that national interests and strategic objectives in the field of security should include the following: introducing an effective pro-family policy; formulating a comprehensive migration policy; improving the innovativeness (effectiveness, competitiveness) of economy; ensuring the financial stability of the state; and improving the energy security as well as ensuring the protection of the environment.

The historical experience which has determined the Polish strategic culture, the diagnoses of the state's strategic potential, and the provisions of the Constitution of the Republic of Poland may all serve as a basis for the formulation of a catalogue of **national interests and strategic objectives in the field of security**.

The starting point is the set of so-called constitutional interests listed in Article 5 of the Constitution of the Republic of Poland, namely: the existence of the independent Polish state within its inviolable borders (state); freedom and security of citizens (citizens and society); sustainable development of the societal (nation's intangible assets) and economic (nation's material assets) potential with the constitutional emphasis on the national heritage and the protection of the environment.

The constitutional interests defined in this way provide the basis for identifying the following national interests in the field of security: development of the effective national security potential (readiness and capability to deter, defend and protect); membership in credible international security systems; freedom of citizens to exercise human rights and liberties without detriment to the security of other persons and the security of the state; individual protection of citizens and collective protection of population against accidental and intentional threats to their life and health as well as against any violation, loss or degradation of the (material and spiritual) assets at their disposal; safe conditions for developing the societal and economic potential; adequate societal and economic support for security, corresponding to needs and capabilities.

The above interests, in turn, serve as the basis for deriving the corresponding sets of strategic objectives of both an operational and preparatory nature.

Outlook for the security environment

One of the key factors shaping the security environment is the globalization and information revolution, which generally help raise the level of prosperity as well as foster the spreading of modern technologies and the improvement of methods of management and manners of financing the economic development. They create, therefore, a major opportunity for democratization as well as enable economic and societal progress in the world, including also in its poorer regions.

Along with positive effects, the processes of globalization and information revolution bring about new challenges and threats to worldwide security, both in the military and non-military aspects. The severity and pace of new divisions in the world accompanying the globalization processes are increasing. The development of technology and the expansion of the world market, in turn, led to the rapidly growing demand for fuels, food and water. These issues are important for worldwide policy, economy, and societal processes.

Global and regional security is also influenced by instability in individual regions of the world. At present, there are a number of hot spots (especially in the Middle East) which can become a source of conflicts on a larger scale. This situation is accompanied by a dangerous phenomenon of proliferation of weapons of mass destruction and means of their delivery. It causes the erosion of disarmament regimes and, as a consequence, may lead to their breakdown.

At the global level, the most important challenge is posed by a group of failed and failing states whose internal structural weakness, lack of an effective control over their territories or even internal breakdowns have a negative impact on the situation in their vicinity.

It is predicted that in the coming decades the scale of transnational and asymmetric threats and challenges will increase. Terrorism will constitute a threat to counteract which the countries will need to prepare themselves not less than to the threat of war. Terrorist activity also spreads to cyberspace, which becomes the area of rivalry and confrontation, including among states.

The faltering role of international organizations presents a serious challenge, which is reflected in their poor ability to launch effective, common mechanisms of security cooperation. It concerns, in particular, the United Nations and, regionally (in Europe), the Organization for Security and Co-operation in Europe.

The process of relative decline of the nearly hegemonic, until recently, power of the United States can be observed. It does not change the fact, however, that during the next two decades the USA will continue to be the most powerful country in the world, both in terms of military potential and the level of domestic product, and from the point of view of their share in global turnover capital and commodity markets. Projections which assume radical and increasingly faster development of the so-called emerging powers (frequently referred to also as BRIC countries: Brazil, Russia, India, and China) as well as the leading position of China take into account the amount of GDP only. The United States, however, is and will remain the issuer of the currency in which the vast majority of global financial reserves have been accumulated as well as the world leader in the development of modern technologies.

The security of **Europe** is basically determined by the following four factors: **NATO, the European Union, the strategic presence of the USA,** and **relations with Russia.**

NATO is and most probably will remain the most powerful and effective political and military alliance on the globe. The organization redefined its tasks in the context of the new international situation after the end of the cold war by adding two other tasks to the core mission of collective defence: crisis management (in Polish terminology also referred to as crisis response) and ensuring security by cooperation (cooperative security). The major challenge facing NATO is to define its role in the "post-Afghan" period. Key in this context will be the answer to the following question: should the alliance after the two decades of post-Cold-War enlargement move onto a new stage of consolidation around its core function of ensuring direct security to its members, or should it continue the operational and institutional development of its global role? It appears necessary above all to consolidate around the defence function, thereby contributing to the strengthening of the sense of security of all member countries of the Alliance and, consequently, increasing their willingness and readiness to engage in *out-of-area* operations which will be also necessary in the future.

Starting from the late 2008, the **European Union** has been facing a crisis and declining dynamics of the common economy. Despite this fact, it tries to adjust itself structurally to the new challenges, from among which the most demanding ones are the crisis of the euro area and difficulties in the development of the Common Security and Defence Policy (CSDP). Another serious challenge for Europe is its low self-sufficiency in terms of raw materials, which is compensated only partially by the production of energy from alternative sources.

The most important challenge for economic security of the European Union pertains to finance. If the EU member states are willing and ready to withstand the rigours of repair and the macroeconomic policy in the euro area is reformed (above all, in order to extend the scope of community fiscal policy), the crisis should be overcome.

A particularly serious challenge facing the EU is an update of the European Security Strategy of 2003.

The **strategic (political, military and economic) presence of the USA** in Europe remains the foundation of European security. There is a number of unknowns connected with the more and more visible strategic reorientation of the USA towards Asia and the Pacific.

An important external factor influencing the state of Poland's security is **relations between Russia and the West**. Today, it is difficult to define its clear perspective. Will Russia stick to its course towards restoration of its power status, ignoring interests of the others, especially its neighbours? Or will it steer a course towards cooperation in building common security? Today, more likely seems the continuation scenario, which is unfavourable to Poland.

Despite the crisis in the euro area and the economic stagnation, discrepancies in living standards, income, and access to goods and services, the escalating demographic crisis, as well as the existence of peripheral hot spots which, in an unfavourable situation, can evolve into conflicts, Europe is still widely perceived as a continent of prosperity and peace. Its centre (the European Union) holds a powerful attraction for other countries.

Challenges for and threats to Poland which arise from the analysis of its external security environment, are mainly of a non-military nature. The most serious non-military security challenges that Poland will have to meet are associated with ensuring the undisturbed economic development of the state, a stable financial situation, and consistent, far-reaching social policies, taking into account the containing of the coming demographic decline. Significant strategic dilemmas facing Poland during the next twenty years also concern the need to ensure security in cyberspace as well as stave off the decapitalization of the industrial and transport infrastructure. The decapitalization and, quite frequently, the devastation of the infrastructure mean that the risk of technical and industrial disasters increases every year.

Military threats still remain significant. They may primarily have the nature of political and military crises provoked to exert a strategic pressure in the current politics, without crossing the brink of war. Such activities might take the form of rapid development of military potential near the Polish borders, practical demonstration of strength or military blackmail. Direct armed threats, however, cannot be excluded. Two kinds of such threats should be identified: first of all – threats which can be most generally referred to as non-territorial (where an opponent does not intend to take control over the attacked territory), i.e. selective, pinpoint strikes, deliberately limited in scale and reach (often hidden, only implicit in the authorship), the aim of which is to blackmail a given state or force it to take specific political steps in isolation from the wider international security system (e.g. without NATO intervention, as a result of creating situations which may be termed "consensus-challenging", in which it would be difficult to reach agreement among member countries on the manner and scope of response); secondly – threats associated with a situation which today seems much less likely but at the same time would be the most dangerous, such as war on a large scale. Such war could take place in an event of a radical change in the current course of international policy, so it would need to be preceded by a rather long-lasting change in the political and strategic situation in the world. As a result, there would be time to prepare a response, including a collective response of the entire Alliance to which Poland belongs.

Poland, as a member state of NATO and the EU, is a beneficiary of positive political and economic transformations in Europe. The predictions concerning internal security conditions should definitely exclude internal military threats (rebellion, coup). There is a risk, however, of the spread of armed organized crime, especially of the transnational character (with the large-scale use of weapons, e.g. in criminal groups' warfare). Tasks of the Armed Forces of the Republic of Poland will probably include, *inter alia,* the provision of traditional support for the other state structures in liquidating the effects of natural disasters and technical accidents or helping the state services to prevent uncontrollable mass migrations of population within the territory of Poland.

The assessment of the security environment and directions of its development at global, regional (European) and national levels during the next two decades allows to outline **three scenarios** of possible development of strategic security conditions: an integration scenario – with prevailing positive and desirable phenomena and tendencies, indicating successive strengthening of the existing international security system; a disintegration scenario – with prevailing unfavourable and dangerous external and internal phenomena, indicating gradual degradation or even breakdown of the existing security system; and an evolutionary scenario – assuming the continuation of the relative balance between positive and negative phenomena, which would mean the continuation of the existing relative instability of international security characterized by irregular outbreaks of crises and attempts to manage them on a short-term basis.

The evolutionary scenario is considered most likely.

Concept of strategic activities (operational strategy)

Poland's security situation, which changes constantly under the influence of both opportunities in the external and internal environment and new challenges and threats, requires an adjustment of the state's strategy of activities (operational strategy), so that it guarantees the optimum attainment of strategic objectives under any conditions.

In accordance with the outlook scenarios concerning the development of the security environment, **three options of Poland's operational strategy** can be outlined: an option of maximum internationalization of Poland's security, which corresponds to the integration scenario; an option of strategic autarky (self-reliance and self-sufficiency) which refers to the disintegration scenario; and an option of sustainable internationalization and autonomy of Poland's security corresponding to the evolutionary scenario.

The third option is recommended, taking into account, however, the readiness to implement the other options, if possible or required. It means that the strategic security activities should focus on the following three main priorities:

- remaining determined and ready to act in the full spectrum of fields, areas, and sectors of national security, including especially these in which the allied operations can be difficult;
- strengthening the international security community by intensifying integration processes in the Euro-Atlantic area, based on shared interests and values, especially within NATO's collective defence system, the EU's Common Security and Defence Policy, and strategic partnerships (including with the USA) as well as – within their frameworks – the strategic neighbourliness;

- supporting and selectively participating in international operations aimed at preventing the emergence of new sources of threats or the spread of existing crises to supra-regional level, based on a explicit international mandate.

The above-mentioned operational priorities should be further developed in the next National Security Strategy of the Republic of Poland and later in the Political and Strategic Defence Directive of the Republic of Poland (or in a Political and Strategic Directive on the National Security of the Republic of Poland, extended to non-military issues).

Concept of preparing the national security system (preparatory strategy)

In accordance with the possible variants of the operational strategy, three options of the preparatory strategy can be formulated: internationalization of the national security system (corresponding to the option of maximum internationalization of Poland's security), an autonomy of the national security system (corresponding to the option of strategic autarchy), and sustainable integration of the national security system (corresponding to the option of sustainable internationalization and autonomy of Poland's security).

The latter option, i.e. the **sustainable integration of the national security system**, is considered the most reasonable. This option consists in preparing the security system both for seizing the opportunities resulting from international cooperation and for the rational development of capabilities in order to oppose military and non-military threats jointly with allies or individually, if need be. A particular strategic specialty of the Polish security system should be its counter-surprise capabilities. This is an extrapolation of the already initiated processes of transforming the security system. Its implementation, however, must also take into account the conceptual and planning preparations for the two other options, if possible or necessary.

Considering the option of sustainable integration of the national security system reasonable and realistic, the following **major tasks regarding the preparation** (maintenance, streamlining, and transformation) of this system can be specified: establishing the legal and organizational basis for the integrated national security system; currently, its subsystems (and their components) function in separation from each other, and the legal bases are incomplete and dispersed; setting the rules and procedures for political and strategic control over the national security system, uniform in all security conditions (the control subsystem). In this way, the synergy of the national security system will be achieved as a result of the integration of the national security control subsystem, professionalization of operational (defence and protection) subsystems, as well as the universal preparation of support subsystems (societal and economic).

The aforesaid objectives for the preparation of the national security system of the Republic of Poland are comprehensive and reflect interests and needs of the state and population. Their aim is to ensure greater effectiveness, remove the duplication of responsibilities, and allow a more rational managing of funds allocated for national security purposes.

The vast majority of recommendations can be implemented within the existing constitutional order. Further–going changes in the national security system would require constitutional changes.

Warsaw,
9 March 2012.
President Bronislaw
Komorowski delivers
a speech during the 4th
plenary conference of
the National Security
Strategic Review.
Photo: BBN

Warsaw,
11 December 2012.
The Head of the National
Security Bureau, Stanislaw
Koziej meets experts
involved in the NSSR.
Photo: BBN

INTRODUCTION

The White Book on National Security of the Republic of Poland has been conceived as a publicly available presentation which popularises the outcome of the National Security Strategic Review.

The obligation to conduct the NSSR was set out in the 2007 National Security Strategy of the Republic of Poland. In accordance with the said document, the President of the Republic of Poland decided to conduct the Review and issued a relevant order on 24 November 2010. At the same time, he entrusted this task to the head of the NSSR Commission. The Commission was chaired by the Head of the National Security Bureau. Pursuant to the order of the President of the Republic of Poland, the Head of the National Security Bureau determined the substantive and organizational details pertaining to conducting the NSSR.

The aim of the Review was to assess comprehensively Poland's national security and formulate conclusions regarding the state's strategic objectives and practices in the field of security as the preparation of the national security system. In accordance with the task defined in such a way, the concept of the Review and the range of issues to be covered were determined.

The concept was based on a holistic approach to security, which allowed to identify its specific areas such as: defence, protection, society, and economy, to which specific sectors were assigned along with entities executing national security strategic tasks (fig. 1). In order to harmonize the approach to the issues analyzed and the manner of presenting them, a catalogue of basic security terms has been prepared. The said catalogue constitutes appendix no. 2 to this publication.

Figure 1. The structure of national security adopted for the purposes of the NSSR

	AREAS OF NATIONAL SECURITY																	
	Defence		Protection			Society						Economy					
	SECTORS OF NATIONAL SECURITY																	
	diplomacy	military	intelligence	counterintelligence	law and public order	rescue	culture	education	social	demography	migration	⋮	finance	energy	transport	critical infrastructure	natural environment	⋮
	Transsectoral areas of security (e.g. cyber security; anti-terrorist security)																	
	National security entities performing strategic tasks (operational–supporting)																	
	MSZ --- MON MSW	MON --- MSW MSZ	AW SWW	ABW SKW	MSW (Police, SG, BOR), MS (SW) MAC, CBA, Public Prosecutor's Office	MSW (PSP OCK) --- MAC, MŚ	MKiDN MEN --- -- public and non-public entities, NGOs	MNiSzW MEN --- MKiDN, public and non-public higher education institutions (schools), NGOs	MPiPS --- MZ, state and local government facilities, NGOs	MPiPS --- MZ, NGOs	UDSC --- MAC, MSW	---	MF --- MG, MRiRW MSP MRR MTBiGM	MG --- MSP	MTBiGM --- MG	MTBiGM --- MG MSP	MŚ --- state and local government entities, NGOs	---

Left vertical labels: National security control; the President, the Council of Ministers

Source: authors' own compilation.

MSZ – Ministry of Foreign Affairs, MON – Ministry of National Defence, MSW – Ministry of Interior, AW – Foreign Intelligence Agency, SWW – Military Intelligence Service, ABW – Internal Security Agency, SKW – Military Counterintelligence Service, SG – Border Guard, BOR – Government Protection Bureau, MS – Ministry of Justice, SW – Prison Service, MAC – Ministry of Administration and Digitization, CBA – Central Anti-Corruption Bureau, PSP – State Fire Service, OCK – Civil Defence, MŚ – Ministry of the Environment, MKiDN – Ministry of Culture and National Heritage, MEN – Ministry of National Education, MNiSW – Ministry of Science and Higher Education, MPiPS – Ministry of Labour and Social Policy, MZ – Ministry of Health, NGOs – non-governmental organizations, UDSC – Office for Foreigners, MF – Ministry of Finance, MG – Ministry of Economy, MRiRW – Ministry of Agriculture and Rural Development, MSP – Ministry of Treasury, MRR – Ministry of Regional Development, MTBiGM – Ministry of Transport, Construction and Maritime Economy

The review covered four problem areas corresponding with the four stages of the strategic cycle of analyses and studies in the field of security (fig. 2).

Figure 2. Strategic cycle of analyses and studies in the field of security

Strategic self-identification of the entity: the diagnosis of the state as the security entity (the basis of national security) as well as the definition of national interests and strategic objectives in the field of security

Outlook for security environment: outlook for internal and external security conditions – assessment of future conditions for the pursuit of national interests and attaining strategic security objectives

Operational strategy projection: formulation of the concept of strategic activities – ways of achieving strategic objectives under given conditions of the security environment

Preparatory strategy projection: formulation of the concept of strategic preparations – the ways of maintaining and transforming the national security system pursuant to future operational needs

Source: authors' own compilation

The first stage involved the diagnosis of Poland as a national security entity, on the basis of which a catalogue of national interests and strategic objectives in the field of security was drawn up (the diagnosis was supported by an analysis of fundamental legal acts on national security – a list of these acts is contained in appendix No. 3). The second stage consisted in the comprehensive analysis of the security environment at global, regional, and national level, taking into account its military and non-military spheres, as well as in the determination of possible strategic scenarios of the development of future security conditions in Poland. During the third stage, possible and desirable options for the concept of strategic activities (operational strategy) were prepared: the rules and ways of achieving strategic security objectives were indicated and the tasks associated with strategic activities in specific security sectors were outlined. The fourth stage focused on the designing – in accordance with the tasks and requirements defined during the third stage – of the strategic options for the state's preparations in the field of security (preparatory strategy). The process is synthetically illustrated in fig.3.

Figure 3. The leading concept of the NSSR

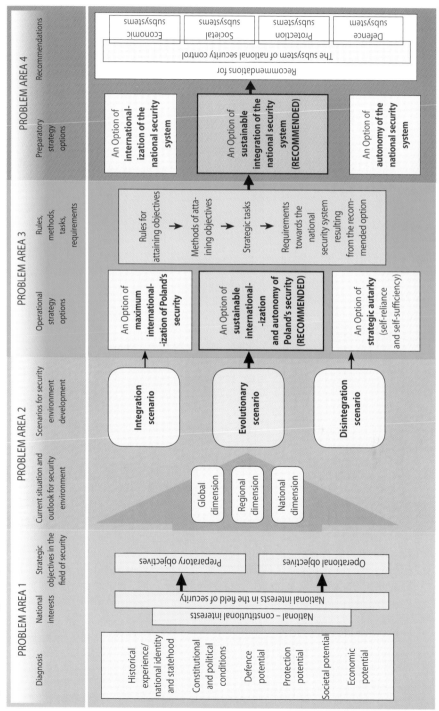

Source: authors' own compilation.

The Commission appointed by the President of the Republic Poland was composed of four problem area teams, the Advisory Team, as well as the Commission Staff (a list of persons involved in the work done by the teams is presented in appendix no. 4).

The basic work was tackled by the problem area teams acting autonomously. The consistency of the work was ensured by feedback loops (fig. 4).

Figure 4. Interactions (feedbacks) among problem area teams during the NSSR.

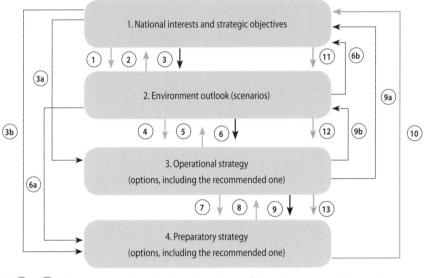

Legend: (1) – (13) subsequent stages of consultations – the exchange of information among problem area teams

→ feedback   → partial results   → final results

Source: authors' own compilation.

The Review has taken into account the results of the government's work on integrated development strategies (including, in particular, the Strategy for the Development of the National Security System of the Republic of Poland 2022) as well as the Long-term and Medium-term Strategy for the Development of the State.

The Advisory Team provided substantial support to the problem area teams by preparing relevant expertise and consultations on results of their respective work. The Commission Staff, which was organized on the basis of the National Security Bureau, provided organizational and substantial assistance to all entities involved in the Review. It was also responsible for the final editing of the Report of the NSSR Commission.

As a part of the commission work, numerous plenary conferences, problem-focused seminars and workshops on the issues assigned to specific teams took place. Their aim was to facilitate the exchange of opinions and help to formulate conclusions, which were later included in the final documents of the Review.

The Review brought together a wide range of representatives of various communities, including the central and local government structures, non-governmental organizations and academic communities dealing with the security issues, parliamentary commissions responsible for security, former heads of the National Security Bureau as well as independent experts in various areas of security. Such a representative group provided an opportunity for professional, comprehensive and open discussion on the national security issues, including the achievements of major scientific and academic institutions and non-governmental organizations in this field.

Proceeding from the analysis conducted, a classified Report of the National Security Strategic Review Commission was drawn up, containing key conclusions and recommendations. In the coming years, these conclusions and recommendations will be used as the basis for the preparation of substantial proposals to be decided by the President of the Republic of Poland and the Council of Ministers and aimed at ensuring security and improving the national security system, including in particular the verification of the National Security Strategy of the Republic of Poland, the Political and Strategic Defence Directive of the Republic of Poland (or the Political and Strategic Directive of National Security of the Republic of Poland, which also covers the non-military issues), as well as other documents of strategic significance.

The Report provided the substantial basis for the National Security Bureau to issue this White Book. It is intended to reach a wide audience, not only institutions responsible for security issues by law or obligation, but also all other state and non-state public and economic entities and citizens for whom, in the globalizing world and "information-absorbing" society, security becomes the area of challenges, threats, and risks which affect them directly. Everyone must therefore, as a minimum, not only feel secure but also understand security and, to an increasingly large extent, both make individual decisions and participate in collective decision-making. That is why the broadly understood education for security has become one of the most critical tasks. The main purpose of the present White Book is to make a substantial contribution to the implementation of the aforementioned task, which is of key importance for the security of Poland.

Chapter 1

DIAGNOSIS OF THE STATE OF NATIONAL SECURITY

The starting point of any comprehensive national security study is a diagnosis of the state's strategic potential as a security entity. This is a basic step allowing to formulate national interests and resulting strategic objectives in the field of national security.

Warsaw,
15 April 2011.
The 1ˢᵗ plenary
conference of
the National Security
Strategic Review.
Discussion of the main
theses developed by
the National Interests and
Strategic Objectives Team.
Photo: BBN

Consequently, when analysing the state of Poland's security, it is necessary first of all to answer the questions about its strategic potential: what characterises Poland as a security entity, what is its strategic potential, and in what way does that influence its national interests and resulting strategic objectives in the field of security? That is why the present chapter takes up three main themes. The first one elaborates on the development of national identity and statehood as well as of their impact on national interests and strategic objectives in the field of security. The analysis covers the period from the origins of the state to the modern times. The second theme broaches the constitutional and political conditions of the Republic of Poland and assesses Poland's strategic potential in four areas: defence, protection, society, and economy. The third theme identifies and formulates a catalogue of national interests and strategic objectives in the field of security. This catalogue serves as a reference point for the discussion of the outlook for the development of security environment at an international and national level as well as for the formulation of the possible and desirable options of the operational and preparatory strategy.

1.1. Historical evolution of Poland's security

From the very beginning of Poland as a state, the decisive factor for its survival and development was – apart from the internal sphere (system, the military, economy, human potential, etc.) – its ability to build a friendly international environment using a wide range of political, military, and economic tools. In this context, what became particularly important for ensuring security was – at an external level – effective diplomatic and military activities (being an important element of skilful foreign policy of the state) and – at an internal level – the shaping of a national identity and statehood.

The contemporary national interests and strategic objectives in the field of security ought to be defined on the basis of historical experience, as it shows the ways in which customs, habits, orientations, and beliefs regarding the needs and conditions for the existence and decent life among other peoples have been engraved in the awareness, memory, and character of the Polish nation. In this way the national policy relating to identity, functioning, and strengthening of the state as well as safeguarding its territorial integrity was formed.

From the early years of statehood to the partition period

The main national interests (in the contemporary understanding of this category) at the dawn of statehood were focused on the survival of the Polish state, especially in the context of the civilization and military pressures coming from the west. These interests were advanced by the adoption of Christianity. The strategic security objectives of Poland under the first, Piast, dynasty were aimed at: maintaining statehood under the rule of the Piasts and, simultaneously, repelling the threat of German expansion; wielding more effective internal control over individual provinces of the state; protecting the integrity of the state in the face of external threats (Baltic tribes, the Mongols, the Teutonic Order); developing the defence infrastructure; creating optimum conditions for legal, administrative, and economic development of the state as well as strengthening of its international position through active foreign policy, often supported with the country's own or coalition-based military operations.

During the Jagiellonian era, the concept of security policy was based on cooperation with neighbours and territorial expansion, finding its expression in the personal union with neighbouring countries (Hungary, Lithuania). The alliances moved the borders and interests to the east, making Poland reorient its interests towards the areas of Rus and Lithuania, but they also were the confirmation of Poland's significant ability to form coalitions (Grunwald, 1410).

The most important strategic interest of Poland under the Jagiellonian dynasty (1385–1572) was concentrated on the integration of different nationalities into one community of the Polish Commonwealth. The main strategic objectives of the Polish state in the field of security included: strengthening the military and demographic potential through the union of Poland and Lithuania; neutralizing and later removing the threat to the autonomy and integrity of the state from the Teutonic Order as well as consolidating the international position of Poland as a regional power, thereby forming a kind of counterbalance to the expansion policy of other regional strategic players in this part of the continent (Germans, the uniting Russia, the Ottoman Empire). At the same time, the Polish gentry gaining new privileges laid down the foundations for the gentry's democracy, which was a phenomenon in Europe, as well as the base for the Polish-Lithuanian Commonwealth's political and military might in the 16th century.

In the 17th century, the security problems of the Polish-Lithuanian Commonwealth were to a significant extent associated with the multi-ethnicity of the state. Conflicts of interests between the Polish nobility and the subjects in the borderlands triggered the Cossack rebellions, weakening the Polish state internally. Additionally, the state was devastated by conflicts with Sweden, Russia, and Turkey. The more limited was the power of elective kings, the weaker was the international position of the Polish Commonwealth (cf. *liberum veto*). The last positive note of effective foreign policy was the rule of John III Sobieski. The personal union with weak Saxony resulting from the election of Augustus II the Strong as the king of Poland (1697), and later of his son Augustus III (1734), did not strengthen Poland which at that time was devastated by wars. The Polish magnates and gentry, who feared strong royal powers and obstructed or contested reforms, objectively weakened the authority and might of the state.

In the 18th century, Poland was successively becoming the sphere of influence of neighbouring powers which, at Poland's expense, advanced their interests. During the Great Northern War (1700-1721), the Polish kingdom was the object rather than the subject of the strategic play in the region and Polish lands became the scene of battles and marches of foreign troops. The dependence on Russia was growing. In that part of Europe it was no longer Poland who fought war with Russia and Sweden, as was the case in 16th and 17th century, but Sweden who fought Russia. The attempts to reform the political system, for which appealed Stanislaw Konarski in the first half of the 18th century, were launched following the ideals of the European Enlightenment under the rule of Stanislaw August Poniatowski. In this period the state authorities placed great emphasis on the development of culture and art, thus strengthening the national identity. The restoration of the Republic of Poland was accelerated after the shock of the first partition (1772). A series of internal reforms (e.g. the establishment of the Commission of National Education and of the Corps of Cadets) was undermined by the factions of gentry and magnates who, defending their interests, even in good faith (protecting themselves against the allegedly absolute power of the king), objectively weakened the state (the Bar Confederation). The favourable international situation (the Russo–Turkish War and disputes among the partitioning powers) was taken advantage of by the patriotic party during the Four-Year Sejm held in Warsaw between 1788 and 1792. It instituted far-reaching reforms, the most important of which was the adoption of the Constitution of May 3, 1791, setting forth the basis for a new political system of the Polish kingdom, as well as the resolution on augmenting the army to 100 thousand soldiers. The reforms were soon brought down by the treacherous Confederation of Targowica (despite the insurgent rebellion – the Kościuszko Insurrection) and partitions executed by the neighbouring powers in 1793 and 1795.

To sum up, after the times of division of the state and the overcoming of it, followed by the period of prosperity, especially in the 16th century, from the mid-17th century on the effectiveness of pursuing national interests was being hampered despite individual, meaningful military successes (the Vienna battle, 1683).

Conclusions from that period from the point of view of current interests and strategic objectives can be summarized as follows: the vital interest is to be capable of organizing and maintaining an effective state; the balance between the freedom of an individual or a group and the responsibility for the country must not be disturbed; the cultivation of national identity must be continuously pursued; and unfavourable commonality of interests among neighbouring powers must be effectively countered.

The period of partitions and regaining of independence

The critical national interest in the period of partitions was to maintain the national identity, cultivate the Polish language and resists the programmes of Germanization and Russification. The problem of Poles' national identity during the period of partitions (between 1795 and 1918) was particularly complex due to the loss of independence. The lack of independence along with the simultaneous transformations of the political and economic systems of the partitioned areas led to a gradual disappearance of the "nobility nation". The emergence of the contemporary Polish nation encompassing all social classes and strata was accompanied by the enfranchisement of peasants (abolition of feudal service and personal serfdom), urbanization and industrialization of partitioned Polish lands (the pace and scale of these phenomena varied among partitions) as well as the inflow of people of various nationalities (Germans, Jews, Russians). Such a situation resulted in a shift from the traditional gentry-only understanding of the Polish national identity towards its interpretation as a modern political community, whether in the national sense (the national movement) or the class sense (social democratic ideas).

The factors which were particularly important for the awakening of national awareness included education and the cultivation of the Polish language against the policies of Russification and Germanization by the respective partitioning powers, as well as the development of art, science, and national culture. The reinforcement of national identity was supported by the patriotic (Romanticism) and social (Positivism) mission of Polish literature.

Both national interests and strategic objectives of the society without a state – the Polish nation building itself on new foundations – were oriented in individual partitions and in various forms towards: regaining independence (a nationwide objective, promoted by secret societies and in subsequent national uprisings); extending the autonomy (the Galicia region); organizing the resistance against Germanization and Russification; egalitarianism and social solidarity as well as improving the level of awareness and quality of life of Polish communities in partitioned areas (the peasants' issue, the idea of organic work, positivism).

The period of World War I (1914–1918) showed particular determination of the nation and its elites to build and strengthen a modern nation encompassing all social groups in every aspect – political, social, economic and cultural – in Polish lands and in exile. It also emphasized the importance of Polish diplomacy efforts to sustain international support for the Polish struggle for independence and self-organization (including the military one – the Polish Legions) in the absence of a sovereign state.

The main conclusion that can be drawn from events of that period concerns the special role of sustaining, cultivating, and developing the culture and national identity in the survival of a nation.

The interwar period and World War II

The main national interest in the interwar period was to build and strengthen the state. After regaining independence under the 1919 Versaille Treaty and as a result of the fight for the borders of the Second Polish Republic, Poland held an important place in the Central Europe region. The international position of Poland was significantly enhanced by the victory in the Polish–Soviet War (1919-1921), which for two decades stopped the expansion of communism to the west and stabilized the political relations in Central and Eastern Europe. However, the situation of the state in terms of security guarantees from other entities in the international environment was difficult. This predicament resulted from the following: geopolitical conditions; submissive and inconsistent policy of western countries (especially of Great Britain) towards Germany, associated with abolishing the constraints imposed on Germany under the Treaty of Versailles; international isolation of the Weimar Republic and the Bolshevik Russia and the resulting closer relations between the two powers, which was unfavourable to Poland (the Treaty of Rapallo, 1922), as well as the policy aiming at revision of the Polish boundaries, exercised by German and Soviet diplomacy. The position of Poland in the region was affected by bad relations with Lithuania and cool relations with Czechoslovakia. The relations with Western Europe (with France in particular) suffered a setback in 1925, when the Locarno Treaties channelled German claims and expansion to the east. The British guarantees for Poland of March 1939 (and the earlier agreement with France) proved to be of little use in the face of German (1 September 1939) and, later, Soviet aggression (17 September 1939). That situation was the source of the betrayal syndrome in the consciousness of the Poles. Such thinking was further reinforced by decisions taken by the Allies "above the heads of Poles" which, after the end of World War II, left Poland in the Soviet sphere of influence (Yalta–Potsdam agreements).

During the interwar period, Poland was a multinational state. Objective and subjective factors in international and national policy antagonized the young state and its minorities against each other.

The effective achievement of strategic objectives in Polish security policy was hampered by the following factors: ineffectiveness of political and military alliances entered into by the authorities of the Second Republic of Poland; the efforts of German diplomacy towards the achievement of their strategic objectives by exerting diplomatic pressure and taking military measures; the collusion between the Third Reich and the Soviet Union at the expense of Poland (the Molotov–Ribbentrop pact of August 1939 and its secret protocol); significant disproportions between the Polish military potential and the German and Soviet potentials; the appeasement policy of western powers towards Germany and difficulties in building a state community on solid foundations, encompassing all citizens. Poland's security was severely affected by the global crisis (1929–1933) and the customs war with Germany, which crippled the economy.

The fundamental Polish national interest during World War II was the physical survival of the nation. The priorities also included regaining sovereignty within its pre-war borders. The main strategic objectives were the following: building and developing the structures of the Polish underground state and the resistance movement at home and the military structures abroad; patriotic and historical education of all social groups; active and passive resistance to the extermination policy and propaganda of the invader, as well as internationalizing the Polish cause and gaining the support of the Allies for Polish claims. The politics of the Soviet Union combined with the elimination of independent political forces in the occupied countries of Central and Eastern Europe prevented the achievement of strategic objectives set by the Polish government-in-exile. The final political defeat of the London-based government in its fight "for government and borders" was the result of non-equitable treatment of the Polish cause by the "Big Three" – the United Kingdom, the United States, and the Soviet Union.

The conclusions from that period in the context of the current interests and strategic objectives indicate that special attention must be paid to the scope and form of cooperation between the two powerful neighbours of Poland: Russia and Germany, as well as to ensuring that the Polish interests are taken into account in critical areas of relations between these two powers. It is also necessary to keep modernizing the state's own defensive capabilities and rationally evaluate the effectiveness of alliances to which Poland is a party.

The post-war period and the People's Republic of Poland

As a consequence of World War II, the continuity of the statehood was broken and the country lost its sovereignty. The resistance against the imposed authorities and political system, although futile, was put up by the military and political underground. From 1945, the London-based government--in- exile was no longer recognized, while the communist government (*de facto* imposed on Poland by the Soviet Union) was getting stronger, while revising the concept of national identity on the basis of class criteria and justifying it also with the national security requirements. At least until 1956, the communist authorities resorted to inhumane practices, and the continuously developed repression system played a major role in these activities.

In the early years of the Polish People's Republic (People's Poland, PRL), the following issues from among the national and state interests were considered to be of prime importance: building an ideologized, "socialist" state in the absence of sovereignty; the permanence of the Oder–Neisse border between Poland and (East) Germany; internal security, which was associated, *inter alia,* with the strengthening of the so-called people's power and provided the basis for deep political, constitutional, social, economic, and other kinds of changes.

The strategic objectives of the Polish People's Republic in the field of security were concentrated, above all, around maintaining power and internal order in the state at all costs (the development of secret services, police forces (*milicja*), surveillance of the society, resorting to solving social problems by force). External activities were dictated by the dependence on the Soviet Union and, comprised, *inter alia,* treaty guarantees for the post-war borders of the state, including especially the integration of the western and northern areas; maintaining the unity of the Eastern bloc, among others, through participation in the Warsaw Treaty Organization (Warsaw Pact) and the build-up of the armed forces in close cooperation with the Soviet army and other Warsaw Pact forces within the USSR's strategic plans (the military dimension), as well as the development of the imposed economic cooperation with the Eastern bloc countries, including within the Council for Mutual Economic Assistance.

Activities in the non-military aspects of security were focused on the reconstruction and development of the state infrastructure; the reconstruction of the demographic potential of Poland, as well as the improvement of the quality of social life through employment, education, health care, and other social activities. The inefficiency of the central planning system hindered the achievement of the majority of these objectives.

Strategic incapacitation of Poland expressed itself, *inter alia*, through the consent of the authorities to interference in internal affairs of the allies of the Warsaw Pact – indirectly, in terms of politics (Hungary, 1956), and directly, through military operations (Czechoslovakia, 1968).

In those conditions, the Polish authorities were interested in easing tensions between the blocs; reducing the military dangers; seeking for itself a margin of political freedom in Europe, which found expression in the plans of Rapacki (1957), Gomulka (1963) and Jaruzelski (1987); and strengthening of Poland's international position, *inter alia*, through its activity in the UN and the Conference of Security and Cooperation in Europe (CSCE).

During that period, the strategic objectives pursued by the Polish independence opposition, which was not acknowledged by the authorities of the Polish People's Republic, included: restoration of sovereignty of the Polish state; real democratization of public life; rejection of the inefficient economic system; striving for the improvement of the living conditions of the population; promoting truly pluralistic attitudes in the society; ensuring the observance of human rights by the authorities; limiting the impact of the state propaganda; establishment and development of organizations defending the interests of persecuted individuals and public groups; perpetrating acts of disobedience versus the communist authorities (strikes, appeals, manifestations) as well as informing the public abroad about the situation in the country.

The inefficiency and stagnation of the national centrally-planned economy system aggravated the national security, leading to the deterioration of the living conditions of the population (social unrests in years: 1956, 1970, 1976) as well as causing resistance of the intellectuals and students (March 1968) and giving rise to the nation-wide movement of "Solidarity" ("Solidarność") (1980). In the face of the deteriorating situation in years 1980–1981, the state authorities did not hesitate to declare martial law (13 December 1981), which impeded the democratic aspirations of the opposition.

In the deteriorating social and economic situation, the security policy of the Polish People's Republic in its final years was focused on the internal sphere, ultimately leading to a "round table" dialogue of the authorities with the opposition (6 February – 5 April 1989). It was agreed that the partially-free contract parliamentary elections would be held on 4 June 1989. As a result of the resounding victory of the opposition, a peaceful transition of power took place and, on 12 September 1989, a new government was formed by Tadeusz Mazowiecki, which initiated the process of transformation of the entire state. The changes were confirmed after the election of Lech Wałęsa as president of the Republic of Poland in 1990 and the first fully free parliamentary election of 27 October 1991.

The advancement of national interests in the post-war period was impossible due to Poland's dependence on the Soviet Union and the country's strategic incapacitation. Although the survival of the Polish nation and state was not at risk, its development and strengthening of the international position were limited and conditioned by the interests and directions of policy and strategy of the Soviet Union. The activity of the opposition groups in Poland, the deteriorating economic situation, the overall "fatigue" (exhaustion) of the communist system, and changes in the geopolitical situation (especially after Mikhail Gorbachev took power in the USSR in 1985) led to a peaceful restoration of strategic autonomy and the change of the state's system.

Despite its satellite role (and domination of the ideology alien to Poles), the Polish People's Republic was seeking every opportunity to mark its subjectivity (e.g. in the CSCE process). Importantly, the territorial integrity of the country was strengthened by the conclusion of a relevant treaty with the Federal Republic of Germany, which normalized mutual relations (1970).

Conclusions from this period in the context of the current national interests and strategic objectives indicate that maintaining national sovereignty remains one of the key tasks of the state, while non-democratic (satellite) political and military alliances may turn out to be not a measure of strengthening the security but rather an instrument of enslavement and strategic incapacitation by the hegemon of such an alliance.

The Third Republic

The collapse of the Cold-War bi-polar international order was a result of the "Solidarity" revolution initiated in Poland in 1980, the transformations in the Soviet Union after the assumption of power by Mikhail Gorbachev and, later, the "Autumn of Nations" in 1989. This process ushered in the change of the political and economic system of the Republic of Poland, while determining its security situation.

After Poland regained its full sovereignty, its main national interests included guaranteeing the security of the state under the new conditions (after the downfall of the Eastern bloc Poland found itself in a "grey security" zone), the sustainable development, and the gradual growth of the international position, including through membership in the most powerful organizations in the world – NATO and the European Union.

The strategic objectives of Poland in the field of security were the following: the strengthening of the state's own defence potential in the conditions of strategic autonomy while simultaneously seeking new strategic partners in the West (applying for membership in NATO and the EU as well as developing relations with the USA), making the Soviet army leave the territory of Poland, and conducting foreign policy in such a way that it contributes to the building of a stable and peaceful international environment. In the non-military sphere, the strategic objective was the development of economy based on free market principles.

As a result of the strategic work in the late 1980s and early 1990s, the Defensive Doctrine of the Republic of Poland was developed and later adopted by a resolution of the State Defence Committee (*Komitet Obrony Kraju*, KOK) of 21 February 1990. It was the first unclassified document in the post--war history of Poland, which determined and publicly declared the basic elements of its national defence strategy.

Later, on 2 November 1992, two other documents were adopted at the KOK's meeting – the Polish Defence Policy Objectives as well as the Security Policy and Defence Strategy of the Republic of Poland. The executive document was the Plan of Defence of the Republic of Poland, outlining specific operational tasks of the state structures in the area of security, including various possible scenarios under the conditions of strategic autonomy.

Other key state documents integrating the strategy of security and defence were adopted after Poland joined the North Atlantic Treaty Organization, including the National Security Strategy of the Republic of Poland (4 January 2000) and the Defence Strategy of the Republic of Poland (23 May 2000). In the aftermath of the events of 11 September 2001 (terrorist attacks on New York and the Pentagon) and subsequent measures taken by the anti-terrorist coalition, and also as a result of the crisis over Iraq in 2002–2003, the said documents became outdated. They were therefore replaced by the National Security Strategy of the Republic of Poland (8 September 2003). In 2007, in turn, the National Security Strategy of the Republic of Poland was adopted, where, for the first time, the issue of security was approached from a broader perspective, taking into consideration not only its military aspects but also the non-military ones. Next, in 2009, an executive document was approved – the Political and Strategic Defence Directive of the Republic of Poland. These aforementioned documents, based on provisions of the Constitution of the Republic of Poland and other legal acts, were the interpretation of the basic strategic tenets in the field of security of Poland as the member of the North Atlantic Treaty Organization and the European Union. In addition, they provided the conceptual basis for further detailed planning, programme, and doctrinal work relating to the preparation and use of the state's defence potential in peace, crisis, and war.

The period of the Polish Third Republic has also marked a break with the ideological approach to national identity. This meant the return to traditional elements, such as the sense of common history, special role of Catholicism and Christian traditions, as well as a strong rooting in history and simultaneous rebirth of cultural and civilization ties with the West. It has found its symbolic expression, *inter alia,* in the restoration of the image of the white eagle wearing a golden crown on the coat of arms of the Republic of Poland.

The process of strengthening the Third Republic is expressed in particular in: the democratization and reinforcement of the free market economy; striving for gradual integration with the countries of Western Europe in the political, economic, social, and military contexts as well as close cooperation with the United States; political activity towards other countries in the region; the promotion of democracy in Ukraine and Belarus; the development of political and military cooperation with neighbouring countries; regional initiatives (the Weimar Triangle: France, Germany, and Poland; the Visegrád Group: the Czech Republic, Hungary, Poland and Slovakia), or efforts to develop partnership relations with Russia on equal terms.

The majority of strategic objectives of the Republic of Poland, which were set after 1989 have been accomplished. Poland joined the North Atlantic Treaty Organization (1999) and the European Union (2004); established strategic partnership with the United States; got engaged in sub-regional cooperation (the Weimar Triangle; the Visegrád Group, the Central European Initiative, the Council of the Baltic Sea States); and became more involved in international stabilization operations, thereby increasing the level of interoperability of the Polish Armed Forces.

The fact that not all of the strategic objectives have been achieved is evidenced by: the mixed balance sheet of relations with Russia (particularly in regarding non-military aspects of security – energy industry, historical policy) as well as the deterioration of relations with Belarus.

* * *

Historically, the geopolitical location of Poland between the East and the West has predominantly shaped the Polish national identity and statehood, determining the nature of national interests and objectives in the field security (fig. 5).

Figure 5. Historical geo-strategic location of Poland on the East-West line

Source: authors' own compilation.

Due to external wars and other crises, the policy and activities of authorities and the population were concentrated around the issues of security for a long time in Polish history. Ignoring such issues led either to marginalization on the international scene (the division into duchies period, the rule of the Saxon Dynasty) or total collapse of the state (the partition period, World War II). The history also shows the importance of right proportions between particular interests (of an individual) and collective interests (of the state) as well as between material interests and intangible (spiritual) interests. The prevalence of individual or particular interests (dynastic interests, the gentry's "golden freedom"/ anarchy, etc.) over the national ones led to a number of crises and undermined the international subjectivity of Poland, as well as resulted in the collapse of the Polish state (fragmentation and partitions).

History teaches an important lesson that the survival of the Polish nation, also in the period when it did not have its own state, was possible owing to the cultivation of the language, tradition, culture, and art, all of them strengthening the national identity.

The history of Poland says also a lot about the reliability of allied and coalition commitments. Simply making or signing such commitments did not guarantee the real help in the time of trial, as evidenced by September 1939. It is therefore critical, on the one hand, to make consistent efforts to maintain the credibility, cohesiveness and strength of organizations of which Poland is a member, and, on the other hand, to strive to build the state's own security potential.

1.2. Poland's security potential

National security system

The national security system is not optimal. The 2007 National Security Strategy of the Republic of Poland does not define the system in full, but merely indicates a number of various partial subsystems.

In the present White Book, the national security system (that of security of the state) is understood as the entirety of resources, means and forces (entities) earmarked by the state for the performance of tasks in the field of security, organized (into subsystems and components), maintained and prepared in a manner adequate to the purpose of performing such tasks. The system consists of a control system (subsystem) as well as a number of executive subsystems (systems), including operational subsystems (defence and protection) and support subsystems (societal and economic subsystems). Its structure is presented graphically in figure 6.

Figure 6. The universal national security system model

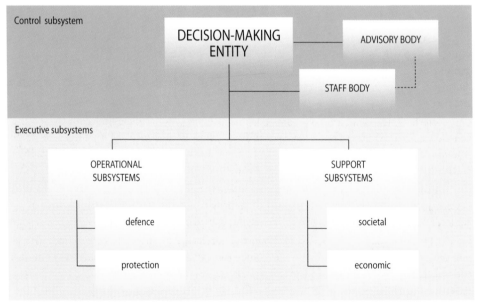

Source: authors' own compilation.

As the entire state, the national security system of the Republic of Poland has a territorial structure. In this sense, the commune (*gmina*), district (*powiat*), and province (*województwo*) subsystems of territorial security can be identified. Given the functional structure of the state, there are ministerial (departmental) security systems.

The nationality security system is multi-layered and multidimensional. It takes into account the shaping of relations within the state and the state's relations with external entities, as well as it covers their different spheres and levels: political, legal, military, economic, social, cultural, scientific and other relations.

Controlling national security is one of the most important functions of the state the aim of which is to ensure its existence and development under the changing conditions of the security environment. There are three basic elements of the national security control: control of defence of the state (the competence of the President of the Republic of Poland acting in cooperation with the Council of Ministers), general security control (the competence of the Council of Ministers), and crisis management (the competence of the Council of Ministers, province governors (*wojewoda*), district governors (*starosta*), commune heads (*wójt*), town mayors and presidents).

The **control subsystem** is the key element of the national security system. It is the part of the national security system designed for the purposes of controlling the functioning thereof, encompassing public authorities and heads of organizational units which perform tasks related to national security (including the command authorities of the Polish Armed Forces), along with advisory bodies and administrative (staff) apparatus as well as operating procedures and infrastructure (control and management positions and centres, communication system). The control subsystem is of vital importance for the entire security system in times of peace, crisis, and war. The subsystem ensures the identification of threats and their analysis, the planning of preparations and activities of the operational and support subsystems and their management (command) during operations.

There are four strategic task areas of the control subsystem. The first one concerns monitoring of threats, including their scale, type, and location. The second one deals with preventing the emergence of threats in the territory of the state and abroad. The third one includes the removal of relevant dangers, if the threats were not prevented. The final task area concerns the control of defence of the state in case of direct military aggression.

The fulfilment of these tasks requires adequate planning, organizational, financial and technical conditions. Such conditions, in turn, are ensured by legal regulations aimed at increasing the defence readiness of the state and preparing a system of command positions for specific public administration authorities, including the Central Control Post of the State Defence.

Executive subsystems (including components) the means and forces earmarked for the performance of statutory tasks in the field of security which remain available to security control authorities. There are two kinds of such subsystems: operational subsystems and support subsystems.

Operational subsystems consist of: the state's defence subsystem (defence, national defence, military security) – designed to seize opportunities, face challenges, reduce risks and counter (prevent and resist) external threats of a politico-military nature – as well as the state and civil protection subsystems (non-military, civil security) – designed to seize opportunities, face challenges, reduce risks, and counter (prevent and resist) external and internal threats of a non-military (civil) nature.

The support subsystems are societal and economic entities, the aim of which is to seize opportunities, face challenges, reduce risks, and counter (prevent and resist) external and internal threats of a socio-economic nature, as well as to support socially and economically the operational subsystems of national security in times of peace, crisis, and war.

As stated before, the security system is not yet organized in an optimal way, the major challenge being the proper integration of its elements.

Political system conditions as the basis of the management potential

The basis for the national security control subsystem is the political system conditions the legal foundations of which are laid down in the Constitution of the Republic of Poland of 2 April 1997. Article 5 which lays down the basic functions of the state, is key in this regard.

In accordance with the said article, the Republic of Poland preserves the independence and integrity of its territory (the state as a national political organization), ensures the freedoms and rights of persons and citizens as well as the security of the citizens (a citizen as the unitary element of the nation), safeguards the national heritage (the intangible potential, the constant component of which is the cultural and historical heritage) as well as provides the protection of the natural environment pursuant to the principles of sustainable development (the material potential, built in the course of the social and economic development, taking into account the need for the protection of the natural environment). These functions determine specific responsibilities and tasks of the state authorities. Preserving the independence and territorial integrity of the state – even in view of the scheme of the basic law – is the state's key function, the implementation of which allows for fulfilling of other functions defined as fundamental in Article 5.

The Constitution of the Republic of Poland of 2 April 1997

Art. 5. The Republic of Poland shall safeguard the independence and integrity of its territory and ensure the freedoms and rights of persons and citizens, the security of the citizens, safeguard the national heritage and shall ensure the protection of the natural environment pursuant to the principles of sustainable development.

As regards preservation of independence, territorial integrity and national security, the provision of aforementioned Article 5 of the Constitution of the Republic of Poland corresponds closely with the standard set in Article 26, para. 1 of the Constitution, which determines the system position of the Polish Armed Forces. By ascribing the Polish Armed Forces the role of safeguarding the independence and territorial integrity of the state as well as of the security and inviolability of its borders, the Constitution of the Republic of Poland entrusts the Armed Forces with the role of the primary executor of the state's most important function.

Within the framework of the political system conditions, the Polish Constitution contains provisions which determine the system founding principles of the Republic of Poland. The following tenets are of particular importance: a democratic state of law realizing the principles of social justice; a unitary nature of the state; the supreme power of the nation; sustainable development; access to national cultural heritage; the rule of law; separation of and balance among public powers (legislative, executive and judicial);

political pluralism; freedom of association; freedom of the press and of other means of social communication; decentralization; a social market economy and the freedom of economic activity; the neutrality of the Armed Forces in political matters and their being subject to civil and democratic control.

The institutional and functional conditions in the sphere of security are determined by the constitutional principle of separation and balance among the branches – the legislative (the Sejm and the Senate), the executive (the President of the Republic of Poland and the Council of Ministers), and the judiciary (courts and tribunals). The structure of the executive in the state is of basic importance for the shaping of solutions in the security system.

The position of the President of the Republic of Poland is defined under Article 126 of the Constitution, in accordance with which the President is the supreme representative of the Republic of Poland and the guarantor of the continuity of state authority, ensures observance of the Constitution, safeguards the sovereignty and security of the state as well as the inviolability and integrity of its territory. The functions performed by the President correspond therefore to Article 5 of the Constitution, making the head of the state the guardian of the basic values of the state such as sovereignty, territorial integrity, and external and internal security. Important in this context is the provision of Article 134 of the Constitution which – by entrusting the supreme command of the Polish Armed Forces to the President – determines the position of the head of the state in relation to the apparatus appointed to perform the most important function of the state. The position of the President of the Republic of Poland in the security system is confirmed under Article 135 of the Constitution, pursuant to which the National Security Council is an advisory body to the President regarding internal and external security of the state. The responsibilities and instruments of the President concerning the issues of security – with the exclusion of extraordinary measures – fall within the general powers provided for in the constitutional and statutory standards. In order for the President of the Republic of Poland to fulfil his constitutional functions, it is essential that the President has the powers to: approve, at request of the Prime Minister, the National Security Strategy of the Republic of Poland as well as to issue, also at request of the Prime Minister and by way of a decision, the Political and Strategic Defence Directive of the Republic of Poland. In addition, the President, by way of a decision issued at the request of the minister of national defence, determines the key objectives of the development of the Armed Forces and their preparation to defend the state as well as, on the motion of the Council of Ministers, decides about the deployment of the Polish military contingents abroad.

It should be stressed that the function of the state regarding security as defined in Article 5 of the Constitution is transferred to the Council of Ministers competence under Article 146 para. 1 of the Constitution. In the light of provisions of this article, the Council of Ministers conducts the internal affairs and foreign policy of the Republic of Poland. Detailed objectives of the Council of Ministers defined in the Constitution and therefore considered particularly important include ensuring the internal security of the state and public order (Article 146 para. 4 item 7 of the Constitution of the Republic of Poland), ensuring the external security of the state (Article 146 para. 4 item 8), as well as exercising general control in the field of national defence and annually specifying the number of citizens who are required to perform active military service (Article 146 para. 4 item 11).

The development of the strategic concept and national security system is guided by the constitutional principles of the rule of law, supremacy and direct applicability of the provisions of the Constitution of the Republic of Poland, as well as observance of international law by Poland. The public authorities shall function on the basis and within the limits of the law.

The contents of the constitutional catalogue of rights, freedoms, and obligations of persons and citizens set a framework for defining the system objectives and solutions in the field of security.

The strategic concept and the national security system must be developed taking into account, in particular, the rights of every person, as listed: protection of life; legal protection of their private and family life; making decisions about their personal life; rearing their children in accordance with their own convictions; not disclosing information concerning them and their philosophy of life, religious convictions or belief; having access to the public service based on the principle of equality; obtaining information on the activities of public authorities as well as foreigners' right of asylum or right to obtain the status of a refugee. It also concerns numerous freedoms, especially the freedom of: communication; movement within the territory of the Republic of Poland and leaving it; choice of place of residence and sojourn; expressing opinions; assembly and association, as well as the prohibition (excluding the cases defined in the Constitution of the Republic of Poland) of extradition of a Polish citizen.

Important circumstances when designing the security-related solutions include: establishing, under the Constitution of the Republic of Poland, of a broad catalogue of measures for the protection of rights and freedoms; identifying clearly which of them can be claimed directly under the Constitution of the Republic of Poland; establishing the rules and procedures for introducing extraordinary measures (martial law, a state of emergency, a state of natural disaster) as well as specifying the admissible degree to which the freedoms and rights of persons and citizens may be subjected to limitation for the duration of extraordinary measures.

In the context of developing the strategic concept and preparing (maintaining and transforming) the national security system, the state of law is a problem in itself. In the field of security, the Polish legal system lacks comprehensive regulations of statutory nature. The regulations are scattered among various acts, lack a systematic character, and do not reflect in a sufficient manner the changing notion of national security associated with the growing importance of its non-military dimension.

Party system. The fundamentals of the party system are laid down by the constitutional principles of a democratic state and political pluralism. The boundaries of the party system are marked by the constitutional prohibition of the existence of political parties and other organizations whose programmes are advocate totalitarian methods and Nazi, fascist or communist practices, as well as those whose programmes or activities assume or acknowledges racial or national hatred, the use of violence aimed at obtaining power or influencing the state policy, or provide for the secrecy of their own structure or membership. The constitutional principle that the financing of political parties is open to public inspection is essential from the perspective of political security.

The characteristic feature of the political scene is its multi-party nature, and this feature appears permanent. At the programme level, apart from the traditional division between the left and the right there is – and will continue to be – a partially overlapping (and even countervailing) division into supporters of solutions leaning toward traditionally-understood interests of the nation-state and, on the other hand, those advocating the broadest possible international and supranational cooperation, including in the framework of the European integration process. The European Union and in particular its institutional and functional consolidation becomes, under such conditions, the subject of dispute between proponents of European integration and Euro-sceptics, which reshapes the political scene.

Local government. An important factor in developing the security strategy is, in accordance with the constitutional principle of decentralization, the share of local government in the exercise of public power as well as the execution by local government of the substantial part of public duties which it is empowered to discharge by law.

The tasks associated with the public security, including public order, and citizens' safety, are carried out by local government units at commune and district level as its direct responsibility. As a result, the coordination and allotting of tasks in this field can be done only in accordance with the provisions of generally applicable law. The strong position of local self-government, particularly at the level of communes and districts – which are the territorial units in which only local public administration authorities of general jurisdiction can function – is further accentuated by the rule of locally combined administration. The supervision by the central administration over the activities of the local government is, in principle, except for a situation when extraordinary measures have been introduced, limited by the provisions of the Constitution of the Republic of Poland to the criterion of legality.

Non-governmental organizations. Non-governmental organizations (NGOs) are an element of public space, which, to a certain extent, affects the national security system. In accordance with the principle of freedom of association, there exist trade unions, socio-occupational organizations, societies, citizens' movements, as well as other voluntary associations and foundations. In addition, on the basis of laws, there are self-governments created within a profession in which the public repose confidence, which concern themselves with the due practice of such professions in accordance with and for the purpose of protecting the public interest. The best chance for the national security system associated with the existence of non-governmental organizations is that they are established, function, and fulfil their statutory objectives spontaneously, at grass-root level, and consequently – that the civil society is being built, whose members feel jointly responsible for important matters, either at the local community or state level.

Poland's experience resulting from NGOs activities is not long enough to allow elaboration of effective cooperation mechanisms between such organizations and the administration. It means that despite the implementation of solutions in the field of public benefit, they are not sufficiently involved in carrying out public tasks, including the measures taken to ensure national security. Above all, the third sector is noticed in the context of security when sudden disasters befall, but its role in daily activity is underestimated.

The activities of non-governmental organizations contributing to ensuring security include both their involvement in the measures **directly improving the security** of the state (e.g. in the case of Voluntary Fire Brigades, for which the security system provides the protective, interventional, educational, and cultural functions) and their **indirect involvement** (e.g. think tanks suggesting directions of security policy of Poland, organizations combating pathological phenomena – such as corruption, foundations supporting families, health, education, etc.).

Authority control mechanisms. The constitutional and legal system provides for solutions aimed at ensuring the control over activities of the public authorities as well as providing these authorities with necessary tools to carry out the control tasks. Regulations in force allow to determine, also in issues relating to national security, the correspondence between the existing situation and the projected or admissible one, establish, the reasons for discrepancies, formulate of conclusions (for an institution being controlled and for other state authorities), as well as improve management support mechanisms.

The said solutions comprise internal and external control mechanisms within the administrative structures, mechanisms of control imposed by state institutions (including the Supreme Audit Office), as well as prosecutorial and judicial control. Political control exercised by legislative entities (using such tools as interpellations, enquiries, desiderata, votes of approval, investigations, activities of parliamentary commissions, including of parliamentary investigation commissions) as well as directly by citizens (e.g. through elections and access to public documents) is of particular significance. The media fulfil an important control function, too. In a growing number of cases to which the provisions of international law and interstate agreements apply, the control function is performed by external entities (including, above all, the bodies of the European Union and of the Council of Europe).

* * *

The political system and legal conditions stipulated in the Constitution of the Republic of Poland provide a general framework for defining the catalogue of national interests and strategic objectives in the field of security, as these interests and objectives should be formulated taking into account both the functions of the state specified in Article 5 of the Constitution and the system-founding rules of the Republic of Poland.

The defence potential

The defence potential is comprised of: the foreign service (diplomacy) whose task is to ensure security, the Armed Forces of the Republic of Poland, military secret services, and defence industry.

The **foreign service tasked with ensuring security** functions and transforms itself in accordance with the contemporary trends and the changing geopolitical and economic situation. Poland has embassies in 89 countries and representations with 9 international organizations. There are 36 consulates general in 19 countries and, in addition, there are consular departments of the Polish embassies. Currently, there are 23 Polish Institutes functioning abroad (as of 31 December 2012).

The support for foreign service tasked with ensuring security is provided by 55 defence attachés at diplomatic missions of the Republic of Poland around the world. They are an important element within the structure of Polish embassies and play a significant role in the development and coordination of international military cooperation.

The task of foreign policy – and of diplomacy as its tool – is to help ensure favourable international conditions, thereby guaranteeing, as much as possible, the security of the Republic of Poland and protecting its broadly-conceived security interests. Diplomacy allows the country to express and conduct foreign policy through, *inter alia*, appropriate legal bases, organization, staff, procedures, and methods of operation.

Poland's location as a frontier country of the North Atlantic Treaty Organization and of the European Union places a special responsibility on diplomacy. Polish diplomacy represents the interests of a major state in central Europe, having ambitions to play a significant role on the continent. Its activities include creating a stable international security environment at regional and global level through international cooperation, particularly within the North Atlantic Treaty Organization, the European Union, the United Nations, the Organization for Security and Co-operation in Europe and other international organizations as well as in relations with its nearest neighbours and main partners.

The Permanent Representation of the Republic of Poland to NATO plays a particularly important role within the foreign service tasked with ensuring security and participates in the decision-making processes of the North Atlantic Treaty Organization on an ongoing basis. Essential tasks in the field of security are also implemented by the Permanent Representation of the Republic of Poland to the European Union. Their value is that they can seek, within the Alliance and the EU, to have Polish national interests and strategic objectives taken into account in activities of the two organizations. It is achieved through participation in the work and meetings of various committees and working groups.

The Polish Military Representation to the NATO Military Committee and the EU Military Committee as well as the representations to the NATO strategic commands are the liaison cells between the national and NATO military authorities. Activities of the Polish MilRep are mainly concentrated around the issues of military security of the Euro-Atlantic area as well as military cooperation between the allies and the partners from NATO and the EU. The strength of the Polish Military Representation lies in its ability to influence the ongoing operation of NATO and the EU through participation in the processes of defence planning, crisis management, command structure transformation, exchange of information and of reconnaissance and intelligence data, as well as in their ability to develop military and civil cooperation with international security institutions.

As the globalization process advances – leading, *inter alia,* to a relatively weakened role of the state, a broader notion of security, the quickening pace of the dissemination of information and the multitude of its resources – diplomacy will become even more significant. Moreover, the functions of diplomacy will change as well. For instance, the significance of development policies in the activities of the Polish Ministry of Foreign Affairs will increase – as an expression of aspirations to enjoy the status of a developed country and an instrument to stabilise crises after the conflict stage is over.

Changes in the foreign service which have taken place in recent years included: the introduction of new standards for formulation and assignment of objectives; the categorization of missions abroad; the introduction of project management; the informatization and streamlining of consular services; the reform of the diplomatic security system; the modernization of the IT platform as well as focusing on promotion of the image of Poland and Polish foreign policy through modern forms of communication, mainly *via* the Internet.

There are two common models of recruitment of diplomatic personnel functioning in the world: the American model (where top diplomatic positions are given to activists and persons who made significant contributions to a winning party, and the executive positions – to professional diplomats with best qualifications) and the European model (where diplomatic positions are held only by specialists selected in competitions from among the personnel of the department of foreign affairs). In Poland, there is a mixed model in place. Positions in diplomatic missions are partially assigned to unprepared party activists, partially – through "external recruitment" – to personnel from ministries and central offices, and partially to staff employees of the Ministry of Foreign Affairs. The picture is completed with military attaches and liaison officers of uniformed services as well as employees of the Polish Institutes who are newcomers in the field of diplomacy. From among the above categories, only the professional diplomats, military attaches, and liaison officers always receive sufficient preparation to undertake diplomatic service.

The **Armed Forces** of the Republic of Poland remain the key instrument in implementing Polish security policy. Their constitutional task is to safeguard the independence and territorial integrity of Poland, and to ensure the security and inviolability of its borders.

The Armed Forces of the Republic of Poland maintain readiness to perform three types of missions: guaranteeing defence of the state and ward off aggression; participating in the process of stabilization of the international situation and in crisis response and humanitarian operations; and supporting the internal security and rendering assistance to the population.

The Polish Armed Forces comprise the following four types of forces: the Land Forces, the Air Force, the Navy, and the Special Forces. The Polish Armed Forces staff comprises 120 thousand military posts, including 100 thousand posts for soldiers on active duty and 20 thousand posts for soldiers of the National Reserve Forces (*Narodowe Siły Rezerwowe*, NSR). The number of posts in the Polish Armed Forces and their internal structure is shown in figure 7.

Figure 7. Number of staff and internal structure of the Polish Armed Forces (2012)

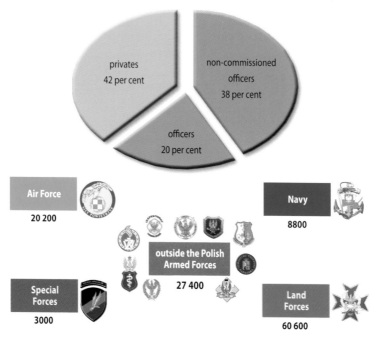

Source: authors' own compilation based on data from the Ministry of National Defence.

For more than two decades the Polish Armed Forces have been undergoing deep systemic transformation. The starting point of this process was more than 400-thousand mass army based on conscription, which concentrated its efforts on preparations for major armed conflict within the forces of the Warsaw Pact. Large and costly reserves were an inherent element in the system. Further maintenance of such potential in completely different geopolitical conditions not only did not fit the defence needs, but also substantially exceeded the economic capabilities of the state. The initial stage of the transformation consisted, in fact, in a rather chaotic reduction of the personnel and of significant amounts of military equipment and armaments. Only between 1989 and 1993, the armed forces were reduced by 25 per cent.

The organizational and structural reforms carried out in accordance with the changing concepts, led, ons the one hand, to certain savings, but on the other – resulted in the loss of certain capabilities (as a consequence of withdrawing from service of large quantities of outdated equipment and armaments, including destruction means) as well as in the technical degradation of (mainly post-Soviet) armament, equipment and military infrastructure.

Photos: 1, 2, 3. Adam Roik/ Combat Camera Reporter Team of the Armed Forces Operational Command. Photo: 4. Archives of the Special Forces Command.

Another negative consequence of the transformations was uneven and ineffective deployments of military units (often in isolation from training ranges) as well as the unfavourable change of proportions between the combat components and the broadly understood supply base (support units, training and education system potential, overextended command structures, etc.). All these factors affected directly the level of defence capabilities.

The second stage of transformations as well as an attempt to organise this process began with Polish efforts to join the North Atlantic Alliance. The standardization process was launched and efforts were made to achieve compatibility and interoperability of the Polish Armed Forces with the forces of other NATO members. Moreover, the number of garrisons was successively limited and, in order to meet social expectations, the duration of conscript military service started to be gradually reduced.

An important turning point marking the beginning of the third stage of the armed forces transformations was the Act on the Restructuring, Technical Modernization and the Financing of the Polish Armed Forces adopted on 25 May 2001. The act introduced a systemic solution new to the Polish legal system, namely: each year not less than 1.95 per cent of the GDP from a preceding year shall be allocated for defence purposes.

The said solution was adopted by agreement among political elites above the party lines. In accordance with the act, the "Programme of Reconstruction and Technical Modernization of the Armed Forces of the Republic of Poland in years 2001–2006" was prepared and launched – the first of the series of the Polish Army transformation programmes adjusted to NATO's defence

The Act of 25 May 2001 on the Restructuring and Technical Modernization and the Financing of the Armed Forces of the Republic of Poland

Article 7 para.1. The defence needs of the Republic of Poland shall be financed from the state budget and the amount of funds assigned each year for this purpose shall not be lower than 1.95 per cent of the Gross Domestic Product from a preceding year.

planning cycle, owing to which it was possible to reach and later exceed the level of 20 per cent of capital (modernization) expenditure under the defence budget. Substantial modernization projects were launched as well (fig. 8), as a result of which F-16 multi-role aircraft, CASA transport aircraft, Spike anti-tank guided missiles, and Rosomak wheeled armoured vehicles (*kołowy transporter opancerzony*, KTO) all entered into service. The major process of computerization and IT advancement of the army commenced.

Figure 8. Primary modernization programmes of the Polish Armed Forces

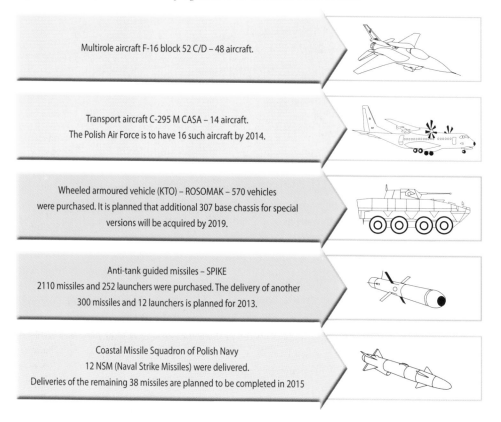

Multirole aircraft F-16 block 52 C/D – 48 aircraft.

Transport aircraft C-295 M CASA – 14 aircraft.
The Polish Air Force is to have 16 such aircraft by 2014.

Wheeled armoured vehicle (KTO) – ROSOMAK – 570 vehicles were purchased. It is planned that additional 307 base chassis for special versions will be acquired by 2019.

Anti-tank guided missiles – SPIKE
2110 missiles and 252 launchers were purchased. The delivery of another 300 missiles and 12 launchers is planned for 2013.

Coastal Missile Squadron of Polish Navy
12 NSM (Naval Strike Missiles) were delivered.
Deliveries of the remaining 38 missiles are planned to be completed in 2015

Source: authors' own compilation based on data from the Ministry of National Defence.

The next stage of transformation of the Polish army was marked by the adoption of the "Programme of Professionalization of the Armed Forces for the years 2008–2010" by the Council of Ministers on 5 August 2008. The professionalization of the armed forces was the most important transformation decision of the past two decades. As a result, the military service is completely voluntary, with all consequences of this fact.

Thanks to the stable and predictable investments allocated for defences purposes starting from 2001 as well as the above-mentioned principle on the share of capital expenditure in the budget of the Ministry of National Defence at the level not lower than 20 per cent of defence spending the process of technical modernization of the Polish Armed Forces has accelerated. Owing to the planned purchases and the successive entry into service of modern military equipment and armaments, certain segments of the Polish Armed Forces have already been sufficiently modernized, while other require further investments.

In the defence budget for 2012, the share of capital expenditure once again exceeded, as planned, the level of 20 per cent of defence spending, reaching exactly 24.4 per cent (as shown in fig. 9).

Figure 9. The Polish defence budget for year 2012 (in millions PLN)

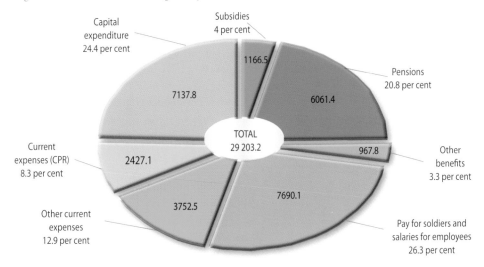

Source: authors' own compilation based on data from the Ministry of National Defence.

Despite the deep transformation that the armed forces have undergone for many years, there are still a number of shortfalls resulting from both the above-mentioned historical conditions of the process and the lack of consistency in introducing the changes (particularly from the initial period of reforms in early 1990s), which still significantly affects the level and efficiency of Poland's defence capabilities. As a consequence of substantial reductions of the number of posts, many valuable soldiers left the ranks and their skills and experience are not easy to replace in the short term. This has led to a kind of a "generation gap" in various areas. The withdrawal of the bulk of Warsaw Pact-vintage armaments, as well as the "ageing" of the equipment and armaments, in particular of the missile and artillery systems, have greatly limited the striking capabilities, which is especially palpable in the area of air defence. In a situation when missiles have become the key carrier of the striking force, the Polish Armed Forces have currently no anti-missile defence capabilities. The lack of purchases, inconsistency in the implemented programmes (cf. the Gawron corvette) and the changing concepts undermined also the potential of the Polish Navy.

The organization of the control and command system at the strategic level is hardly effective. Overblown and frequently duplicated functions of the command structure do not meet the needs of allied cooperation/collaboration or of the considerably reduced army, thereby complicating the strategic planning and ongoing implementation of tasks. The major weakness of the current command and control system of the armed forces lies in inefficient supervision of the execution of the decisions and the lax implementation discipline. This results from the defective organization of the system, in which the minister of national defence has limited possibilities to fully control the armed forces (in terms of decision-making, implementation, and accountability). In fact, the minister is dependent on the General Staff which, in its capacity as the staff/command entity, holds all the command functions: it is responsible for planning the tasks (as the staff), their implementation (as the command of the armed forces), as well as for the assessment of execution (again as the staff).

A number of problems emerged in the area of enlistment and reserves. Forming the National Reserve Forces (NSR), with the target number 20 thousand soldiers, began on 1 July 2010. The Ministry of National Defence initially divided this process into two stages. It was planned that 10 thousand of the National Reserve Forces would be enlisted by the end of 2010, and the other 10 thousand – by the end of 2011. Currently (as of the end of 2012) there are less than 10 thousand soldiers in the NSR. The concept was that the NSR soldiers would fill in the full-time posts for specialists in deficient specialities as well as will staff the posts in military specialities which do not require everyday military training.

The military education system, despite successive reforms, remains dispersed and far too large. Moreover, it focuses more on the needs of the civil market rather than the army, which is contrary to the idea of professionalization of the armed forces. At present, there are three military academies: the National Defence Academy, the Military University of Technology, and the Naval Academy, as well as two military higher education institutions: the Polish Air Force Academy and the Military Academy of Land Forces.

The health care system faces some problems, too. The health service is understaffed and finds it difficult to secure the operations of the Polish military contingents (PMCs, *polskie kontyngenty wojskowe*) abroad. Both the state of the battlefield medical technology and the system of training and bettering qualifications of medical personnel are unsatisfactory.

Photo 1.
Sebastian Kinasiewicz /
Combat Camera Reporter
Team of the Armed Forces
Operational Command;
Photos: 2, 4. Adam Roik/
Combat Camera Reporter
Team of the Armed Forces
Operational Command;
Photo 3. Sylwia Guzowska/
Press Department, Military
Gendarmerie Headquarters

The IT systems used in the army, both in the logistics and support area and the automated command systems, are often incompatible, which makes it difficult to use data effectively, particularly in the real time, hampers joint operations, and complicates the decision-making processes. The armed forces do not make sufficient use of unmanned aerial vehicles as well as use the satellite technologies – which ensure effective communication over long distances and an offer informational advantage – only to a limited extent. The potential of the country's arms industry and research base is not exploited enough.

A positive result of the transformation of the armed forces is the fact that, since Poland's entry into NATO, the country has become not only the consumer of security, but also its "producer". This finds its confirmation in the participation of Polish military contingents in missions abroad, which is highly assessed by allies and partners (fig. 10). A turning point in this regard was the PMC participation in the stabilization mission in Iraq, during which Poland took the command of the Centre-South Multinational Division responsible for security in the central region of the country, and in the ISAF operations in Afghanistan, where Poland was tasked with ensuring security in the Ghazni province. Tens of thousands of soldiers and military staff have gained invaluable experience in those missions.

Experience gained so far in the course of the transformation process confirmed that professional armed forces – flexible, mobile, as well as adequately armed and trained – are more effective and efficient and, consequently, are of greater operational value and better guarantee the security of the state and its citizens than a conscript army. It was therefore an important achievement of the previous transformations of the Polish Armed Forces that, irrespective of minor shortfalls, the professionalization programme was completed. This process needs to be continued and appropriately adjusted taking into account the experience of the last few years during which the Polish army functioned in accordance with the new scheme.

The armed forces successfully fulfil their tasks connected with assistance provided to the population in crisis situations, including during natural disasters (this is one of the reasons why the army enjoys the undiminished confidence of the public). The bond between the army and the population is of particular importance in the conditions of the professional army.

In conclusion, the condition of the Polish army is systematically improving. The process of further transformation of the Armed Forces of the Republic of Poland, is underway, aiming at increasing the military potential and operational capabilities. The modern equipment is successively provided to the army while the ongoing organizational consolidation helps gradually improve the operational capabilities of the Polish armed forces. There are still some areas, however, which require special attention and further modernization effort.

Military intelligence and counterintelligence. The *Military Intelligence Service* (*Służba Wywiadu Wojskowego*, SWW) carries out intelligence operations for the Polish Armed Forces. It is a secret service tasked with ensuring protection against external threats to the state's defence, security, and combat capabilities of the Polish Armed Forces and other organizational units reporting to or supervised by the minister of national defence. The SWW was established after the liquidation of the Military Information Service in 2006 and operates on the basis of the Act of 9 June 2006 on the Military Counterintelligence Service and the Military Intelligence Service. The chief of the SWW is responsible to the minister of national defence, on the stipulation of the powers of the Prime Minister or the minister-coordinator of the secret services, in case one is appointed.

The aforesaid formation is a member of the international intelligence community. It participates in the exchange of information and experience among intelligence services of members of NATO

Figure 10. The participation of the Polish military contingents in security operations (since Poland's entry into NATO in 1999)

2004 – present
EUFOR Althea
Bosnia and
Herzegovina

1996–2004
SFOR
Bosnia and
Herzegovina

2006, 2008,
2010, 2012,
Baltic Air Policing
Estonia, Lithuania,
Latvia

1999 – present
KFOR
Kosovo

2003 Concordia
Macedonia

2005, 2006,
2006/07, 2008,
2008/09, 2010/11, 2011
Active Endeavour
Mediterranean Sea

1999
AFOR
Albania

1974–2009
UNDOF
Syria

2004 – present ISAF
Afghanistan

1992–2009
UNIFIL
Lebanon

2002–2007
Enduring Freedom
Afghanistan

2008–2009
EUFOR
Tchad/RCA
Tchad

2005–2006
Swift Relief
Pakistan

2009
MINURCAT
Chad

2006
EUFOR RD Congo
Gabon,
Democratic Republic
of the Congo

2003–2008
Iraqi Freedom
Iraq

2005–2011
NTM-I
Iraq

2013 – present
EUTM
Mali

Source: authors' own compilation.

and the EU. The SWW carries out its tasks outside the territory of the Republic of Poland. The activity of SWW within the territory of Poland can be conducted only in association with its operations abroad. The statutory tasks of SWW officers include the preliminary reconnaissance as well as analytical and informational activities. They are authorized to use firearms and have the powers under the act on protection of people and property as regards officers and soldiers handling tasks relating to physical protection of the SWW facilities.

Some of the key tasks systematically performed by the Military Intelligence Service include: collection and processing of information critical for the safety of the defence potential, combat capabilities and implementation of tasks by the Polish Armed Forces; identifying and counteracting military threats against Poland's defence capabilities as well as international terrorism threats; identifying threats associated with illicit international trade in arms, ammunition and explosive materials, trade in goods, technologies and services of strategic importance for the state's security as well as the proliferation of weapons of mass destruction; participating in planning and controlling the implementation of international disarmament agreements; identifying and analyzing threats in regions of international tensions, conflicts, and crises, which affect the national defence and operational ability of the Polish Armed Forces, as well as taking steps to eliminate those threats; carrying out electronic intelligence activities for the Polish Armed Forces and projects in the field of cryptanalysis and cryptography.

The counterintelligence activities for the Armed Forces of the Republic of Poland are pursued by the **Military Counterintelligence Service** (*Służba Kontrwywiadu Wojskowego*, SKW) – a secret service responsible for ensuring protection against internal threats to the defence capabilities of the state, security and combat capabilities of the Armed Forces and other organizational units responsible to or supervised by the minister of national defence. To this aim, the SKW carries out a number of activities associated with counteracting espionage, corruption in the area of dangers to the defence capabilities of the state as well as threats to units, facilities and installations important from the point of view of defence, and also ensuring cyber security of the Polish Armed Forces. Moreover, the SKW performs tasks associated with ensuring security and conducting scientific research, development work, the aim of which is to enhance the military security of Poland.

Defence industry. The defence industry potential (*przemysłowy potencjał obronny*) is made up of tangible and intangible assets of the Polish industry which meet the defence needs of the state, including the needs of the Polish Armed Forces as regards armaments and military equipment (AME). At present, the defence industry potential comprises, *inter alia,* the companies conducting business activity for the needs of security and defence of the state, the majority shareholder of which is the state treasury; enterprises founded by the minister of national defence; R&D units as well as companies engaged in foreign trade in goods, technologies, and services of strategic importance for the state's security. Moreover, the importance of non-state-owned companies on the domestic defence market is growing.

The system of procurement of armaments and military equipment for the Polish Armed Forces, i.e. selection of a supplier or manufacturer of a specific product or service, is based on principles set forth in the Act of 29 January 2004 – Public Procurement Law as well as relevant decisions of the minister of national defence. The selection process takes the form of open tenders and every bidder can take part in those ones. Due to the competitiveness of the European market and the consequences of Poland's membership in the European Union, tenders are open also to foreign suppliers.

The procurement of armaments and military equipment for the Polish Armed Forces is based on specific future and current needs, as well as on urgent operational requirements. Future needs result from operational requirements defined in long-term plans and programmes, aimed at achieving or streamlining specific operational capabilities of the Polish Armed Forces. The current needs, in turn, necessitate reaching specific operational capabilities, the aim of which is to ensure that the Armed Forces function systematically, as intended. The urgent operational requirement means immediate acquisition of AME due to the necessity of using the Polish Armed Forces, which could not have been foreseen during the planning stage given reasonable diligence.

According to the objectives of the Strategy for Consolidation and Support of the Development of the Polish Defence Industry, the defence industry potential is one of the basic elements of security and defence of the state. The strategy of activities relating to the defence industry potential provides for the consolidation based on, *inter alia,* the commercialization of state enterprises and selected research and development (R&D) units, the reorganization of the defence industry potential, and cooperation with strategic investors.

The current condition of the defence industry potential is unsatisfactory. The defence industry is not competitive enough to participate extensively in the process of technical modernization of the Polish Armed Forces, as well as to effectively compete on foreign markets. Companies in this sector – especially those which are directly or indirectly controlled by the State Treasury – are not sufficiently resistant to effects of fluctuations on the defence market while they cope with a number of structural problems. This results in their strong dependence on orders from the government; their insufficiently attractive market offer in terms of the product range, costs, and technological advancement; their weak position on foreign markets as well as the lack of activity in the field of R&D and in obtaining funds for this purpose.

The current experience with the restructuring of the sector has indicated that division of responsibilities among a number of ministries (the Ministry of National Defence, the Ministry of Treasury, the Ministry of Economy), which results, *inter alia,* from the previous ownership structure of the DIP, excessively lengthens the decision-making process and is not conducive to the effectiveness of activities related to the acquisition, manufacture and promotion of armaments and military equipment. From the perspective of technical modernization of the Polish Armed Forces, ensuring of the state's security should be understood as a need to develop and introduce modern armaments and military equipment as well as to maintain the state's own production capabilities. Guaranteeing the safety of supplies of armaments and military equipment to the armed forces and the effective operation of the equipment supplied (the warranty period, overhauls, servicing) are a constant challenge for the state's administration.

* * *

The defence potential of the Republic of Poland is systematically growing. The improvement of operational capabilities of the professional Polish Armed Forces has a positive effect on the level of Polish ambitions and, therefore, on the scale and nature of national interests and strategic objectives in the field of security.

The protection potential

The protection potential comprises: the judiciary; secret services; services, guards, and inspections specializing in providing security and public order; rescue and civil safety services; elements of crisis management; border guards and other institutions whose direct or indirect task is to safeguard public security.

The judiciary. A properly operating system of justice guarantees a stable functioning of the state and ensures the security of the population and citizens. The judicial power is one of the three elements of the systemic separation of powers. Pursuant to Article 175 of the Constitution of the Republic of Poland, the justice in the Republic of Poland shall be administered by courts only. These include: the Supreme Court, common courts, administrative courts, and military courts. Apart from courts, the judicial powers are also vested in two tribunals – the Constitutional Tribunal and the Tribunal of State.

Special courts, competent for a specific group of cases, are outside the system of common courts. They include administrative and military courts. The rules applicable in proceedings held before special courts are the same as in common courts. Administrative courts control the legality of activities of the public administration.

One of the most serious problems of the Polish judiciary is the lengthiness of court proceedings. This situation affects the certainty and stability of business activity, the freedom of which is one of the pillars of the economic system of the Republic of Poland. In addition, the authorities conducting proceedings frequently demand exorbitant bail bonds and unjustified security on property, which may lead to bankruptcy of companies and consequential loss of jobs even before the court verdict is issued.

The unsatisfactory effectiveness of the Polish judicial system is also associated with its insufficient computerization, the process of which has in fact just started and requires intensification. The weakness of the judiciary lies in the insufficient flow of information among various entities due to the lack of a common electronic database. For instance, the National Court Register, in which data on members of companies' governing bodies are held, has no access to the criminal record base and therefore is unable to verify whether the function of a member of management board or supervisory board of a given company has been entrusted or not to a person with a criminal record.

Institutions of the system of justice closely cooperate with legal protection bodies, including the public prosecutors and the Prison Service.

Public prosecutors. The role of public prosecutors is to ensure the observance of the law and to combat crimes. They comprise: the public prosecutor general and subordinate prosecutors of common and military organizational units of as well as prosecutors of the Institute of National Remembrance – Commission for the Prosecution of Crimes against the Polish Nation.

Prosecutors of common organizational units of the prosecutor's offices are prosecutors of the General Public Prosecutor's Office, appellate public prosecutor's offices, regional public prosecutor's offices, and district public prosecutor's offices.

Prosecutors of military organizational units of prosecutor's offices are prosecutors of the Chief Military Prosecutor's Office, regional military prosecutor's offices, and garrison military prosecutor's offices.

In terms of substance, military prosecutors are responsible to the public prosecutor general, whose one of the deputies is the chief military prosecutor. In terms of structure and organization, military organizational units of the prosecutor's offices are part of the Polish Armed Forces and their activity is financed from separate budgetary funds of the Ministry of National Defence. In terms of military service, the chief military prosecutor reports to the minister of national defence.

The Constitution of the Republic of Poland does not contain any direct provisions stipulating the legal model of the prosecutor's office or its position within the constitutional system of the state. The organization and activity of the prosecutor's office were defined in the Act of 20 June 1985 on the Prosecutor's Office, which later has been amended many a time.

Prosecutors conduct or oversee preliminary proceedings in criminal cases as well as perform the function of a public prosecutor before courts. A detailed range of powers held by prosecutors who participate in such cases and their obligations are regulated by the law of criminal procedure.

Military prosecutors – apart from carrying out their official tasks corresponding to the obligations of prosecutors of common organizational units of the prosecution service – pursue in addition activities directly connected with ensuring the observance of law and maintaining an appropriate level of military discipline both in military units and institutions and in military contingents abroad.

In 2010, the functions of the public prosecutor general and of the minister of justice were separated.

The **Prison Service** (*Służba Więzienna*) pursues penitentiary, protection, and social rehabilitation activities towards persons sentenced to imprisonment. It is also responsible for temporary detainment in a manner ensuring the proper conduct of criminal proceedings. The basic tasks of the Prison Service include: protecting the public against the negative impact of offenders identified by the system of justice; fending off threats by deterring potential perpetrators of offences; isolating sentenced persons from the rest of the society with respect for human dignity and humanitarian principles, as well as social rehabilitation of offenders.

The Prison Service consists of the following organizational units: the Central Board of Prison Service, regional inspectorates of the Prison Service, correctional facilities, and remand centres as well as of in-service training centres for personnel. Nearly 27 thousand officers serve in the Prison Service. In addition, there are approximately 3 thousand civilian employees in the sector.

The biggest challenge for the Polish penitentiary system in recent years was overcrowding of correctional facilities and remand centres. Such a situation was a result of the increase in crime, especially in 1990s and at the turn of the century. Overcrowding in Polish prisons was the subject matter of decisions of the European Court of Human Rights and the Polish Tribunal of State.

Prison overcrowding is still a problem in certain units but, in general, the situation has lately improved. In November 2012, the population in penitentiary units did not exceed their normative capacity and reached 96.7 per cent. Penitentiary facilities held 85.2 thousand convicts, while nearly 47 thousand persons waited to serve their prison terms (as of March 2012).

Photos: Archives of the
Prison Service

Another problem that the Prison Service faces is the chronic lack of adequate funding. The assets owned by the Prison Service are constantly declining. Three-quarters of the 160 penitentiary units were erected before World War II. The aged infrastructure, especially taking into consideration the large numbers of convicts, may have a negative effect on efficient performance of the isolating function or social rehabilitation.

In order to improve the functioning of the Polish prison system, a new act on Prison Service was adopted on 9 April 2010, which established the Penitentiary Policy Council – an advisory body to the minister of justice. The act tidied up a number of issues relating to the employment of the Prison Service officers. It is assumed that certain problems connected with overcrowding will be solved by the electronic probation system.

Secret services. There is no definition of secret services in Polish law. Although Article 11 of the Act on Internal Security Agency and the Intelligence Agency refers to the Internal Security Agency (*Agencja Bezpieczeństwa Wewnętrznego*, ABW), the Foreign Intelligence Agency (*Agencja Wywiadu*, AW), the Central Anti-Corruption Bureau (*Centralne Biuro Antykorupcyjne*, CBA), the Military Counterintelligence Service and the Military Intelligence Service as special services, it does so only for the purposes of the act. Taking into consideration the fact, that the above services are not the only ones that shoulder the preliminary investigative responsibilities, it is difficult to state without doubt which of them should be considered secret services and what the classification criteria are. Above all, there is no single act which would define and classify the preliminary investigation activities and stipulate, for all services, who, when, and in what circumstances as well as upon whose authority can carry out these tasks.

The main entities who carry out special protection tasks include: the Internal Security Agency, the Intelligence Agency, the Central Anti-Corruption Bureau as well as – already discussed in the section devoted to the defence potential – the Military Counterintelligence Service and the Military Intelligence Service (fig. 11).

Figure 11. Secret services and who they report to

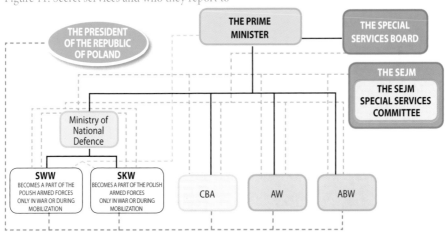

Source: authors' own compilation.

Photo: Internal Security Agency

The ***Internal Security Agency*** is a secret service responsible for safeguarding the internal security of the state and its constitutional order. Its tasks include surveillance, heading off and combating threats against the state's internal security, its constitutional order, and specifically its sovereignty and international position, independence and territorial integrity, as well as national defence. As the national security authority, the ABW implements, within its competence, the tasks relating to protection of classified information. An important element of the Agency's operation is its analytical and informational activity, which involves collecting information that is potentially significant from the point of view of internal security of the state as well as analysing of this information and its provision to competent authorities. The Head of the Internal Security Agency, who leads the Agency's operations, is a central organ of the government administration. The organ reports directly to the Prime Minister and its activity is controlled by the Sejm.

The ***Foreign Intelligence Agency*** is responsible for safeguarding the external security of the state and, in principle, carries out its operations outside the territory of the Republic of Poland. The basic tasks of the AW include: collecting information which is potentially significant from the point of view of security and international position of Poland and its economic and defence potential as well as the analysis of this information and its provision to competent authorities; identifying and combating external threats to the state's security – including international terrorism, extremism, international organized crime groups; operations of foreign secret services and other activities which can be detrimental to the interests of the Republic of Poland. The Agency ensures cryptographic protection of communication with Polish diplomatic and consular missions. Another critical challenge facing the Agency in the age of globalization and the development of cyberspace is electronic intelligence. The Foreign Intelligence Agency is managed by the Head of the Foreign Intelligence Agency who reports directly to the Prime Minister and whose activity is controlled by the Sejm.

The Central Anti-Corruption Bureau is a secret service established to combat corruption in public life and economy, particularly in public and local government institutions, as well as to combat activities detrimental to the State's economic interests. The CBA is managed by its Head, who is supervised by the Prime Minister. The activities of the head of the CBA are controlled by the Sejm.

The Bureau, apart from operational issues and preparatory proceedings, exercises control, analytical, informational, and preventative activities, including the educational tasks.

Corruption is one of offences against the interests of the state and its citizens, which are particularly difficult to detect and prove. Poland is considered a country in which corruption – understood as using one's position or influence for personal gain – is quite common. According to global data from 2012 collected by Transparency International, Poland ranked 41st (out of 176 countries surveyed) and scored 58 points (on the scale of 0-100, where 0 means the highest index of corruption in the public sector) – table 1.

Corruption is not just a problem of criminal behaviour, but also of the quality and transparency of public life, education, and control of the state's socio-economic mechanisms.

Table 1. World corruption statistics – Poland's ranking

Rank	Country / Territory	Score /index	Rank	Country / Territory	Score /index
1	Denmark	90	22	Saint Lucia	71
1	Finland	90	25	Austria	69
1	New Zealand	90	25	Ireland	69
4	Sweden	88	27	Qatar	68
5	Singapore	87	27	United Arab Emirates	68
6	Switzerland	86	29	Cyprus	66
7	Australia	85	30	Botswana	65
7	Norway	85	30	Spain	65
9	Canada	84	32	Estonia	64
9	Netherlands	84	33	Bhutan	63
11	Iceland	82	33	Portugal	63
12	Luxemburg	80	33	Puerto Rico	63
13	Germany	79	36	Saint Vincent and the Grenadines	62
14	Hong Kong	77	37	Slovenia	61
15	Barbados	76	37	Taiwan	61
16	Belgium	75	39	Cape Verde	60
17	Japan	74	39	Israel	60
17	Great Britain	74	41	**Poland**	**58**
19	United States	73	...	...	...
20	Chile	72	...	...	...
20	Uruguay	72	174	Afghanistan	8
22	Bahamas	71	174	North Korea	8
22	France	71	174	Somalia	8

Source: Corruption Perceptions Index 2012 – Transparency International

The services performing tasks the aim of which is to ensure Poland's security also include treasury control authorities that are subordinate to the minister of finance (General Inspector of Treasury Control, heads of treasury control offices) and have certain investigative powers in the field of treasury intelligence.

The assessment of functioning of the secret services is difficult due to the imprecise separation (and overlapping) of responsibilities among civil services as well as between civil and military services.

The existence of many agencies tasked with safeguarding the state's security and its constitutional order, with overlapping responsibilities and subject to various system structures and having investigative and surveillance powers, questions the practicality of the present solution.

Another problem – apart from the overlapping scope of tangible properties – is an inconsistent definition of powers held by the services (e.g. the ABW is entitled to the so-called passive provocation, and the CBA and the Police – are also authorized to active provocation, while the SKW has limited powers in this field). Moreover, the overly extensive use of the secret services by the prosecutors in the course of their investigations and proceedings raises many doubts.

Safety and public order. The aim of the subsystem of safety and public order is prevention and prosecution of perpetrators of attacks on life, health, and property of Polish citizens and other persons staying within the territory of the Republic of Poland as well as against the state's interests. The said subsystem consists of public authorities, services, guards, and inspections specializing in safeguarding security and public order. It is also a sector in which – apart from the medical rescue subsystem – certain tasks, which were previously fulfilled by the state, are now partially privatized.

The tasks of the public authorities in the field of safety and public order are set forth in relevant acts, *inter alia,* those regarding secret services, the Police, the Border Guard, the Customs Service, and the Government Protection Bureau.

In recent years, the number of disturbances of safety and public order has been decreasing, but it still remains a problem, especially during mass events.[1] It is important to note, however, that mass-

Photos: Marek Krupa/KGP

---

[1] In recent years, the number of mass-scale events during which the police guarded security has dropped from nearly 11 thousand in 2008 to approximately 8 thousand in 2011 and 3699 in the first half of 2012. At the same time, the numbers of offences and misdemeanours connected with these events have increased (in 2010, 701 offences and 1690 misdemeanours were committed; in 2011 – 901 offences and 6791 misdemeanours, and in the first half of 2012 – as many as 735 offences and 3905 misdemeanours were recorded). The vast majority of these is related to football matches (1065 misdemeanours and 530 offences in 2010, or 2209 misdemeanours and 574 offences in the first half of 2012).

-scale violations of the law in the context of public gatherings, social protests, strikes and blockades have been slightly on the rise.

A negative phenomenon in Poland is that organizers of mass-scale events, in particular those who organise political or public events, often lack basic knowledge about their duties relating to ensuring security, binding procedures, and associated consequences. On the other hand, the services who, under the law, are responsible for ensuring security and public order during such events are frequently the subject of public accusations. Such a situation has a negative influence on decisions regarding the engagement of the said services, in consequence of which the measures are taken under conditions of legal uncertainty.

The Police, as a uniformed and armed formation, are tasked with protecting citizens, and ensuring security and public order. The main responsibilities of the Police include: protecting human life and health as well as protecting property against violent attacks which might cause damage to these assets; protecting security and public order; initiating and organizing activities aimed at staving off offences and misdemeanours. The Police's organizational structure is made of officers working in the following services: criminal service, prevention service, as well as the service providing support for the Police activities in the areas of organization, logistics, and technology. The Police also consist of the court police, prevention units and anti-terrorist subunits.

Figure 12. The structure of the General Police Headquarters

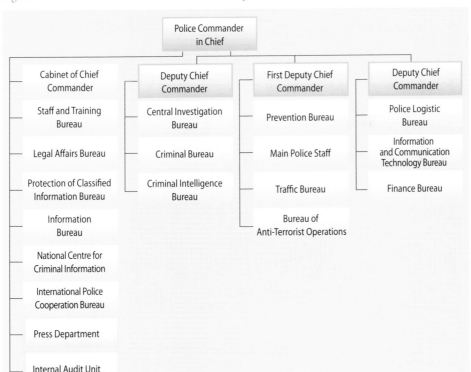

Source: The General Police Headquarters.

Police training facilities include the Police Academy in Szczytno, the Police Training Centre in Legionowo, the Police Academy in Piła, the Police School in Słupsk, the Police School in Katowice, and research institutes. The Police are one of the largest formations among all uniformed services. As of 1 November 2012, 95 997 officers served in its ranks, along with 24 792 civilian employees. All Police officers ultimately report to the Police Commander in Chief (the structure of the General Police Headquarters is shown in fig. 12), who in turn reports to the minister for the interior.

It is essential to properly utilise the forces and resources at the Police's disposal – make sure not to disperse them, but to concentrate them on tasks that are deemed priorities. The Police's potential should be adjusted to real or most probable threats.

The **Government Protection Bureau** (*Biuro Ochrony Rządu*, BOR), a uniform, uniformed and armed formation functioning within the ministry of the interior, is tasked with protection of the highest authorities and public administration bodies. Responsibilities of the BOR include protecting the President of the Republic of Poland, the Marshal (Speaker) of the Sejm, the Marshal of the Senate, the Prime Minister, the Deputy Prime Minister, the minister of the interior, and the minister of foreign affairs, as well as: other persons important for the state's security; former presidents, official foreign delegations during their visits to Poland; Polish diplomatic representations; consular offices and representations to international organizations. It is also responsible for ensuring security of facilities and installations of special importance.

A number of problems faced by the BOR result from inadequate budgetary funding for the scale of activities as well as the multi-stage decision-making path in the course of carrying out the tasks.

Photos: Government
Protection Bureau

There are also procedures in place aimed at ensuring the protection of the most important persons in the state, concerning their transportation and movement, in particular regulating the performance of HEAD flights. Changes in this regard were introduced by virtue of the decision No. 19/MON of the Minister of National Defence of 2 February 2012 on the implementation of the "Instruction on Organization of HEAD Flights in Aviation of the Armed Forces of the Republic of Poland"[2]. The adoption of the aforesaid changes was the result of conclusions drawn from the tragic TU-154M plane crash on 10 April 2010 near the city of Smolensk, resulting in death of the President of the Republic of Poland, Lech Kaczyński, and of 95 other persons, including all top military commanders. One of the most important provisions of the aforesaid decision concerns separate air travel of persons particularly important from the point of view national security control.

Crime prevention refers to heading off any acts prohibited by law, which have been defined as offences committed by individuals or organized groups.

For several years, after a significant decline in the number of offences recorded in years 2004–2008, a relatively stable level of crime can be observed in Poland, as well as a slight fall in the common crime rate (table 2). Moreover, the improvement of the detection rate has been noted. This situation is reflected in the lesser sense of threat from crime among Poles (fig. 13).

The continuation of this trend will depend on effective cooperation between individual entities responsible for combating crime and the population, as well as on the active implementation of preventative measures – particularly the measures aimed at minors – by, *inter alia,* non-governmental organizations. Education for security, including the sensitization to the significance of reporting offences, is of key importance. The "dark number of offences" is still relatively high, because not all offences are reported and, thus, recorded. Crime prevention activities must be correlated with programmes of support for victims and their relatives.

Appendix to the Decision No. 2/MON of the Minister of National Defence of 4 January 2013 on the Implementation of the "Instruction on Organization of HEAD Flights in Aviation of the Polish Armed Forces"

Par. 21 sect. 2. The organizer of a given flight, when preparing a list of passengers, shall apply the following principles and limitations:

1) the following persons must not travel aboard the same aircraft at the same time:
   a) the President of the Republic of Poland and the Marshal of the Sejm of the Republic of Poland;
   b) the President of the Republic of Poland and the Prime Minister;
   c) the Prime Minister and the first Deputy Prime Minister;
2) no more than half of the following can stay aboard the same aircraft during the same flight:
   a) members of: the Council of Ministers, the National Security Council, the Special Services Board;
   b) military commanders;

---

[2] Decision No. 19/MON quoted above was later replaced with decision No. 2/MON of 4 January 2013.

Table 2. Proceedings initiated, criminal offences established, and crime detection rate in years 2000-2012.

Year	Proceedings initiated	Offences ascertained – in total	Number of suspects	Detection rate (per cent)
2012	950 860	1 119 803	500 539	67.8
2011	981 480	1 159 554	521 942	68.7
2010	964 614	1 138,523	516 152	67.9
2009	994 959	1 129,577	521 699	67.1
2008	968 620	1 082,057	516 626	65.9
2007	1 014 695	1 152,993	540 604	64.6
2006	1 156 031	1 287 918	587 959	62.4
2005	1 235 239	1 379 962	594 088	58.6
2004	1 296 356	1 461 217	578 059	56.2
2003	1 248 082	1 466 643	557 224	55.2
2002	1 277 420	1 404 229	552 301	54.9
2001	1 275 418	1 390 089	533 943	53.8
2000	1 169 185	1 266 910	405 275	47.8

Source: The General Police Headquarters.

Figure 13. Degree of personal perception of being under threat from criminal activity

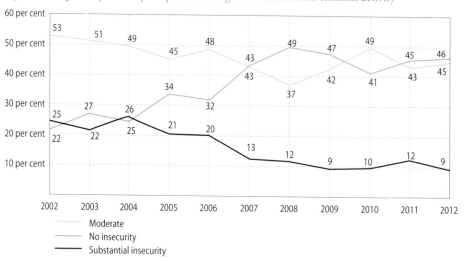

Source: CBOS, survey report BS/62/2012, „Opinions on security and the threat of crime".

Cyber-crime prevention. The development of the so-called information society as well as new and emerging technologies in data communication systems bring not only obvious benefits but also threats both to security of the systems themselves and to information processed or sent using these systems.

The real scale of cyber-crime is difficult to measure. The attempts made in this regard focus on material losses sustained during a short period. The offenders, however, usually work for a longer pe-

riod of time, and their actions also cause substantial intangible damage. The Polish procedures and regulations pertaining to the exchange of information on practices and tactics employed by such offenders are not perfect. Consequently, it is difficult to develop uniform methods aimed at detection, monitoring and prevention of such offences in cyberspace and, therefore, to adequately prepare the law enforcement agencies. Due to the fact that information technologies quickly become obsolete, that means earmarked on ensuring proper security of IT and data communication systems are constantly growing.

At present, the protection of cyberspace is one of the key strategic tasks in the field of security in practically every country. With the rapid development of technology observed in recent years, in particular of telecommunication technologies, as well as a very rapid computerization of virtually every sphere of life, information becomes the most valuable asset. It is a key to success not only in politics and business, but also in planning and carrying out military operations. What is also important is the fact that the proper flow and availability of information is a condition for ensuring efficient economy, administration, and specialist services in any state.

In order to meet challenges connected with the development and wide application of data communication networks, a Ministry of Administration and Digitization (*Ministerstwo Administracji i Cyfryzacji*, MAC) was established on 21 November 2011. The new ministry assumed full responsibility for the computerization and communication areas. It is responsible for the computerization of public administration and its data communication networks, information techniques and technologies, IT standards, the support for IT investments, the application of IT technologies in information society; the development of information society, a well as the fulfilment of Poland's international commitments concerning computerization, mail, and data telecommunication.

It must be stressed that modern data communication systems and in particular the systems which are part of the so-called critical infrastructure and are of key importance for the state's security should be most reliable. These systems must also ensure a high level of integrity and confidentiality of information processed and sent through them. This is all the more important as systems and information they store are liable to become a target of attacks by e.g. foreign secret services or even private users, as evidenced by WikiLeaks and hacker attacks in response to Poland's signing of the international ACTA agreement.

The responsibility for appropriate response in the case of attacks on data communication systems lies with the Governmental Computer Security Incident Response Team CERT.GOV.PL, which functions within the ABW.

Technically, the creation of an absolutely secure data communication system is practically impossible. The effectiveness of even best designed and most costly security systems depends mostly on their users as well as on their awareness, training, and knowledge of the regulations.

Another serious problem faced by institutions tasked with ensuring data communication security are difficulties in finding specialists, in particular IT engineers knowledgeable about data communication security issues. They belong to a group of professionals who are very much in demand. What negatively impacts the security of telecommunication systems is also the lack of sufficient skills and awareness of threats to the information processed, both at the level of users and of administrators or organisers of data communication systems.

Yet another problem may arise from the dispersion of responsibility for data communication safety and improper flow of information between entities obliged to tackle with problems. Lack of

a stable coordination system as well as of procedures for collaboration and exchange of information hampers or even sometimes makes impossible effective response to attacks on data communication systems and services they offer.

The acts on extraordinary measures which were amended in 2011, including the Act on Martial Law and the Competences of the Commander-in-Chief of the Armed Forces and the Rules of His Subordination to the Constitutional Authorities, were an important contribution to ensuring cyber security. For the first time in the Polish system the aforesaid acts referred to events in cyberspace as premises for taking extraordinary measures.

The solutions adopted in these acts translate into the system of functioning of the authorities responsible for the entire sphere of national security and its individual segments. They also provide a legal basis for activities which allow for planning, preparing, and implementing specific projects that are necessary to eliminate threats occurring in cyber space. The contents of these acts neither change the rules and procedures for taking extraordinary measures nor do they provide for additional curtailing of rights and freedoms of citizens. They rather allow the constitutionally authorized entities to take into consideration additional circumstances resulting from the rapidly growing use of cyberspace in public activity when making decisions, if any, on taking the aforesaid measures. The acts do not constitute a full system of cyber security, because they contain only certain elements necessary in the state's response to situations which may potentially require taking the specific extraordinary measures. The aforementioned solutions, however, are suitable for the policy on protection of cyberspace of the Republic of Poland, which is currently under development, at the same time opening the way for further legislative initiatives.

> **Act of 29 August 2002 on Martial Law and on the Competences of the Commander-in-Chief of the Armed Forces and the Rules for his Subordination to the Constitutional Authorities**
>
> **Article 2 para 1b.** Cyberspace (...) shall be understood as the space for processing and exchange of information, made up of data communication systems specified in Article 3 para 3 of the Act of 17 February 2005 on the Computerization of the Activities of Entities Performing Public Tasks (Journal of Laws No. 64, item 565, as amended), including their mutual connections and relations with users.

Combating terrorism. The global reach and scale of the phenomenon of terrorism pose a serious challenge for the majority of international and national authorities. National and international authorities responsible for the analysis and exchange of information on terrorist threats are still being shaped both in terms of responsibilities and the manners of operation. This concerns the strategic and operational levels in particular.

Poland has at its disposal the necessary forces and resources (services and institutions) to combat terrorism; nonetheless these forces and resources are scattered. The imprecise definition of obligations and responsibilities of specific entities within the security system that are responsible for combating terrorism as well as the insufficient coordination of activities are a major impediment to cooperation and collaboration at national and international level. An example of this situation is the National Crisis Management Plan (adopted by the Council of Ministers on 6 March 2012). In accordance with this document, there are four stages of activities performed by services in the field of crisis management – including a crisis arising from a terrorist threat: prevention, preparation, response, and recovery. The responsibility for each type of these activities lies with different services (fig. 14).

Figure 14. Tasks and obligations of participants in the event of a crisis situation – terrorist threats

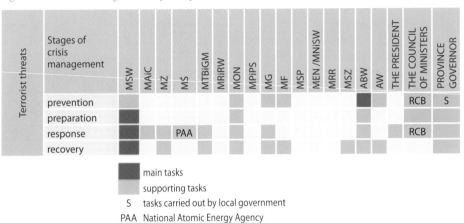

Terrorist threats	Stages of crisis management	MSW	MAiC	MZ	MŚ	MTBiGM	MRiRW	MON	MPiPS	MG	MF	MSP	MEN /MNiSW	MRR	MSZ	ABW	AW	THE PRESIDENT	THE COUNCIL OF MINISTERS	PROVINCE GOVERNOR
	prevention																		RCB	S
	preparation																			
	response			PAA															RCB	
	recovery																			

■ main tasks
■ supporting tasks
S tasks carried out by local government
PAA National Atomic Energy Agency

Source: The National Crisis Management Plan adopted by the Council of Ministers on 6 March 2012.

The problem of the lack of coordination was alleviated to a certain extent by the establishment of the Inter-ministerial Team for Terrorist Threats, which functions as an auxiliary body of the Council of Ministers. The Team provides for cooperation of the governmental administration in the area of detecting, preventing, and responding to terrorist threats.

The Anti-Terrorist Centre (*Centrum Antyterrorystyczne*, CAT), a unit of the Internal Security Agency, plays one of the central roles in the Polish anti-terrorist system. It performs coordination and analytical functions, supporting the process of the exchange of information between various participants of the anti-terrorist system and enabling the joint implementation of response procedures in event of a threat.

Preventing and combating the financing of terrorist activity is a crucial task which, in Poland, is carried out by such financial bodies as the General Inspector of Financial Information and the Customs Service. Another important actor in the anti-terrorist security system is the Governmental Security Centre.

As regards the sphere of regulations concerning terrorist activity, the Polish law – apart from international and European law – is based on acts stipulating responsibilities of specific services involved in combating terrorist threats, the provisions of the Penal Code which define a terrorist offence (Article 115 para. 20), as well as on provisions of acts on money laundering and financing of terrorism.

Penal Code

Article 115 para. 20. A terrorist offence is a prohibited act subject to penalty of imprisonment of up to at least 5 years, committed with the purpose of:

1) Serious intimidation of a large number of persons;

2) Compelling the public authorities of the Republic of Poland or of another State, or a body of an international organization, either to perform or abstain from performing any act;

3) Causing serious disorder in the system of government or the economy of the Republic of Poland, another State or international organization – as well as a threat to commit such an act.

Rescue and civil protection services. The ***State Fire Service*** (*Państwowa Straż Pożarna*, PSP), a professional formation set up to fight fires, natural disasters and other local threats, plays the leading role among rescue and civil protection services. Within the rescue and civil protection subsystem, the PSP is supported by other services, guards, and state institutions as well as a network of non-governmental organizations. The PSP's scope of duties has been significantly expanded since its establishment. It is no longer limited to fighting fires, as it used to be in the beginning, but covers also the organization and execution of rescue mission in crisis situations, including disasters and traffic, construction, or chemical accidents. Moreover, the formation oversees compliance with fire regulations, carries out the scientific and research work in the field of fire protection and civil protection, as well as cooperates with the head of the National Criminal Information Centre. Nearly 30 thousand officers serve in the State Fire Service. The head of the formation is the Chief Commandant of the National Fire Service, who is subordinate to the minister of the interior.

In practice, the PSP often coordinates rescue operations at the site of a disaster, including the work of policemen and ambulance service. In recent years, the fire service underwent technical modernization. Both its vehicles and rescue and fire-fighting equipment have been systematically replaced with new ones. Moreover, the PSP procedures have been revised and adjusted to meet new challenges. The PSP works particularly closely with the voluntary fire service (*Ochotnicza Straż Pożarna*, OSP), which counts nearly 17 thousand units with ca. 500 thousand active volunteer fire fighters (of which 3815 voluntary fire fighting units with 126 thousand fire-fighters are a part of the National Fire Fighting and Rescue System (*Krajowy System Ratowniczo-Gaśniczy*, KSRG)).

The responsibility for building the National Fire Fighting and Rescue System lies with the Chief Commandant. The objective of this task was to create an integrated system which would bring together various interrelated rescue units and enable carrying out operations in the field of rescue and civil protection. At present, the KSRG is an integral part of the state's internal security system and covers operations aimed at protecting life, health, property, or environment against fires, natural disasters and other local dangers.

Photos: Archives of Polish
Medical Air Rescue

It should be pointed out in this context that insufficient cooperation of the rescue and civil protection services with the population poses a problem. On the one hand, it concerns the evolution of methods applied previously to inform the population about dangers. On the other hand, however, certain shortcomings associated with the establishing of emergency call centres need to be addressed. The centres do not serve the population of the entire country in a proper and uniform manner, and people calling 112 do not always receive adequate assistance. Nonetheless, the previous emergency telephone numbers are still valid and active.

An important element of operations in the field of rescue and civil protection is the functioning of the civil protection system in time of war (civil defence).

Under the current state of the law, the Chief of the National Civil Defence, as the central government administration authority for civil defence matters, is responsible for the implementation of tasks involving the preparation of draft objectives and principles of civil defence operations, determination of general rules of performing civil defence tasks, as well as coordination of specific projects and control over the performance of civil defence tasks by government administration and local government authorities. According to the law, the Chief of the National Civil Defence may issue dispositions, guidelines, instructions and regulations on matters within his competence.

Other challenges in the context of efficiency of civil defence include the lack of definition of tasks in this field (which is required by a ratified international convention[3]) as well as the issue of release of the OSP members (this issue is referred to in the Council of Ministers regulation of 21 September 2004 on releasing from the obligation to do active military duty in case of mobilization or during war – Journal of Laws of 2004 No. 210, item 2136) from the obligation to do military duty in the event of resuming of conscription under imminent threat to the state's security (or militarization of the entire KSRG).

Elements of the crisis management system. The issue of crisis management deserves special attention when discussing the national security potential. In the Polish model, a crisis situation refers only to non-military threats, although crisis management takes place both in emergency and in wartime.

In Poland, the responsibility for crisis management at the central level lies with the Council of Ministers, which is supported in this task by the Government Crisis Management Team (its composition is shown in fig. 15). In accordance with the law, in special situations, the said tasks can be carried out by the minister competent for the interior, although replacing this position with the minister for public administration should be considered.

At the province level, crisis management is in the hands of province governors, who use the province crisis management teams and centres. At the local government level, crisis management is the responsibility of: in districts – of district governors; in communes – of heads of communes, town mayors and presidents. Again, support in this field is provided by relevant crisis management teams and centres.

---

[3] Additional Protocol to the Geneva Conventions of 12 August 1949 relating to the Protection of Victims of International Armed Conflicts (Protocol I), drawn up in Geneva on 8 June 1977 (Journal of Laws of 1992 No. 41, item 175) and adopted by the Republic of Poland on 19 September 1991.

Figure 15. The composition of the Government Crisis Management Team

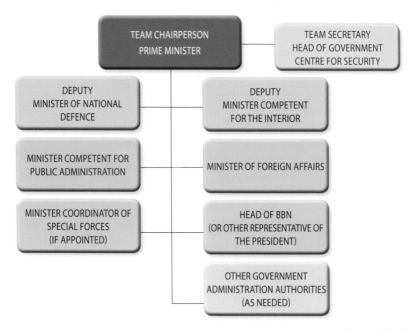

Source: authors' own compilation.

Border services. After Poland's entry to the EU and the Schengen area, the Polish subsystem of state border protection was revised, thereby becoming an element of the joint European strategy for EU protection of external borders and migration control. Consequently, the subsystem affects the security of the Republic of Poland as well as of the other EU member states in the fields of freedom, security, and justice. The lack of control of the internal EU/Schengen border means that it is necessary to enhance controls on the Union's external border as well as to intensify actions taken within the country, *inter alia*, through closer cooperation, exchange of information, and collaboration between services in Poland and in other EU member states (fig. 16).

The state border protection model adopted in Poland is the result of external and internal environment and international commitments. The responsibility for protection of the state's land and sea borders as well as for border traffic control lies with the minister competent for the interior, who performs these tasks with the assistance of the Chief Commander of the Border Guard. The protection of the air space borders is the responsibility of the minister of national defence.

The **Border Guard** (*Straż Graniczna*, SG), a uniform, uniformed and armed formation, plays the leading role in the state border protection subsystem. It is a specialized administrative unit subordinate to the Ministry of the Interior, with 15 thousand officers and 4 thousand civilian employees. The SG performs tasks associated with the protection of state borders and control of border traffic. Moreover, it is responsible for issuing of permits for crossing of the state border, including visas, as well as for preventing of transport of dangerous substances without a required permit. The Border Guard's responsibilities also include the identification, prevention and detection of offences and

Figure 16. The Schengen system countries in the EU

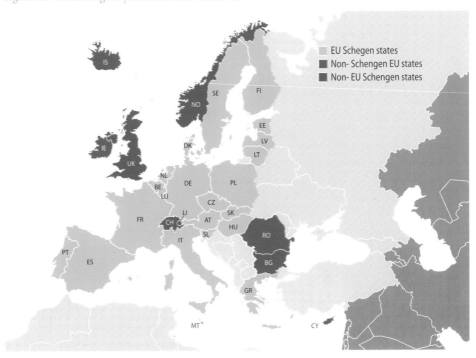

EU Schegen states
Non- Schengen EU states
Non- EU Schengen states

Source: the European Commission.

Photos: Border Guard

misdemeanours concerning illegal crossing of state borders, as well as the control of legality of doing work and conducting business activity by foreigners or of allowing foreigners to have work.

Apart from its standard equipment the Border Guard has at its disposal the following equipment: aircraft for patrolling of land and sea areas, vessels, as well as land and mobile infrared and night-vision observation systems.

Customs Service. The other component in the broadly understood subsystem of state border protection is the Customs Service, which is subordinate to the minister of finance. The Customs Service is a uniform and uniformed formation tasked with ensuring protection and security of the EU customs territory, including compliance with the law on import and export of goods. In addition, it performs duties specified in separate regulations, in particular on excise tax and gambling tax. The Customs Service is also involved in fighting the smuggling and illegal production of cigarettes and tobacco products, gambling, infringement of intellectual property, and cyber crime. There are nearly 15 thousand officers employed in the Customs Service.

The comparison of duties and powers reveals that certain tasks of individual institutions overlap. For instance, the Border Guard and the Customs Service have duplicative powers as regards fighting fiscal offences and misdemeanours as well as preventing movement of excise goods, dangerous substances, radioactive materials, weapons, etc. across the state borders.

The transfer of responsibility for the state border protection in the event of armed aggression against the Republic of Poland is another issue that needs to be regulated. Today, there are no legal regulations which would determine the point at which the state borders cease to be protected by the Border Guard and its role is taken over by the Polish Armed Forces. The manner in which the responsibility for the state border protection would be transferred to the Armed Forces is not regulated either.

Photos: Customs Service

Poland's accession to the European Union and the integration of the legal framework for foreigners led to the establishing of the **Office for Foreigners** (*Urząd do Spraw Cudzoziemców*), which replaced the previous Office for Repatriation and Foreigners. The Head of the Office for Foreigners is the central authority of governmental administration competent with respect to entry of foreigners in the territory of the Republic of Poland, their transit through the territory, residence in the territory, and leaving of the territory, as well as granting to foreigners the refugee status, asylum, permit for tolerated stay, and temporary protection (excluding matters reserved for other authorities). The activities of the Head of the Office for Foreigners are supervised by the minister of the interior.

Important actors in the Polish immigration policy – especially in terms of collaboration in controlling the legality of stay and employment – are province governors. They conduct various proceedings relating to foreigners, concerning, *inter alia,* the issues of residence, i.e. issuing of decisions on granting (or cancelling) a permit to stay for a definite period of time (temporary residence up to 2 years), a permit to settle (unlimited residence), a permit to stay as a long-term resident of the EU (unlimited residence), extending, upon a foreigner's application, of a national visa and Schengen visa in urgent and exceptional circumstances, such as for humanitarian reasons.

Subsystem of secret information protection. The Act on Protection of Secret Information adopted on 5 August 2010 (which repealed the previous act of 1999) led to the creation of a uniform, comprehensive, and effective system of protection of information both at national and international level. What is important, the act has ensured both the simplicity and flexibility of functioning of the entire classified information security system.

At present, the protection specified by the provisions of the act covers only such information, the disclosure of which would be detrimental to the interests of the Polish state. The remaining information resources, which are also important from the point of view of the state's interests and concern such spheres as economy, social and economic relations, and security of citizens, are regulated by other acts.

The protection of personal data of Polish citizens is ensured by the Act on Personal Data Protection of 29 August 1997. The act is implemented by authorized bodies, institutions, organizational units, entities or persons who take decisions on the purposes of processing information and the means used to this end. The implementation of the act is overseen by the Inspector General for the Protection of Personal Data.

The state's information security becomes a new area of the comprehensive national security system. It introduces the standards regarding data and information protection as well as on the selection of measures and technical parameters for processing of information and data depending on the required level of confidentiality. This also concerns the security of information processed in the strategic sectors, such as industry, banking, telecommunications, energy industry, and health care.

Other protection subsystems. In Poland, there numerous institutions directly or indirectly tasked with protecting public security. Regrettably, these institutions do not form a fully structured system. Three types of these institutions, however, can be identified, depending on their hierarchical position, organizational structure and scope of tasks, namely: ***central institutions, local government institutions, and private institutions***.

The ***central*** institutions include, *inter alia,* the following ones :
- The Road Transport Inspection (*Inspekcja Transportu Drogowego*). It has been established to control the compliance with regulations on road transport and on the transport of passengers and goods; its activities are aimed at eliminating any negative phenomena in road transport;

- The State Sanitary and Epidemiological Inspection (*Państwowa Inspekcja Sanitarno-Epidemiologiczna*), the Veterinary Inspection (*Inspekcja Weterynaryjna*), and the Agricultural and Food Quality Inspection (*Inspekcja Jakości Handlowej Artykułów Rolno-Spożywczych*) perform tasks in the field of civil protection. They are supervised by ministers competent for health or agriculture. In addition, the first two of them implement tasks for the subsystem of state border protection;
- The Office of Competition and Consumer Protection (*Urząd Ochrony Konkurencji i Konsumentów*) and its subordinate State Trade Inspection (*Państwowa Inspekcja Handlowa*) pursue activities aimed at improving the well-being of consumers by creating adequate conditions for competition and its protection;
- The General Inspector of Building Control (*Główny Inspektor Nadzoru Budowlanego*) carries out activities in the field of construction safety, including: fire safety, evacuation routes, and users' safety. These activities overlap to a certain extent with tasks implemented by other security institutions (e.g. PSP), sometimes at the expense of operational activities;
- meteorological and hydrological services, tasked with warning about potential natural disasters;
- control services at the disposal of specific ministries and province governors, as well as security services established at certain research or production facilities which are key for national security;
- The Railroad Guard (*Straż Ochrony Kolei*) – a uniformed, equipped with direct coercion means and partially armed protection formation at the disposal of the Polish State Railways (PKP, *Polskie Koleje Państwowe*), a commercialized company owned by the State Treasury. Similar tasks are performed by company guards in certain production enterprises.

Public security institutions, subordinate to or supervised by local government, include municipal (city) guards and voluntary fire brigades.

Municipal (city) guards are a uniformed formation, equipped with means of direct coercion, and serve as a tool of commune governments in maintaining public order. Municipal guards are optionally established by the commune decision-making bodies. The commune councils decide, *inter alia,* about the organization status of the guards, their structure, and number of posts. The decision to establish or dissolve the guards requires consultation with the Police and notifying the province governor.

Responsibilities of the municipal guards include in particular: preserving peace and order in public places, controlling road traffic, co-operating with entities responsible for saving life and health of citizens, helping to remove technical breakdowns and consequences of natural disasters and other local threats. Relevant legal standards impose on the municipal guards and on the Police the obligation to cooperate and coordinate activities in the area of local security and in particular regarding preventative actions. This involves, *inter alia,* the exchange of information, joint control, and joint trainings.

Municipal guards are equipped with means of direct coercion, including handcuffs, batons, pepper spray, and electroshock weapons. In order to restore order, the guards may apply these means as well as other technical means, impose fines, and detain persons who disturb order to hand them over to the Police. In cases of misdemeanours, they have also the trial rights.

Voluntary fire brigades within the rescue and fire fighting system traditionally carry out fire fighting and prevention activities. Their functions, however, have evolved in recent years. The brigades have become more commonly involved in other types of rescue operations, including primarily technical or road incidents, where various rescue methods and measures are applied. Quite often voluntary fire fighters are the first to appear at the site of an accident and take measures to save people's life, health, and property. Voluntary fire brigades also play an important role by participating in educational and charity events of local communities.

Private protection institutions are commercial entities which ensure security of individuals and property (Specialized Armed Security Formations (*specjalistyczne uzbrojone formacje ochrony*, SUFO); Internal Security Service (*Wewnętrzna Służba Ochrony*, WSO) security companies protecting people and property). The development of the private sector of people and property protection services in Poland dates back to the early 1990s. The first permits for conducting this type of business activity were issued on the basis of regulations on business activity. In 1998, however, the Act on Protection of People and Property was introduced into the Polish legal system, which comprehensively regulated the activities of private security institutions.

The private security sector in Poland offers a wide range of services: physical protection of facilities and sites; escorting money and valuable assets; personal, physical protection of people, as well as protection during sports and artistic events. The protection of people and property is provided also in the form of technical protection. It is estimated that in Poland there are approximately 110-150 thousand security officers.

* * *

The protection potential is now confronted with a number of difficult challenges, which result from the high crime rate (although slightly declining), including organized crime, the threat of terrorism, including cyberterrorism, as well as a higher rate of illegal immigration. In addition, there are certain shortcomings in the rescue system, as the coordination of activities of central and local administration is insufficient. Another noticeable problem is the lack of funds for preventive activities and weaknesses of the warning system. Moreover, the excessive number of services and dispersed supervision complicate the coordination and weaken the effectiveness of the protective potential. These weaknesses substantially limit the possible level of ambitions in defining national interests and strategic objectives in the field of security.

The societal security potential

The societal potential of security is conditioned by national identity and cultural heritage. It is also predicated on social safety, the demographic potential, as well as the intellectual, scientific, and technological potential. Important factors in the development of the societal security potential include education, training, R&D in the field of security, health service, or media.

National identity and cultural heritage. Every nation develops and cultivates values and the memory of its history, which distinguish it from other nations and constitute a foundation of a belief in its distinctiveness, on the one hand, and of the sense of belonging to a given community which shares the same historical awareness and experience, on the other hand. This is called national identity and its determinants are national heritage (national culture) and the belief in the necessity of its commemoration and of passing it on to future generations.

The national identity of the Polish nation has been shaped over centuries on the basis of such elements as: language, historical tradition, religion, customs, literature, culture, art, and national symbols, including in particular the coat of arms, national colours, and the national anthem. Depending on the times and the social and political situation, this was an open phenomenon, to a lesser or greater extent susceptible to external cultural influences and substantially affected by cultural patterns from Western Europe (and, to a certain extent, from the East), including the common tradition of philosophy, culture, science and law. This is also from where the main philosophical trends, art styles, upbringing and education models, or even economic models and legal and political systems were received and adapted. At the same time the process was often accompanied by the cultivation of cultural distinctiveness and national identity. This was particularly evident in the times of enslavement, wars, and partitions.

The historical tradition connected with struggles for independence, including the commemoration of the glory of the Polish Army (e.g. the 1410 battle of Grunwald, the Napoleonic Wars and insurrections) as well as the care for the sites of national remembrance, in particular of military and insurgents' cemeteries, have also played an important role in the development of Poles' national identity.

Social safety. Social safety is one of the fundamental values and citizen's rights. Measures taken by the state to eliminate or reduce the uncertainties and threats associated with a life situation are an important tool used to maintain the social order. The state's policy includes its commitments to citizens who are in difficult or exceptional situations, guaranteeing aid and securing minimum benefits.

The changes which took place in Poland after 1989 led to a deep stratification of the society. The number of people with the lowest income grew dramatically, as did the number of persons permanently unemployed. One of the consequences of this fact was the expansion of the group of people suffering from poverty. In the long-term perspective, these persons having low income, no job, housing, access to culture, health care, and not rarely, to education, have their chances for changing their situation wrecked and get marginalized. This situation brings serious social consequences, such as higher crime rates or pathological phenomena e.g. drug abuse, alcoholism and prostitution. It should be noted that the process of poverty alleviation is extremely difficult, and children born and brought up in such an environment usually remain in there.

As a result of the current financial crisis, the number of people who cannot cope with the difficult economic situation has grown additionally. This phenomenon is associated not only with events on financial markets, but also with the insufficient engagement of the state in providing social support for those most in need. Higher unemployment and the increasing number of people who are poor, excluded or at risk of social exclusion automatically result in growing expectations towards the state. The situation also gives rise to extreme views and positions as well as leads to greater susceptibility of the crisis-stricken population to populist propaganda. This may stir social unrest and weaken internal security of the state.

Recent years have also witnessed a change in the family structure, which is reflected in the decreasing number of marriages, the growing divorce rate, and the declining birth rate. In this context, young people who face decisions about starting a family and having children require special assistance from the state. At present, there are an insufficient number of nurseries and kindergartens, and prospects in the labour market after having a child are unsatisfactory. The deteriorating value of family may lead to weakening of interpersonal bonds and, as a further consequence, of social bonds.

Demographic potential. Demography is a component of national security, which determines Poland's position in the European balance of power. In recent years the European countries, including Poland, have witnessed adverse demographic changes.

At the end of 2011, Poland's population was 38 million 482 thousand, which ranked Poland in the 8th place in Europe and the 6th place in the European Union. It was the second year since 1997, in which the population growth was recorded. Despite the natural increase in the number of population, the birth rate remains low – it was 1.3 in 2011. This causes a number of social and economic problems: further deformation of the age structure of the population and acceleration of depopulation processes as well as the ageing of society (fig. 17).

Figure 17. Population by gender and age for year 2011 (in thousands, as of 31 December 2011).

Source: Demographic Yearbook 2012, Central Statistical Office.

The number of births is not sufficient to stop the ageing of society (fig. 18). In 2008, the number of elderly people, aged over 65, grew again[4]. In 2011, these persons accounted for 13.8 per cent of the entire population, i.e. 5.3 million. The eldest group (aged over 80) accounts for 3.6 per cent of population.

Figure 18. Number of births in Poland in 2011 (as of 31 December 2011) and in previous years

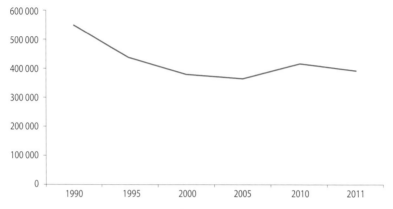

Source: authors' own compilation based on data from the Central Statistical Office.

Societal capital. The essential components of the societal security capital include: the shape of the social and demographic structure, existing inequalities and social conflicts, and the activity of civil society. Another important factor is the population's awareness of national security issues.

The societal capital refers to the potential accumulated in the society in the form of standards of conduct, trust, and commitment. An active society, possessing high qualifications and competences, adequately prepared for contemporary security threats and challenges, is a condition *sine qua non* for ensuring the social and economic development, including the development of the civil society and further improvement of the quality of life and security of citizens.

Assessing the standards of conduct is an extremely complex process. The key factors which determine the development potential of Poles and of Poland include: cooperation, independent thinking, subjectivity and integrity. Other factors are: trust and entrepreneurship, and lastly, leadership and energy. The level of trust is additionally correlated with the competitiveness of the economy.

National security in the public opinion[5]. Nearly three-quarters of respondents (72 per cent) consider Poland a safe country to live in (fig. 19). Less than one-fourth of respondents have the opposite views (24 per cent). The opinions on this issue are the most positive in the entire period of the Third Republic (fig. 20).

---

[4] The age of 65 years (the same for females and males) is used as the so-called elderly threshold in documents prepared by the UN.

[5] This section has been prepared on the basis of the report of the CBOS entitled: Assessment of the State of National Security. The Report from the Survey Conducted by the CBOS at Request of the National Security Bureau, January 2012. The survey was conducted on 1–8 December 2011 on a representative random sample of 950 Polish citizens by direct interviewing of respondents at their homes.

Figure 19. Answer to the question: Do you think that Poland is a safe country to live in?

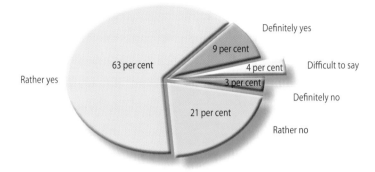

Source: *Assessment of the State of National Security ..., op.cit.*

Figure 20. Answer to the question: Do you think that Poland is a safe country to live in? (years 1987-2011)

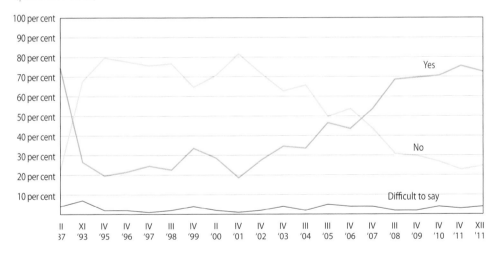

Source: *Assessment of the State of National Security ..., op.cit.*

The conviction that Poland is a safe country to live in is predominant in all social and demographic groups. It is less common, however, among people with lower financial status. At this point it is worth noting that the question whether Poland is a safe country to live in may rather make the respondents think of "daily" threats (such as crime) rather than in terms of "global" national security. Nevertheless, this does describe an important psychosocial context of national security.

The public awareness surveys show that there is a relatively high sense of security among Poles and generally a low level of anxiety about a loss of sovereignty and independence. The dangers experienced in recent years, such as the economic crisis, social unrest, and crime, are perceived as the most real. The hierarchy of threats in terms of their perceived reality is shown in table 3.

Table 3. Answer to the question: What, and to what extent, may currently and in the near feature constitute a real threat to the security of the Republic of Poland?

What, and to what extent, may currently and in the near feature constitute a real threat to the security of the Republic of Poland?	Average on the scale from 0 to 10
Serious financial and economic crisis in Europe, in the world	6.43
Growing poverty, poor living conditions	6.41
Social unrest and protests associated with the need to cut state spending and reforms introduced by the government	5.87
Crime increase in Poland	5.40
Sensitive data being stolen from computers of state institutions	5.05
Development of organized crime and mafia activity	5.03
Development of political organizations with extreme views	4.92
Threats to the state's energy security – fuel and energy supply shortages	4.67
Serious conflicts among various social groups in Poland	4.52
Environmental disaster, dangerous environmental changes	3.76
Terrorist attack in Poland	3.50
The spread of an infectious disease, epidemic	3.49
Fall of the government in Poland, political chaos	3.25
War in Europe	2.49
Military attack on the territory of Poland	2.02
Nuclear attack on the territory of Poland	1.67
Poland's losing its sovereignty or independence	1.47
Disconnection of a part of Poland's territori	1.27

Source: Assessment of the State of National Security... op.cit.

According to Poles, the most real threats are the ones they are familiar with. This is therefore, in some sense, a picture of "fears tamed". The social and economic threats are more real than the one associated with disasters and military operations. Also the threats resulting from unintended events are considered more real than the ones being a consequence of intentional actions. It is a paradox that, despite the generally positive assessment of the institutions responsible for the state's security, the level of the state's preparedness to face terrorist, military, or environmental threats or natural disasters is perceived as low. Apparently, Poles assess these institutions more in terms of trust/sympathy that in terms of efficiency (we like the army, which does not mean that we trust it will defend us).

In the opinion of the public, the state's security depends largely on the activity of numerous institutions, primarily national and international ones (table 4). Interestingly, the majority of respondents did not say about any of the institutions mentioned that their activity has a major impact on the state's security.

Table 4. Hierarchy of perceived impact on security.

EU	68
NATO	67
State authorities	66
Military	63
European and world leaders	62
Worldwide financial and economic organizations	59
The Police	58
Secret services	56
Fire service	32
The media	31
All citizens	11
Local government authorities	-1
Entrepreneurs	-32

Note: the above are net indicators being the difference between the following proportions:
(major impact + high impact) – (minor impact + no impact)

Source: authors' own compilation based on the "Assessment of the State of National Security..." op.cit.

Worth noting is a relatively high position of the media, as well as the comparison to previous results concerning the probability of specific threats. These threats were mostly of economic and social nature, and those who may be important from the point of view of such threats have, in the respondents' opinion, the least impact on them (citizens, local governments and entrepreneurs).

In the eyes of the public, all important institutions which are significant from the point of view of Poland's security perform their role well. From among these institutions, the activity of the fire service is assessed most positively (82 per cent of positive opinions). Approximately three-quarters of Poles are satisfied with the activity of the army (77 per cent) and the Police (74 per cent). Similarly, three-quarters of those surveyed believe that NATO serves well the security of Poland.

More than two thirds of respondents (69 per cent) are of the opinion that Polish authorities perform their role well in ensuring security of Poland. The same proportion of people (68 per cent) appreciate the importance of Poland's membership in the European Union for the security of the state. The majority of respondents (61 per cent) are satisfied with the activity of the secret servicess. More than the half surveyed (58 per cent) assess positively the role of local government authorities.

The most obvious relationship for respondents exists between security and having a modern army and being a member of military alliances. The vast majority of people (80 per cent) also recognize the importance of the economic development level for security of the state.

In the opinion of respondents, all that can be called a high level of the societal potential serves the strengthening of security (fig. 21): citizens' trust in authorities (72 per cent), authorities' trust in citizens (69 per cent), and the existence of the strong civil society (66 per cent). The majority surveyed

(59 per cent) also believe that the existence of a democratic system in the country strengthens the security (as apparently – in the opinion of the public – democratic countries are less likely to engage in armed conflicts than the non-democratic ones).

Most respondents (75 per cent) think that the occurrence of strong social conflicts may contribute to the weakening of national security. The largest proportion of respondents (43 per cent) deems the existence of a multicultural and ethnically diverse society to be a factor rather negatively affecting the level of security.

Figure 21. Answer to the question: In your opinion, what does the security of the country depend on? Please state the significance for state security of each of the issues mentioned.

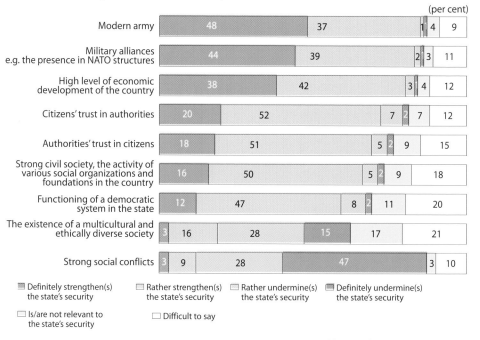

(per cent)

	Definitely strengthen(s) the state's security	Rather strengthen(s) the state's security	Rather undermine(s) the state's security	Definitely undermine(s) the state's security	Is/are not relevant to the state's security	Difficult to say
Modern army	48	37	1		4	9
Military alliances e.g. the presence in NATO structures	44	39	2	1	3	11
High level of economic development of the country	38	42	3	1	4	12
Citizens' trust in authorities	20	52	7	2	7	12
Authorities' trust in citizens	18	51	5	2	9	15
Strong civil society, the activity of various social organizations and foundations in the country	16	50	5	2	9	18
Functioning of a democratic system in the state	12	47	8	2	11	20
The existence of a multicultural and ethically diverse society	3	16	28	15	17	21
Strong social conflicts	3	9	28	47	3	10

Source: Assessment of the State of National Security..., op.cit.

The majority of factors which affect the state of national security are – in the opinion of respondents – rather strongly or very strongly correlated. The public believe that the military power of the state is connected with the level of its economic development. What is more, the economic power (so indirectly the military power) is, according to the public, related to a specific model of social cohesion which is based on trust and democratic mechanisms for the elaboration of social consensus. One of the elements of this model, which is also connected with the high degree of economic development (and – perhaps – with the low level of social inequality), is low intensity of social conflicts.

The existence of a multicultural, ethnically diverse society is poorly correlated with other factors. The analyses show only a strong relation between functioning of the multicultural society and the perceived high intensity of social conflicts.

The majority of Poles (75 per cent) believe Poland's independence is not threatened at the moment. At the same time, 13 per cent surveyed are convinced that such a danger exists.

The only period since the beginning of Poland's political system changes when most respondents saw a threat to its sovereignty was early 1991; the Soviet Union still existed then. After its collapse, the majority of respondents were no longer concerned much about independence. With time, the proportion of people concerned about the curtailment or loss of sovereignty has gradually been dwindling.

The belief that at present Poland' independence is not threatened prevails among all social and demographic groups (fig. 22). Most of the respondents concerned about Poland's independence are among the religious population – who participate in religious activities every week (31 per cent), as well as among those who claim to have right-wing views (22 per cent). Moreover, people who are not satisfied with their living conditions, pensioners (23 per cent), and unemployed (21 per cent) tend to express their concerns about Poland's independence more frequently.

Figure 22. Answer to the question: In your opinion, are there currently any threats to the independence of the Republic of Poland?

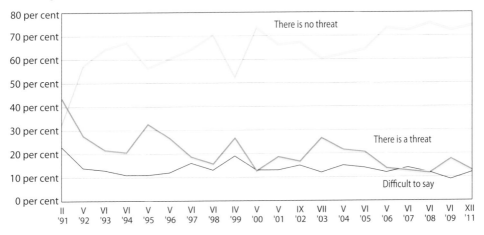

Source: Assessment of the State of National Security....op.cit.

People who saw a danger of Poland losing or having its sovereignty curtailed were further asked what – in their opinion – this threat was. What is it that threatens Poland's independence?

Respondents indicated in their answers both the kinds and possible sources of threats. Generally, the external threats were mentioned more frequently than the internal ones, although in some cases it was difficult to distinguish one from another. Nearly one-fifth surveyed (19 per cent) see a threat to the sovereignty of the state from its neighbours; however – in their opinion – the threat comes mostly from Russia. The problem which was raised more often was the energy dependence on Russia. Just slightly fewer respondents (17 per cent) pointed to the risks associated with membership in the European Union. The concerns stem mainly from federalization of the European Union and the associated processes of the transfer of the state's competence to the Union authorities.

A large portion of comments referred to economic threats: on the one hand, associated with the presence of foreign capital in Poland and associated economic dependence (13 per cent in total) and, on the other hand, with the financial crisis and the excessive debt of the country (9 per cent).

Nearly one in eight people (12 per cent) pointed to military threats, such as an outbreak of war, an international conflict, or a terrorist attack. The danger connected with the potential deployments of the US missiles was also mentioned. Some respondents (8 per cent in total) mentioned threats resulting from the inappropriate – in their opinion – policy of the government or simply pointed to the menace to Poland's political sovereignty or the lack of sovereignty in the government's decision-making.

Various internal threats were also mentioned (7 per cent) such as, *inter alia*, conflicts and tensions among various social groups, immigration, separatist tendencies, the progressing loss of national and cultural identity by Poles, as well as the weakening of traditional values.

Generally, people who saw a threat to Poland's independence and sovereignty most frequently indicated that the threat is of the economic nature and is associated with the dependence on other states as well as on the financial and economic institutions (50 per cent). Nearly one in three people (31 per cent) saw a threat to the state's sovereignty in Poland's political dependence and the lack of autonomy of Polish authorities in decision-making. Poland's military security causes least concern – only one in ten respondents who saw threats to the state's independence considered an attack on Poland's territory a serious possibility. The above is shown in fig. 23.

Despite the positive assessment of the role of institutions in ensuring Poland's security, the prevailing conviction is that the country is not prepared adequately to act in emergency and unforeseen situations (fig. 24) – whether caused by the forces of nature or negligence on the part of people, or planned and organized by forces hostile to Poland. Such situations include e.g. floods, which were experienced by Poles several times in recent years. This is probably the reason for the particularly severe criticism of the state's preparedness to encounter natural disasters (61 per cent of negative answers, and 23 per cent of the positive ones).

Figure 23. Answer to the question: What is the primary nature of the current threats to the independence and sovereignty of the Republic of Poland?

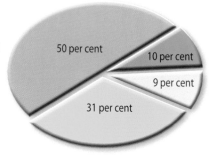

An economic threat, associated with Poland's dependence on other countries and on financial and economic institutions

A military threat, associated with the possibility of an attack on the territory of Poland by another country

Difficult to say

A political threat, associated with dependence and lack of autonomy of Polish authorities in decisions-making

Source: Assessment of the State of National Security…, op.cit.

In recent years Poles have not experienced any of the other situations aforesaid, such as an environmental disaster (on a large scale), a military attack on the territory of Poland, or a terrorist attack, That is why it is all the more difficult for them to fully assess the state's preparedness for any of these situations. Most of respondents, however, are concerned with Poland not being well prepared for such events.

Figure 24. Answer to the question: Is the Republic of Poland sufficienty (or insufficiently) prepared to take action in the event of:

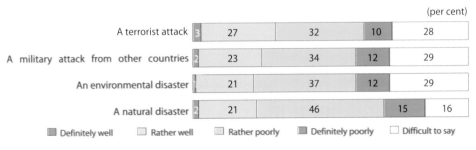

(per cent)

| | Definitely well | Rather well | Rather poorly | Definitely poorly | Difficult to say |

A terrorist attack: 3, 27, 32, 10, 28
A military attack from other countries: 2, 23, 34, 12, 29
An environmental disaster: 1, 21, 37, 12, 29
A natural disaster: 2, 21, 46, 15, 16

Source: Assessment of the State of National Security.... op.cit.

In conclusion, Poles consider themselves to be rather poorly prepared to deal with threats and believe to be relatively less prepared to deal with the unintentional threats than the intentional ones. In the areas in which threats are considered more real there are weak actors. What is also important is the discrepancy observed between the favourable assessment of institutions responsible for security and the weak assessment of their preparedness to face threats. One of the explanations for this may be that the assessment is made considering the trust/sympathy rather than the perceived effectiveness (we value these institutions, which does not mean that they will be effective).

It is important to be prepared to face new social phenomena which are important from the point of view of national security. This concerns above all the new areas of conflicts, their new participants, as well as the new forms of expressing discontent[6]. As far as the forms of discontent are concerned, these may include not only open rebellions but also numerous strategies for "going beyond the system" in the form of refusal to participate, emigration, and escape into the unofficial zones. Even today a greater threat to security results from the lack of civic activity then from some forms of mass, radical and non-civic participation. The new areas of conflict, on the other hand, are the consequence of the evolution from the traditional industrial patterns to the post-industrial era, where the reason is not so much the frustration over the lack of access to material goods but rather the intangible goods which are increasingly critical for social success – such as health, education, culture, and information. The third feature concerns the participants: mainly the groups of professionals. The protesters include university students, school students, patients, doctors, and not just industrial workers. The authorities (the entire state system), however, still seem to be better prepared to face conflicts and threats to the security of the old type.

---

[6] Admittedly, these are not recent phenomena. Their occurrence was already signalled in the study entitled "Threats to Social Stability" prepared for the Economic Advisory Team of the President of the Republic of Poland to the "Memorandum on Economic Threats to Social Life in Poland" drawn up by the team in October 2002.

With the emergence of new social phenomena, the activity of the civil society becomes particularly important. The new threats and conflicts, including these perceived by the public as the most real, are of social and economic nature. The nature of conflicts of the post-industrial era makes the civil society, as it were, a natural actor, important from the point of view of regulating and resolving these conflicts (note that the civil society does not mean only the official organizations of the third sector, but also the local unofficial self-help neighbourhood network; such ties are also created through the Internet network, which is free from any geographical constraints). Incorporating this type of local communities and bonds into the national security system constitutes a challenge for its architects.

Institutions of education for security. In accordance with the present conceptual solutions, the organization and provision of education for security is in the hands of a number of ministries. These include: the Ministry of National Education, the Ministry of Science and Higher Education, the Ministry of National Defence, and the Ministry of the Interior. The educational tasks in the area of security are also performed by the formations subordinate to the Ministry of the Interior (the Police, the State Fire Service, and the Border Guard) as well as to the Ministry of National Defence (the Military Centre for Civil Education, *Wojskowe Centrum Edukacji Obywatelskiej*).

Apart from the central institutions, education for security is also provided in local government centres at the level of province, district, commune, and town, as well as in companies important from the point of view of the security and defence of the state.

Important elements of the system of education for security are public and non-public higher education institutions. Higher education institutions offer the first-, second-, and third-degree courses on national security and internal security. According to the data of the Ministry of Science and Higher Education, there are 83 higher education institutions offering such courses.

As far as the defence education is concerned, the National Defence Academy (*Akademia Obrony Narodowej*) continues to play the major role in this area. Among other things, it offers education in the field of defence to representatives of the central and local government administration in the form of defence courses (*wyższe kursy obronne*).

Other important institutions in the system of education for security include the non-governmental organizations and associations. The organizations which are most engaged in these activities include, *inter alia,* the Polish Scouting and Guiding Association (*Związek Harcerstwa Polskiego*), the Scouting Association of the Republic (*Związek Harcerstwa Rzeczypospolitej*), the Riflemen's Association "Strzelec" (*Związek Strzelecki "Strzelec"*), the Police Sports Association (*Policyjne Towarzystwo Sportowe*), the Association of Military Tradition and Culture (*Stowarzyszenie Kulturalne i Tradycji Wojskowej*), the Association of Soldiers of the National Armed Forces (*Związek Żołnierzy Narodowych Sił Zbrojnych*), the Association of War Invalids (*Związek Inwalidów Wojennych*), veteran associations, the National Defence League (*Liga Obrony Kraju*), and the Polish Red Cross (*Polski Czerwony Krzyż*). The educational activities of organizations specializing in mountain (Mountain Volunteer Search and Rescue, *Górskie Ochotnicze Pogotowie Ratunkowe*, GOPR, and Tatra Volunteer Search and Rescue, *Tatrzańskie Ochotnicze Pogotowie Ratunkowe*, TOPR) and water rescue (WOPR) are worth noting.

When evaluating the education for security in Poland one concludes that it attains an increasingly higher level in lower and upper secondary training. Nevertheless, the present educational processes use various curricula and capabilities. In order for these processes to be effective, the educational activity should be controlled centrally by a single institution. Consequently, this area requires structural and organizational changes.

The effectiveness of the education for security depends largely on the adjustment of its objectives, contents, and organization to the constantly changing needs in the field of structural and personal security, as well as on rational linking of the factor of attractiveness of this education with the proper preparation of the teaching staff and securing the material and financial base.

Moreover, there is no supra-ministerial academic centre in the group of state higher education institutions, which could be tasked with providing education in the field of integrated security (external and internal; military and non-military) and encompass all didactic activities in this area, going beyond just the specialist and professional (ministerial) or general academic scope.

R&D in the field of security. The Ministry of Science and Higher Education is the main centre for the promotion of Polish science policy. The 2010 reform of the science system allowed the Ministry to assume the role of a coordination centre in this scope. The financing of scientific studies and research projects was entrusted to the National Science Centre (*Narodowe Centrum Nauki*) and the National Centre for Research and Development (*Narodowe Centrum Badań i Rozwoju*) as the executive agencies of the Ministry.

The National Science Centre supports the scientific activities regarding basic research undertaken primarily to acquire new knowledge about the underlying foundations of phenomena and observable facts, without any direct practical application or use.

The applied research, oriented towards practical application, is the domain of the National Centre for Research and Development, which is responsible for the management of strategic programmes of scientific R&D work (including R&D work for the purposes of the state's security and defence). It also finances or co-finances such programmes.

In Poland, the basic and applied research and the developmental work are conducted mainly by higher education institutions (basic organization units of higher education institutions), scientific institutes of the Polish Academy of Sciences (*Polska Akademia Nauk*, PAN), as well as by research institutes, R&D centres, and enterprises.

Basic research in the field of security and defence of the state is just being developed. It is mainly due to the fact that the science of security and the science of defence, which constitute the subject of the research, were created in 2011.

At present, only two higher education institutions can award the degree of *doctor habilitatus* in the aforementioned disciplines. These institutions include: the Academy of National Defence and the Naval Academy (*Akademia Marynki Wojennej*). The Police Academy in Szczytno can award the doctoral degree in the discipline of security science. The academies also conduct basic research as part of financing of the statutory activity (the National Science Centre does not finance the basic research in the field of security and defence). Other higher education institutions and science centres concentrate on research and developmental work in the field of security and defence only in the aspect of technical sciences.

The applied research in the field of national security and defence are, in turn, conducted mainly to the order of the Ministry of National Defence and the Ministry of the Interior. Proposals concerning research projects and programmes to be financed by the National Centre for Research and Development are submitted also by the Internal Security Agency.

The priority areas in the realm of R&D work for security and defence of the state include:
- For the Ministry of National Defence (MON): information and network technologies; sensors and observation; precision weapons and armaments; unmanned (autonomous) platforms; protection and survival in the battlefield; and modern materials, including high-energy and smart materials;
- For the Minister of the Interior (MSW): modern technologies and innovative solutions for detecting, combating, and neutralizing threats; forensic technology; individual protection means and equipment; social prevention, victimology, criminology, and social research; organization and management.

The diagnosis of existing solutions in R&D work in the field of national security and defence indicates that at present the sectoral system of planning and implementation of research activities prevails. As a result, we face a situation where the limited financial resources are allocated for strictly ministerial projects instead of the capital being accumulated in cross-ministerial programmes and projects which would integrate the defence (military) and protection (non-military) spheres of the national security system.

In this context, it is important to note the amount of funds spent on the R&D activities. In 2012, the funds allocated for science amounted to PLN 6.4 billion. R&D work in the field of national security and defence were financed in the amount of PLN 300 million (which is more than PLN 118 million less than the subsidy allocated for this purpose in 2011).

Another weakness of the current solutions regarding programmes and developmental work aimed at improving the security and defence capabilities of the state is the lack of a well-developed cooperation platform between the final recipient (end user) and the scientific team and industry, especially during the key stages of implementation of such programmes and projects.

The intellectual, scientific and technological potential. The national security of contemporary countries depends to a large extent on their intellectual and technological potential. According to studies analysing the changes taking place in the countries with most dynamic technological and intellectual capacities, the potential of these countries is strongly linked to "knowledge institutions" such as: universities, research centres, technological parks, as well as innovative educational and social programmes. The transition to the networked economy, IT development, as well as social stability and extending the spheres of democratization of public life goes hand in hand with the strong innovativeness by national knowledge institutions.

Some of the indicators of the IT potential include: the number of students on given types of courses, the scale of research and patents. Referring to the OECD report[7] presenting the number of students of specific disciplines we can say that Poland has reached a high level of potential associated with education in social, pedagogical, and economic sciences, and a low level of potential in disciplines which are nowadays considered crucial, i.e. technology and engineering.

At present, one of the problems connected with the Polish IT potential is migration of researchers to centres located in Western Europe and the USA. It is worthwhile to note that not only the best scientists but also representatives of the world of culture and art choose easier careers abroad, which effects the image of Poland as a peripheral country.

The media in the national security system. The media, broadly understood as means of public communication, undergo deep changes. The previous development of the media was associated with the emergence of new media – from large-circulation newspapers and magazines, through radio to television. The current changes are connected with digitization, as a result of which the former media are transformed and the new ones appear. Digitization has led to the emergence of network media (the Internet), which use various services – data transmission, electronic mail, web pages, and community portals.

There are multiple relationships between the media and national security. The media, both factually and potentially, help identify threats. Moreover, they inform the public about the threats and about the ways of repelling them. The media also stimulate pro-public attitudes, which is an essential premise of the democratic order, including the formation of "democratic security".

---

[7] OECD Reviews of Tertiary Education: Poland 2007.

Effective cooperation of the media with entities responsible for crisis management appears extremely important – most frequently the media shape public awareness of a given threat. Therefore, they can widely educate the public about preventing and effectively coping with threats as well as about cooperation with crisis management authorities responsible for the area inhabited by a given community.

The media should show the population the topics and problems deserving public interest. Meanwhile, in recent years, due to business requirements, the media have been undergoing the process of tabloidization – in pursuit of the widest possible audience the media subordinate the information to sensation which is supposed to attract the interest of the largest possible group of recipients. In case of accumulated negative information this may greatly arouse the general sense of security collapse. Media reports too often dramatise and personalise the message – both in terms of form and contents. That is why common themes in the media are violent events or human tragedy such as catastrophes or acts of terrorism.

The health service in the national security system. The Ministry of Health is responsible, *inter alia,* for the organization of the health care system, health policy, and drug policy. Legal tools at the disposal of the minister of health allow him to carry out policy as part of the state's constitutional obligation which consist, among other things, in providing each citizen with the right to protection of health, equal access to health care services financed from public funds, ensuring special health care for children, pregnant women, the disabled, and elderly persons, as well as fighting epidemic diseases and preventing negative health consequences of environmental degradation. In the current legal framework, when fulfilling the constitutional obligation to provide access to medical services, including in crisis situations, it is important to consider the fact that all activities of entities authorized to provide medical services and the organizational and logistic support result solely from the authorities' competence under the law, while effective, fully modern and competent medical assistance should be the result of collaboration and cooperation of all units and emergency, technical, medical, and administrative services. When referring to the state authorities responsible for ensuring the required level of health care, it should be noted that this competence is not only in the hands of the minister of health, but also of central and local government administration bodies.

One of the challenges for health care in the context of security tasks of the state is the shortfall of clear rules concerning cooperation and collaboration with the minister of national defence, resulting, *inter alia,* from the so-called precedence of the needs of the armed forces over other needs, as well as the lack of a consistent policy on management and administration of staff reserves. Lacking are also uniform and consistent rules (including of financing) adjusting health care units to efficient implementation of tasks for uniformed services as well as the readiness of these units to carry out specific defence tasks. In a situation where more and more health care entities undergo restructuring by changing their legal form (non-public health institution, *niepubliczne zakłady opieki zdrowotnej*), the issue of financing or refinancing the implementation of certain defence tasks creates a number of issues for the authorities responsible for the organization of the assignment and launching of such tasks.

Another problem is that there is no possibility to isolate patients suffering from infectious diseases transmitted from person to person. Individual provinces had designated places for isolation and quarantine, but after inspecting them more closely it was found that these facilities could be of use for quarantine purposes only and were not suitable for isolation. Consequently, the chances to prevent the spread of particularly dangerous diseases do not look good. Once the local stocks are exhausted, the logistics of launching and securing the supplies of new medicines, medical materials and equipment from the state reserves to sites of events would pose a problem.

* * *

When analyzing Poland's societal potential, it is important to stress its numerous weaknesses which do or will affect national security. It concerns, in particular, the social, demographic, educational and cognitive, media and health care areas.

At present, Poland has a significant demographic potential. However, if the low birth rate continues, the situation will start changing in the near future. The resulting phenomena such as the deformation of the age structure of the population and the ageing of society will directly result in problems in the socio-economic sphere.

The stratification of society, including large areas of poverty, remains one of major problems in Poland. This phenomenon, along with the high level of unemployment and the noticeable change of the traditional family structure, leads to the deterioration of social bonds, the growth of extreme and populist attitudes, and, as a consequence, to social unrest, which directly undermines national security.

When assessing the societal potential, attention should also be paid to the shortcomings in disseminating the knowledge about security. As a result, the awareness of needs, conditions and tasks in the area of security among citizens and social structures is insufficient. The level of such awareness among the major state structures that are not directly responsible for security is not satisfactory either, in particular in terms of their relevant responsibilities. All these elements have, to a certain extent, a limiting effect on the definition of national interests and strategic objectives in the field of security.

The economic security potential

Security and development are two fundamental aspects of functioning of the state. They are also inextricably linked with each other. On the one hand, without an appropriate level of security, it is not possible to ensure stable and long-term development of economy. On the other hand, without development a continuous necessary improvement of the national security potential would not happen.

The economic security potential (in combination with the political will of the decision makers) constitutes the basis for defining the power, effectiveness and international position of a state.

In 2011, in terms of the gross domestic product calculated at purchasing power parity, Poland took the twentieth place among the world's biggest economies with GDP estimated at USD 768 billion.

It accounted for ca. 5 per cent of the value of economy of the entire European Union, but 25 per cent of the German economy, 33 per cent of the economies of Russia, France or the UK, as well as more than 40 per cent of the economy of Italy, and 50 per cent of the economy of Spain. In the same year, however, the level of economic development measured by GDP per capita at purchasing power parity accounted for more than 43 per cent of the average for the United States and approximately 64 per cent of the average for the entire EU. At the same time it represented ca 52.8 per cent of the value of this indicator in Germany, 58.7 per cent in Great Britain, 59.2 per cent in France, 64 per cent in Italy, and 65.3 per cent in Spain. It is important to note, however, that in years 2001–2011 the relative GDP per capita in Poland increased by ca. 16 per cent in relation to the European Union and about 13 per cent in relation to the USA[8]. It was due to the continuous growth of GDP during that period, in particular after 2008, i.e. during the global crisis (fig 25).

Figure 25. The gross domestic product per capita in select EU member states and the USA (EU 27=100)

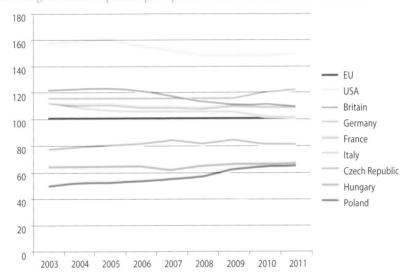

Source: authors' own chart based on Eurostat data.

From the global point of view, Poland can be considered a relatively highly developed country; nevertheless, there is still a large gap between Poland and the most developed countries, as evidenced, *inter alia*, by the structure of economy and the corresponding employment structure – 13 per cent of the population work in agriculture (the EU average is 5 per cent, while in some of the countries, e.g. USA, it is even less than 2 per cent) and only 57 per cent in the sector of services (the EU average – 68 per cent). A relatively large number of people work in industry (30 per cent, while the EU average is 26 per cent), which is a legacy from the period of centrally planned economy.

A major problem of Polish economy is a persistent high unemployment rate (at present, the rate of unemployment is about 13.4 per cent – as of December 2012), but there is no clarity as to the methods of its estimation (it is difficult, e.g. to determine the scale of hidden unemployment in agriculture). A better indicator of professional activity of the population is the proportion of working age population that is employed. In Poland this ratio is approximately 59 per cent, which differs from the European average of 64 per cent, and even more from such countries as the Netherlands – 77 per cent, and Denmark – 75 per cent. Select indicators presenting macroeconomic changes in Poland are shown in fig. 26.

---

[8]   On the basis of Eurostat data.

Figure 26. Selected macroeconomic indicators for the Republic of Poland in years 2000–2011 (expressed in percentages)

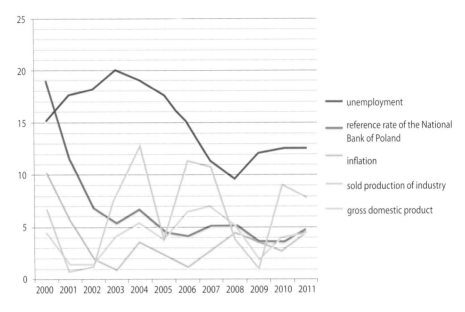

Source: authors' own compilation based on data from the Central Statistical Office and the National Bank of Poland.

Poland in international economic relations. An important dimension of the economic status consists not only in the size of economy or the level of its development, but also in the share in foreign trade, and particularly in the export competitiveness. When analysing the competitiveness of Polish economy in this field, it is important to note, primarily, the systematic growth of Polish export value. In years 2000–2011, exports increased almost three and half times from EUR 39 billion to EUR 139 billion, while at the same time imports increased by nearly 3.5 times from EUR 52 billion to EUR 149 billion (fig. 27). The large increase in exports in the last decade was to a large extent associated with the inflow of direct foreign investments in processing industries. It is evidenced by the fact that from 2000 to 2008 the most noticeable export increase was in the sectors of economy in which the largest direct foreign investment inflow was noted.

Regarding the development of competitiveness in foreign trade, particularly important is the analysis of the export structure and indicators of revealed relative advantage, carried out with the use of various quality classifications of processing industries, including the technological level, the use of material and intangible input, and workforce qualifications. When analysing the changes in the Polish export structure, from the technological point of view it should be noted that the key positive change in the last decade was the decline in the share of exports in low-tech industries accompanied by the increase in the share of export of medium-high technology industries and, during the last two decades, also of high-tech branches. During this entire period the largest share in exports of Polish processing industries was noted in medium-high technology sectors.

When analyzing Polish exports in terms of the classification of industries and according to the use of tangible and intangible factors of production, it is important to note the positive trends, such as a substantial decline in the share of labour-intensive industries, as well as – although to a moderate extent – strengthening of the position in other industries, in particular those based on research and marketing. Moreover, Polish workforce qualifications are also improving.

Figure 27. The import and export of goods in Poland (in millions EUR)

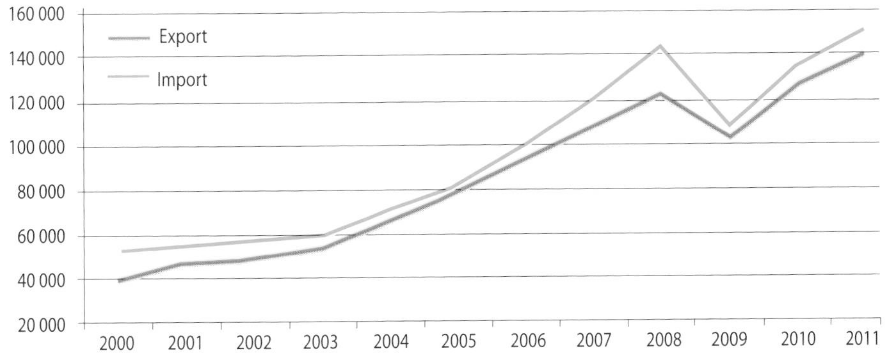

Source: authors' own compilation based on data from the National Bank of Poland.

The inflows of direct foreign investment in Poland grew significantly after its accession to the European Union. The value of direct foreign investments located in the Polish economy has increased by EUR 84 billion and at the end of 2011 reached EUR 147.7 billion. The sectoral structure of foreign investments in Poland has changed since then as well. Initially, in the 1990s most of foreign investment inflows were concentrated in production sectors as well as in trade and less advanced services. With time, however, the investments in financial services and, since 2004, also in real estate and company services, especially in various business services, started to grow. Poland attracted more investors not only due to lower costs (owing, *inter alia*, to inexpensive workforce), but also due to the higher quality of rendered services and qualified workers.

Financial security. The most important aspects of the financial security of the state are: stability of the financial sector, the size of the public debt, as well as the size and structure of the state's foreign currency reserves.

Financial security institutions. The financial sector, including the banking sector, plays a significant role in the economic development of the country. Financial sector institutions perform the role of an intermediary, transforming financial savings of citizens into investment needs of economy. Transformation of savings into investments is a very complex and risky process. Wrong investment of funds by financial intermediaries leads to their bankruptcy, which causes further bankruptcies of those who entrusted their financial resources to them. Due to this specificity of financial intermediation, the sector is regulated and supervised by various public institutions which form a financial security network. The most important financial security institutions in Poland include: the Council of Ministers, the Ministry of Finance, the Polish Financial Supervision Authority, the National Bank of Poland, and the Bank Guarantee Fund.

The Polish government has two important crisis response tools at its disposal. Pursuant to the Act of 12 February 2009 on the State Treasury Support for Financial Institutions, the government can provide liquidity support to banks and certain financial institutions. On the basis of the Act of 12 February 2010 on the Recapitalization of Certain Financial Institutions, the Council of Ministers can provide capital to certain financial institutions or take them over. The aforementioned instruments are associated with the use of public funds. They are also of temporary nature, depending on the European Commission's approval for their use.

The Polish Financial Supervision Authority (*Komisja Nadzoru Finansowego*, KNF) plays a significant role in ensuring financial security. It is tasked with the supervision of the financial market, including, *inter alia,* the banking, pension, and insurance supervision as well as the supervision over the capital market. The aim of the supervision is to ensure proper functioning of the financial market, its stability, security and transparency, to build trust in the market as well as to ensure protection of its participants' interests. The supervision by the KNF is focused on the secure functioning of individual institutions and thereby indirectly on security and stability of the entire financial market.

In turn, the National Bank of Poland (*Narodowy Bank Polski*, NBP) promotes the stability of the banking sector and – provided appropriate security is established – ensures liquidity of the banks. The National Bank of Poland contributes to financial stability also indirectly – by taking responsibility for the stability of prices as well as supporting the government's economic policy, unless its policy contradicts the objective of the stability. The monetary policy of the NBP has been implemented since the end of 1998 as part of the direct inflation targeting strategy. One of its elements is the floating exchange rate regime.

Another important financial security institution is the Bank Guarantee Fund (*Bankowy Fundusz Gwarancyjny*). The Fund's fundamental tasks include: payment of the guaranteed funds up to the amount determined by the law (at present, an equivalent of EUR 100 thousand) in the event of a suspension of a bank's activity as well as the provision of financial help to banks at risk of insolvency.

The aforementioned financial security institutions, within their competence, are responsible for the stability and security of the financial system in Poland. They enjoy a broad mandate and have a range of crisis prevention and management tools.

The experience of the current global financial crisis as well as the financial security standards introduced around the world indicate that the financial security network in Poland needs to be supplemented. One of the threats might be also that the activities of non-bank organizations, i.e. companies performing banking activities and providing financial services, which do not have the legal status of a bank, are poorly regulated. The accumulation of large, multi-billion savings outside financial supervision increases the risk of speculative bubbles. A crash caused by the bursting of such a speculative bubble can lead to a significant decline in the value of savings and, as a further consequence, to an economic downturn.

Foreign currency reserves of the National Bank of Poland. Foreign currency reserves, their accumulation, management, as well as ensuring the security of foreign exchange dealing are some of the major tasks of the NBP as the central foreign exchange banking institution of the state.

Under the floating exchange rate regime the aim of foreign currency reserves is to strengthen the financial credibility of the state by reducing the costs of financing on global markets and the likelihood of withholding access to this source of financing, as well as by limiting the risk of sudden capital outflows (including speculative attacks). Foreign currency reserves can also be used to support the stability of financial markets and of the banking sector, *inter alia*, by ensuring currency liquidity in conditions of disfunctionalities of financial markets.

The accumulated reserve assets of the National Bank securely cover the potential joint needs as regards financing the banking sector in foreign currencies, corresponding – in an extreme scenario – to all currency liabilities vis-à-vis foreign financial institutions as well as to open balance sheet currency position. At the end of November 2012, the official reserve assets of the Bank reached EUR 82.7 billion, increasing by EUR 6.7 billion (8 per cent) since the beginning of the year, and by EUR 38 billion (85 per cent) over the past five years.

The strategy of managing the foreign currency reserves ensures an appropriate level of security and liquidity of funds. It is therefore reasonable to continue to follow this strategy taking into consideration the market conditions, in particular the financial risk profile, as well as changes taking place in the global economy and the international financial system.

Public debt. In Poland, the limitations of the public debt amount are specified in the Constitution of the Republic of Poland and the Act on Public Finance. The constitution sets the limit of the public debt at the level of 60 per cent of the GDP. The Act on Public Finance, in turn, determines the method of calculating the public debt – the so-called prudence limits – at the levels of 50 per cent, 55 per cent, and 60 per cent of the GDP, as well as sanctions resulting from exceeding such limits.

The level of public debt is still close to the constitutional limit (fig. 28). This situation results, to a large extent, from the general imbalance of the public finance sector. It combines a large – although not so disturbing as in other countries – public debt and the deficit of the public finance sector, which is strongly correlated with the economic cycle.

Figure 28. State public debt in years 2005 –2012 (nominal value in billions PLN and expressed as a per centage in relation to the GDP)

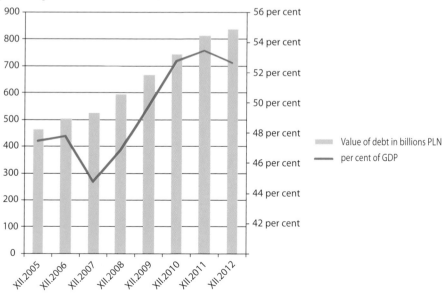

Source: authors' own compilation based on data from the Ministry of Finance.

The pension system. In the next few years, the stable functioning of the pension system is threatened by the unfavourable demographic changes. The system rests on three pillars: the first one is the Social Insurance Institution (*Zakład Ubezpieczeń Społecznych*); the second one includes Open Pension Funds (*Otwarte Fundusze Emerytalne*, OFE) – with 15.7 million accounts as of June 2012; the third one consists of Individual Pension Accounts (Pol. *Indywidualne Konta Emerytalne*, IKE), Individual Pension Security Accounts (*Indywidualne Konta Zabezpieczenia Emerytalnego*, IKZE), and Employee Pension Accounts (*Pracownicze Programy Emerytalne*, PPE) – with more than 1.18 million accounts as at the end of March 2012. The total value of the OFE assets as of June 2012 was PLN 241.1 billion. In the first pillar, the money to pay out pensions is funded by the contributions paid today, in the second pillar, the money from contributions is invested by the OFE, while in the third pillar the future pensioners decide on their own the amount of contributions paid. In accordance with the amended Act on the Organization and Functioning of Pensions Funds which entered into force in the 2nd quarter of 2011, the major part of the contributions is supposed to be paid to the Public Insurance Institution instead of to the OFE (previously 7.3 per cent of contribution was paid to OFE; at present it is 2.3 per cent).

In addition, in Poland there is a separate social insurance system for farmers, based on the Agricultural Social Insurance Fund (*Kasa Rolniczego Ubezpieczenia Społecznego*, KRUS). At the end of 2011, there were 1 516 318 people insured by the KRUS, while 1 326 638 people collected benefits. The number of insured by the KRUS falls every year. The payment of benefits under this scheme is based, to a large extent, on subsidies from the state budget.

Energy security. The legal basis of the Polish energy security system is the act of 10 April 1997 – the Energy Law. The act is continuously amended, which is mainly due to the dynamics of legislative changes at the European level. The energy law sets forth the principles for the development of the state's energy policy, the rules and terms of the supply and use of fuels and energy, including heating, and the activity of energy companies, as well as it specifies the bodies responsible for fuel and energy management.

Over the past decades, a series of strategic documents determined the main directions of development of the Polish energy policy. In principle, the documents were rather general and treated the diversification policy of natural gas supplies from abroad as a priority. Their political implementation, however, proved to be extremely difficult. The lack of proper analyses which would summarise previous studies should be assessed critically. The currently binding document is the Energy Policy of Poland until 2030, which was adopted on 10 November 2009. The document was elaborated before the first information on potential shale basins in Poland appeared.

Additionally, in 2011, the Ministry of Economy and the Ministry of the Environment presented a draft document entitled: "The Strategy: Energy Security and the Environment", which is one of nine development strategies being prepared. It focuses on three fundamental objectives: sustainable management of environmental resources, ensuring safe and competitive energy supply to the domestic economy, and improving the condition of the environment.

Energy security entities. The most important institutions which have the impact on the energy security policy are: the Council of Ministers, the minister of economy, the president of the Energy Regulatory Office (*Urząd Regulacji Energetyki*, URE), province governors, as well as province and commune local governments (district local government has only indirect impact on the state's energy security, *inter alia,* by responsibilities associated with the spatial planning, connected with the implementation of all lines investments such as power transmission lines, gas pipelines, as well as crude oil and petroleum products transmission infrastructure).

According to the Act of 4 September 1997 on Government Administration Departments (*działy administracji rządowej*), the minister of economy is responsible for the implementation of the energy policy and is the main government administration authority in matters relating to this policy as well as is the guarantor of maintaining energy security. The tasks of the minister of economy include, among others: drafting the energy policy of the state as well as coordinating its implementation; planning and overseeing the fuel and energy supply to the state; exercising control over the security and stability of supplies of gaseous fuels, electric power, as well as control of the state energy system; cooperating with province governors and local governments in planning and implementing the supply of fuels and energy as well as coordinating cooperation with international organizations.

The Energy Regulatory Office is subordinate to the minister of economy. The president of the URE is tasked with implementing tasks relating to the regulation of the fuel and energy management as well as supporting the competitiveness of the energy sector. It is also assigned to regulating the work of energy enterprises in such a manner so as to balance their interests with interests of fuel and energy consumers.

Other departments which play an important role in this regard include:
- the Ministry of Treasury, which is qualified for appointing and dismissing the governing bodies of gas industry companies (production, distribution, trade), oil industry and the power industry, as well as plays an important role in privatization process;
- the Ministry of the Environment, which is responsible for rational use of natural energy resources, including for issue of concessions for the exploration and exploitation of energy resources;
- the Ministry of Transport, Construction and Maritime Economy, competent, *inter alia*, in matters of transportation policy.

The group of entities that fulfil direct and indirect tasks relating to energy security includes also province governors and governing bodies of local governments. The local governments of provinces provide opinions on the development plans of energy enterprises as well as the draft assumptions for heating, electric power and gaseous fuel supply plans prepared by the communes. The task of the province local governments is to assess the compliance of the above documents with the Energy Policy of Poland until 2030. The Energy Law, in turn, imposes on the municipalities tasks associated with: the development of spatial management plans; planning and organizing the provision of heating, electric power and gaseous fuels; and planning and financing public lighting.

Energy raw materials and the storage capacities. According to the data published by the Polish Geological Institute (*Państwowy Instytut Geologiczny*, PGI), in Poland there are 84 documented deposits of oil of total exploitable balance resources of 26.29 million tonnes, 279 conventional natural gas resources – of 146 billion cubic metres, nearly 100–120 thousand tonnes of natural uranium, 44 billion tonnes of hard coal and 14 billion tonnes of lignite. In March 2012, the Institute estimated that the national shale gas resources are at the level of 346.1–767.9 billion cubic metres. In effect, the deposits of hard coal and brown coal in Poland are sufficient to ensure its energy security; however oil and natural gas need to be imported.

Poland has geological structures which can be utilized for storing energy raw materials. Salt caves (e.g. in Pomerania) which can be used for construction of tanks for crude oil and natural gas, are particularly important in this regard. Poland has now eight underground storage sites for natural gas, which belong to *Polskie Górnictwo Naftowe i Gazownictwo* company (PGNIG). Their total capacity is 2.06 billion cubic metres of natural gas, thereby allowing to storage this raw material for 45 days of average consumption. It is planned that the storage capacities will reach the level of 3 billion cubic metres of natural gas by 2015.

Poland also has an adequate infrastructure for crude oil storage. The company PERN "Przyjaźń" has three bases with a total capacity of 3 billion cubic metres of crude oil, but the capacity allocated for intervention stocks is nearly 1.4 million cubic metres. PKN Orlen Capital Group operates crude oil storage sites of total capacity of 6.4 million cubic metres, of which 5.8 million cubic metres is intended for storage of crude oil and fuels.

The fuel and energy sector is characterized, *inter alia,* by uneven development, delays in modernization, obsolete technology, the ill-arranged structure of production assets, underinvestment (it concerns mainly the production capacities and transmission infrastructure), and the lack of transborder connections.

Diversification of energy raw material supplies. The national economy is dependent on supplies of certain energy raw materials from external producers. More than 95 per cent of crude oil and 60 per cent of natural gas consumed in Poland is imported. Currently, the majority of these raw materials come from the Russian Federation.

Aiming at improving its energy security, Poland has taken measures at two levels: through the process of physical diversification of sources and routes of energy raw material supplies, and through political activities supporting the creation of a legal and institutional environment in order to build a free energy market within the European Union.

Work on the previous project of diversification of crude oil supplies via the Odessa-Brody-Płock (Gdańsk) pipeline was focused on establishing a consortium (with 24.75 per cent of shares held by the company PERN "Przyjaźń" S.A.) and putting it on the list of co-financed projects. Natural gas from Russia is supplied from two directions – nearly 3/5 of the contracted raw material is supplied via Ukraine, while the other 2/5 is collected at two supply points of the Yamal pipeline.

According to the Yamal contract and its annex, starting from 2022 the PGNIG company will purchase from the Russian Gazprom 10 billion cubic meters of natural gas per year, with a possible deviation of 15 per cent from the contracted amount. Moreover, the PGNIG company has concluded a contract with VNG-Verbundnetz Gas AG on natural gas supply to Lasowo in years 2006–2016 at the level of 400 million cubic metres per year and with Vitol – on natural gas supply to Cieszyn in years 2011–2014 in the amount of 550 million cubic metres per year.

Polish shale gas deposits provide a great opportunity to gain independence from external suppliers. It is expected that the non-conventional gas deposits may contribute to a geopolitical change in the region, becoming significantly competitive for the current monopolists on European markets. The experience of the United States connected with the utilization of shale gas in the economy indicated that this raw material may have a substantial influence on the currents directions of supplies. It is also estimated that Polish shale formations may contain as much as 215–268 million tonnes of liquid hydrocarbons, the so-called shale oil. The Ministry of Environment has obligated the state-owned companies to extract 400 million cubic meters – up to 1 billion cubic meters of shale gas by 2015. The biggest Polish energy companies have invested a lot in the exploration and extraction of this raw material. However, a threat to shale gas extraction in Poland may be the attempts being made within the European Union to limit or prohibit the exploitation of shale gas deposits with the use of the available technologies, as well as the possible withdrawal of foreign companies from Poland which have thus far been involved in the project and which hold the majority of exploration concessions issued by the Polish authorities (fig 29). Another difficulty in shale gas extraction may also be the environmental regulations in force in Poland (e.g. the Natura 2000 programme).

Energy infrastructure. The energy infrastructure is understood as a set of devices which include the following subsystems: electricity, CHP, gas, solid fuels, and liquid fuels. For the sake of state security, the subsystems of electricity, gas, solid fuels, and liquid fuels are the most important.

Electricity is supplied to its recipients with the use of the national electricity system, which is comprised of the following:
- electricity generating devices;
- transmission devices and networks;
- distribution networks;
- power stations;
- devices which receive and convert electricity;

Analysis of the electricity sector infrastructure gives rise to concerns about its technical condition. The major weakness of the electricity system is the high voltage transmission lines (400 kV), both in terms of their technical capacity and the lack of the network coverage in northern Poland. Despite the fact that the transmission lines are on average 35 years old, their reliability looks good. The technical condition of distribution networks is similar to that of the transmission networks; one of The challenge, however, is the necessity to modernize and develop them in the context of connecting the new power generation capacities.

The quality of the electricity networks and their security are verified by natural weather conditions which pose a threat of system failure. The biggest failure of this type was the blackout in 2008 in the West Pomeranian Province, which was classified as an event of extraordinary nature. In the succeeding years, similar events unfolded in other provinces, but on a smaller scale. The high degree of exploitation of the electricity infrastructure, however, contributes to its overload and affects its resistance to extraordinary factors and events. As a consequence, the risk that such failures will occur more frequently increases.

Power generation facilities are located mainly in central and southern Poland. Most of them were built decades ago and are characterized by low energy efficiency. The uneven arrangement of power generation capacities puts at risk the continuous power supply in northern regions of the country. The power is distributed via transmission networks, and the energy security of that part of Poland depends of the quality of these networks.

The gas system infrastructure is operated by a transmission system operator – Gaz-System. The company manages the transmission system comprised of more than 9.7 thousand km of high-pressure gas pipelines, 15 compressor stations, 56 nodes, and 970 exit points.

The technical capacity of receipt points of imported natural gas (excluding its domestic production) to the transmission system allows for import of as much as nearly 18 billion cubic metres of natural gas per year.

Figure 29. Areas with long-term potential for the presence of natural gas and crude oil in lower Palaeozoic shale formations (according to P. Poprawa)

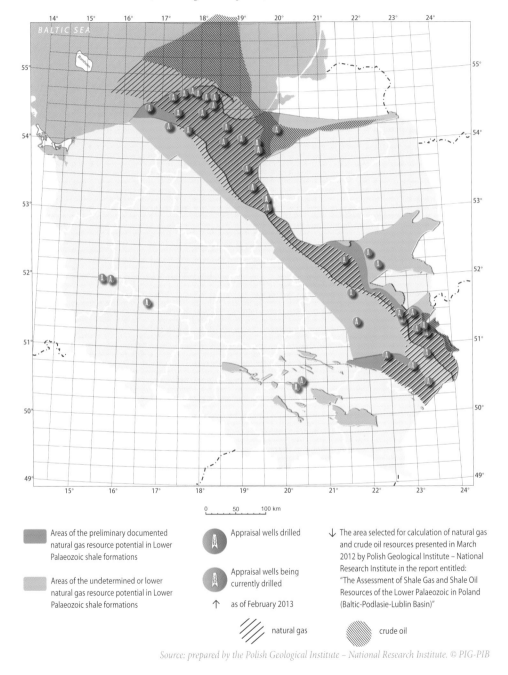

Areas of the preliminary documented natural gas resource potential in Lower Palaeozoic shale formations

Areas of the undetermined or lower natural gas resource potential in Lower Palaeozoic shale formations

Appraisal wells drilled

Appraisal wells being currently drilled

↑ as of February 2013

/// natural gas

crude oil

↓ The area selected for calculation of natural gas and crude oil resources presented in March 2012 by Polish Geological Institute – National Research Institute in the report entitled: "The Assessment of Shale Gas and Shale Oil Resources of the Lower Palaeozoic in Poland (Baltic-Podlasie-Lublin Basin)"

Source: prepared by the Polish Geological Institute – National Research Institute. © PIG-PIB

After commissioning of the LNG terminal in Świnoujście, the transmission capacity will increase by 5 billion cubic metres per year. Another increase in the receiving capacities is associated with the launching of the so-called virtual and real reverse flow on the Yamal gas pipeline. It will allow for importing gas from the West. The development of input capacities of the system is accompanied by the extension and construction of new transmission networks.

Infrastructural security institutions. The responsibility for continuous and effective functioning of the infrastructure lies with the central and local government administration. The earliest legislation in this matter dating back to 1997 was the Act on Protection of Persons and Property, which defined the areas, facilities, equipment and transports of importance for national defence and economic interests, public security and other essential interests of the state, which were required to be protected by SUFO or proper technical protection.

All facilities listed in the register are protected on the basis of protection plans of such areas, facilities and equipment, agreed upon with a competent province police commissioner.

The critical infrastructure protection system is a relatively young but at the same time the most comprehensive system of this kind.

The critical infrastructure includes the following systems: energy supply, energy raw materials and fuels; communication; data communication networks; financial; food supply; water supply; health protection; transport; rescue; systems ensuring the continuity of operation of public administration, as well as production, stockpiling, the storage and use of chemical and radioactive substances, including dangerous substance pipelines.

The previous legal situation provided conditions for the protection of the state's critical infrastructure. The current system, however, has a number of defects, the most critical of which include:

> **The Act of 26 April 2007 on Crisis Management**
>
> **Article 3.** Any reference in this act to the (...) critical infrastructure shall be construed as a reference to the systems and functionally interrelated facilities which are part of these systems, including structures, equipments, installations, and services of key importance for the security of the state and its citizens, as well as serving to ensure efficient functioning of public administration authorities, institutions, and entrepreneurs.

- the lack of factual criteria for the identification of facilities of key importance for the security of the state and its citizens (this does not concern the Act on crisis management). Fulfilment of the function indicated in the act or regulation does not always indicate the important role for security of the state and its citizens. This leads to a significant discretion in deciding which facilities should be on the lists;
- the focus on physical protection of facilities indicated in the act on protection of persons and property as well as in the regulation on facilities of particular importance for the security and defence of the state and on their special protection;
- the remarkable dispersion of responsibilities of specific authorities as regards the organization and control of protection tasks;
- the existence of a number of systems for protection of the critical infrastructure results in inefficient utilization of the forces and resources, as well as frequent cases of misapplication of the regulations and resulting obligations fulfilled by persons responsible for the protection of these facilities;
- the lack of real incentives from the state for owners of the critical infrastructure to invest in its safety;

- the lack of regulations which would enable efficient collection of information on persons managing the state's critical infrastructure;
- the lack of difference between the terms "the critical infrastructure of the state" and "the critical infrastructure of a province, district, and commune".

Violations of secured areas[9] show that despite strong legal regulations, the system of physical protection of critical infrastructure facilities is not always effective.

The geographic potential, the natural environment and agriculture. Poland is a country located in central Europe, along the east-west and north-south axes, which creates good conditions for international cooperation. The country is also characterized by territorial compactness – its shape resembles a circle, which is positive in defence terms.

The Polish state lies at the crossroads of transit routes, which is of key importance for economy. It is a country with access to the Baltic Sea, owing to which it has an opportunity to diversify the raw materials supplies by sea. Moreover, the Baltic Sea region has good climatic conditions for the development of wind power engineering. Poland has also its own natural resources, including hard coal, lignite, copper and shale gas.

Poland is one of the poorest countries in Europe in terms of water resources. The current water consumption generated mainly by the industry increase every year. Poland is also one of the most forested countries in the European Union (in 2010, forests covered more than 29 per cent of the country's area). Forests have the production (economic), environmental (protection) and social function. They are also strategic assets which shape the environmental security of the state – they stabilize the water cycle in the environment, prevent floods, avalanches and landslides; shape the climate; increase the accumulation of carbon; and even improve the health and living conditions of the population.

Poland is also a country with high environmental pollution (of atmosphere, water, soil, and forests). As a result of numerous economic and social phenomena and, above all, political decisions, the environment steadily deteriorated until the end of 1980s. The processes which took place in Poland after 1989, such as limiting the role of heavy industry, the growing environmental awareness and Poland's international commitments, reversed the negative trend. Nevertheless, there are still areas of substantial environmental degradation on the Polish territory (e.g. areas of Upper Silesia).

At present, the nature conservation activities in Poland include the creation of national parks (there are 23 such parks on the territory of Poland), nature reserves, landscape parks, and natural monuments as well as species protection. Since 2004, there is a new act on nature conservation in force in Poland, which made it possible, *inter alia,* to join the EU Natura 2000 network, forming a comman European system of environmental protection. In Poland, Natura 2000 covers a dozen or so per cent of the country's area, which helps improve the natural environment. On the other hand, it limits the possibility of exploitation of natural resources and the development of infrastructure (including the power infrastructure).

The potential of Polish agriculture, used through adequate investments and agro-technical development, ensures a stable situation in terms of food self-sufficiency. Analysis of the flows of agricultural and processed products shows that Poland has a surplus of food production.

---

[9] In July 2009 in Bełchatów, the Greenpeace activities entered the premises of the power station, climbed the cooling tower and painted a slogan on it, reading: "Stop CO_2." In December 2008 in Konin, environmentalists broke into the power plant, climbed a chimney, and began a protest against greenhouse gas emission.

One aspect indirectly related with food production is the use of the results of research carried out in the BIO[10] category, which enable prevention or earlier detection of diseases that threaten the population. Besides its influence on public health, conducting such research and implementing its results will help improve the innovativeness and, as a consequence, the competitiveness of food.

Strategic reserves. At present, the strategic reserve system functions on the basis of the Act of 29 October 2010 on Strategic Reserves. The act sets forth the principles for the creation, storage, sharing, liquidating, and financing of strategic reserves, as well as determines the tasks and organization of the Material Reserves Agency (*Agencja Rezerw Materiałowych*, ARM). The Agency is an executive body, as defined in the Act on Public Finance, which carries out the state's tasks relating to strategic reserves and state stocks of crude oil and petroleum products. The regulations regarding the functioning and organization of the Agency are not basically different from those adopted for other similar entities – state legal persons.

A rational, efficient, and transparent system of strategic reserves is to support the implementation of tasks in the field of security and defence of the state, reconstruction of the critical infrastructure, mitigation of disturbances in the continuity of supplies serving the functioning of economy and meeting the basic needs of citizens, saving life and health of citizens, as well as fulfilling the international commitments of the Republic of Poland.

The most important system solutions include: the obligation to develop a government strategic reserves programme which is adopted by the Council of Ministers; the principle that a proposal to establish certain reserves must be preceded by an analysis of risks and uncertainties regarding threats, for the fighting or prevention of which the reserves would be used; the introduction of one type of reserves – the strategic reserves – without determining their specific range or amount; authorizing one body – the Minister of Economy – to create, share, and liquidate the strategic reserves, as well as allowing the possibility of maintaining strategic reserves which are not owned by the State Treasury.

The range and amount of strategic reserves is defined in the Government Strategic Reserves Programme. Its main basis is the analysis of risks and uncertainties regarding threats to security and defence of the state, safety, law and order, natural disasters and crisis situations, as well as the assessment of the economic and social situation of the state, and of the outlook for the world economy. The programme is developed for the period of five years and may be updated annually, if the conditions under which it was developed have changed. Owing to this solution, the system is able to dynamically respond to any change in security conditions. Moreover, the act provides a possibility to plan the budgetary funds to finance operations in the event of threats which could not have been foreseen and in particular to finance the costs of making the reserves available in crisis situations.

The ARM can carry out its tasks on its own or entrust the storage of reserves to another entity, with pay, on the basis of a storage agreement, the elements of which are defined in the act.

Institutions responsible for planning economic support for security purposes. Planning of economic support for national security purposes is indirectly reflected in a number of legal acts. It concerns, *inter alia,* special acts, which form the basis for implementation of economically important investments in the country. However, there is no single comprehensive regulation in this regard.

---

[10] Research carried out in the field of biology, ecology, medicine and agriculture – in accordance with the classification of the Innovative Economy Operational Programme.

Another problem is the lack of consistent policy of the state with regard to a broadly under-stood planning of economic support for national security purposes, including a clear definition of responsibilities and tasks as well as the provision of appropriate powers and tools. Such a problem is evident in the field of energy security and in particular of the protection of the critical infrastructure, where, on the one hand, the responsibility for energy security– according to the act – lies with the minister, and, on the other hand, the powers and appointment of security officers – due to the owner supervision – is in the hands of the minister of treasury.

* * *

This analysis of the Polish economic potential reveals its diverse influence on the shaping of national security and the definition of national interests and strategic objectives. The development of economy is a positive factor. Despite the current crisis, Poland has managed to maintain the growth of its gross domestic product. Moderation in defining interests and strategic objectives, however, stems from the condition of public finances resulting from the general imbalance of the financial sector. Its main causes are the public debt and deficit in the public finance sector.

Ensuring energy security is another challenge for Poland. The shale gas resources provide an opportunity in this regard. However, Poland is one of the poorest countries in Europe in terms of water resources. Current water consumption rates (mainly in the industrial sector) grow year by year. Aga-inst this background, a positive element is forests, which are a strategic asset determining the environ-mental security. The condition of the infrastructure is unsatisfactory. Maintaining the necessary level of food self-sufficiency of the country, the bio-security of food products, as well as the drinking and industrial water resources is another challenge which must be taken into account when determining the national interest and strategic objectives in the field of security.

The diagnosis of the Poland's economic potential indicates that national interests and strategic objectives in the field of security should include the following: the improvement of innovativeness, effectiveness and competitiveness of economy; ensuring the financial stability of the country and its energy security; and ensuring the environmental protection.

1.3. National interests and strategic objectives in the field of security

The events of the late 1980s and early 1990s led to significant changes in the international situation in Europe and in the world. As a consequence, Poland became a sovereign and democratic country in constitutional and political terms. Its position was additionally strengthened after its acces-sion to the North Atlantic Treaty Organization (1999) and the European Union (2004). Poland's direct surroundings witnessed some positive changes, too. The fact that Poland and Germany are members of NATO and the EU, their close bilateral collaboration, including within the Weimar Triangle, and the practical military cooperation (including between Poland, Denmark and Germany within the Multi-national Corps Northeast), all they made it possible to fully normalise mutual relations, thus opening up a new good-neighbourliness chapter. Slovakia's and the Czech Republic's memberships in the EU and NATO as well as cooperation within the Visegrád Group have consolidated the rapports among southern neighbours. Strengthening of Poland's position through memberships in NATO and the EU enabled to develop the partnership cooperation with Russia. In addition, Poland has consistently supported the existence of independent and sovereign Ukraine.

As a result, Poland's security situation has greatly improved. A menace in the form of a large, conventional conflict in Central Europe is currently very unlikely. Poland's territorial integrity is not called into question, its constitutional system ensures democratic, political independence and internal stability, and the economic development helps improve the quality of life of citizens.

A diagnosis of Poland's potential is necessary in order to correctly define its national interests and strategic objectives in the field of security. This constitutes the starting point for elaboration (taking into consideration the outlook for the development of external and internal security) of a comprehensive concept of the national security system, including the operational and preparatory options of the system.

The starting point of the proposed catalogue of interests and objectives is a set of the constitutional interests, i.e. the fundamental functions of the Republic of Poland set forth in Article 5 of the Constitution, which are as follows: the existence of the independent Polish state within inviolable borders; the free and safe life of its citizens; the sustainable development of the societal and economic potential of the state, with the constitutional emphasis placed on the issues of national heritage and the protection of the environment.

The said functions correspond to the four spheres of the Republic of Poland as a national whole: the state as a political national organization; the citizens as a national community; the intangible (spiritual) potential, an element of which is the historical heritage, including in particular the national identity and culture; as well as the material potential built in the course of the social and economic development, including the need of protecting the natural environment.

The constitutional interests can be specified by referring to the two fundamental spheres of activity of any state, i.e. development and security. Consequently, two groups of national interests can be identified: the development interests and the security interests. This White Book analyses primarily the national interests of the Republic of Poland in the field of security, because the development interests were the subject of analyses carried out as part of the government's work on integrated development strategies of the country.

In practice, there are two dimensions of the implementation of national interests in the field of security (as in the case of an entire security strategy): the operational dimension and the preparatory dimension. In both cases, specific strategic objectives in the field of security can be identified.

Consequently, in the wake of disaggregation of the constitutional interests, while taking into account the above-mentioned procedure, a catalogue of the national interests and strategic objectives in the field of security was compiled, as presented in table 5.

The catalogue can be termed a "constitutional catalogue", as it was drawn up following an analysis of the state's fundamental functions listed in Article 5 of the Constitution of the Republic of Poland in the context of security.

Table 5. The catalogue of national interests and strategic objectives

NATIONAL INTERESTS		STRATEGIC OBJECTIVES IN THE FIELD OF SECURITY	
CONSTITUTIONAL (Article 5 of the Constitution of the Republic of Poland)	IN THE FIELD OF SECURITY (readiness and capability to secure constitutional interests)	OPERATIONAL OBJECTIVES (directions of activities – readiness)	PREPARATORY OBJECTIVES (the scope of preparations – capabilities)
Existence of the independent Polish state within inviolable borders (the state)	Having an effective national security potential (readiness and capability to deter, defend and protect)	Implementing an active policy of seizing opportunities and eliminating preventively risks in the field of security	Developing, maintaining and transforming the integrated national security system, including the control subsystem and the executive (operational and support) subsystem
		Maintaining political, decision-making, planning and training readiness to effectively respond to threats to the independence and territorial integrity of the Republic of Poland	
		Maintaining the constitutional order and internal stability	
	Membership in credible international security systems	Participating in activities undertaken by security organizations, of which Poland is a member, the aim of which is to build and maintain the operational readiness to act in the spheres: political and decision-making, planning and training	Contributing to the improvement of NATO defence capabilities and to the development of the EU defence capabilities
		Participating in international efforts aimed at reducing the sources of threats, including international security operations	Maintaining national capabilities to participate in defence of allies and in international security operations
Freedoms and security of citizens (citizens and society)	Citizens' freedom to exercise their rights and human liberties, without detriment to the security of other persons and the security of the state	Participating in the promotion internationally as well as fostering among the Polish society of the principles and awareness of proper exercise of human and civil rights and liberties	Developing and improving legal regulations and general education on rights and freedoms
		Eliminating the sources of threats to the freedom to exercise rights and liberties as well as consistently prosecuting and punishing offenders against the said freedom	Organizing, equipping and training of services and institutions responsible for ensuring the freedom to exercise rights and civil liberties
	Individual protection of citizens and collective protection of the population against accidental or intentional threats to their life and health as well as against violation, loss, or degradation of (material and intangible) assets at their disposal	Maintaining a high level of planning, training and operational readiness to quickly respond to crisis threats (individually – to persons, and collectively – to population and its assets)	Improving legal regulations in the area of crisis management, civil protection and public security
			Organizational and technical development (modernization) of services and institutions responsible for civil protection, public security and crisis management

NATIONAL INTERESTS		STRATEGIC OBJECTIVES IN THE FIELD OF SECURITY	
CONSTITUTIONAL (Article 5 of the Constitution of the Republic of Poland)	IN THE FIELD OF SECURITY (readiness and capability to secure constitutional interests)	OPERATIONAL OBJECTIVES (directions of activities – readiness)	PREPARATORY OBJECTIVES (the scope of preparations – capabilities)
Development of the societal potential of the state with emphasis on national heritage (intangible resources)	Safe conditions for the development of the societal potential	Protecting entities that are part of the societal potential against the destructive impact of external and internal threats in peacetime, crisis and war	Improving principles, procedures, and capabilities concerning the cooperation between entities that are part of the societal potential with services responsible for their protection and defence in peacetime, crisis and war
	Societal support for security	Informational, educational, scientific, technical and other support for activities undertaken by various operational entities within the national security system	Developing binding strategies, plans, and programmes for the preparation (maintenance and improvement) of capabilities of societal entities of the state to function in an emergency (crisis) situation and in war, including to carry out tasks aimed at providing support to operational entities within the national security system
Development of the economic potential of the state with emphasis on the protection of the natural environment (material resources)	Safe conditions for the development of the economic potential	Protecting entities that are part of the economic potential against the destructive impact of external and internal threats in peacetime, crisis and war	Improving principles, procedures, and capabilities concerning the cooperation between entities that are part of the economic potential with services responsible for their protection and defence in peacetime, crisis and war
	Economic support for security	Financial, energy, infrastructural, material and other support for activities undertaken by operational entities within the national security system	Developing binding strategies, plans, and programmes for the preparation (maintenance and improvement) of capabilities of economic entities of the state to function in an emergency (crisis) situation and in war, including to carry out tasks aimed at providing support to operational entities within the national security system

Sources: authors' own compilation.

It is also important to stress that as far as the typology of strategic objectives in the field of security is concerned, two spheres of security can be additionally considered: the sphere of external relations (external security) and the sphere of internal relations (internal security). What is more, two kinds of activities supporting the national interests can be identified within each of these spheres: strengthening of all that contributes to security (positive relations with other entities, the state's own strengths) and combating all that undermines it (negative international phenomena and the state's own weaknesses). That is why, in more detailed analysis, an additional study of the following four types of strategic objectives in the field of security might be helpful: promoting the positive in the international environment and seizing the resulting opportunities; counteracting external risks and threats; reinforcing the country's own strengths; and eliminating one's own weaknesses.

* * *

Analysis of the process of shaping the national identity and statehood shows that the most critical factors were the following: creating the conditions for the development of the state, nation and society which consolidate the historical heritage and national identity; providing adequate resources and capabilities for the national security system; building and maintaining Poland's strong position internationally through consistent diplomatic activities, including integration ones (alliances).

The principles set forth in the constitution – of the democratic rule of law, upholding the principles of social justice, the protection of freedoms and rights of persons and citizens; the unitary nature of the state; the supreme power (sovereignty) of the nation and political representation; separation and balance among the public authorities; the decentralization of the state administration and local government as well as the function of ensuring security and inviolability of the state's borders – all determine the constitutional and political conditions of Poland and provide the framework for the formulation of the catalogue of interests and strategic objectives in the field of security.

The defence potential is systematically reinforced. Its key element is the fully professionalized Polish Armed Forces which are being gradually modernized. This potential has a positive impact on the level of Polish strategic ambitions.

The protection potential (services and guards) plays an important role in defining the national interests and strategic objectives. It faces, however, a number of difficult challenges. These include: the broadly understood organized crime, terrorism (including cyber-terrorism) and illegal migration. The excessive number of the services and dispersed supervision complicate the coordination and undermine the coherence of their operations.

The societal and economic potential of Poland affects the process of defining the national interests and strategic objectives in the field of security in various ways. The sustainable socio-economic development of Poland ensures adequate resources and capabilities for the state's security system. The development of economy is a positive factor. The state of public finances, resulting from the general imbalance of the financial sector, has a restrictive impact. The country's demographic situation may also have negative consequences.

The analysis of the above elements of Poland's security potential made it possible to compile a catalogue of national interests and strategic objectives in the field of security. To the constitutional national interests in the spheres such as: the state, citizen, and society, intangible resources and material resources, relevant national security interests were assigned, within which, in turn, strategic (operational and preparatory) security objectives were identified. The catalogue of the national interests and strategic objectives in the field of security provides the basis for discussions in subsequent chapters.

Chapter 2

THE SECURITY
ENVIRONMENT
OUTLOOK

In this chapter, the present state of affairs is presented as well as forecasts regarding the strategic security environment in external (international) and internal (national) as well as military and non- -military terms are outlined. The analysis comprises opportunities, challenges, risks and threats the Republic of Poland will face during the next 20 years.

It is assumed that in the two decades to come, the conditions of external and internal security of Poland shall evolve very dynamically, therefore forecasting should also reflect the dynamic – and sometimes difficult to predict – behaviour of actors of international relations in global and regional dimensions, as well as the development of national factors. Consequently, this should allow to outline possible scenarios of development of Poland's security conditions.

Warsaw, 16 June 2011.
2nd Plenary Conference of the National Security Strategic Review. Discussion on main theses developed by the Security Environment Assessment Team.
Photo: BBN

2.1. The global dimension

The security of a nation on the international arena is a combination of its internal power and capabilities that can be shaped depending on the possibilities and needs as well as the external factors the influence of which can be modified only to a limited extent.

Effects of globalization. Globalization processes have yielded both positive and negative re- sults. On the one hand, they have enabled the global flows of thoughts, people, capital, technology, etc. at an unprecedented scale. This had a positive impact on the acceleration of development processes across the globe. On the other hand, this led to the dissemination of a wide range of negative phenome- na. Internal political, economic and financial crises, international terrorism, cyber-threats, organized crime, corruption, trafficking in human beings and drugs, money laundering, maritime piracy and similar phenomena spread quickly across the globe from one region to another. Adaptation to globa- lization is uneven and entails turbulences in international relations.

The role of the state as the main player on the international arena is waning. This trend is palpable all over the world. The regulatory role of the state towards external entities is being limited. This phenomenon is beneficial in some areas, as it stabilizes the situation through the voluntary delegation of certain sovereign rights onto the international level. It increases the predictability of states' behaviour and offers better opportunities of coordinating activities, and enforces the harmonization of the law (the condition of EU membership). However, states are now facing more serious and more varied challenges stemming from the presence of powerful non-state players – supranational corporations, organized crime, terrorist organizations, and even private paramilitary companies. In unfavourable circumstances these organizations may, albeit to a varied degree – become factors of instability.

The changing role of main international actors. In recent years, the gradual constraining of the United States of America as a global superpower has become visible. However, the USA remains a global military power. In the previous decade, the public debt of the USA soared, which was in part the result of the wars in Afghanistan and Iraq, as well as the problems of the American economy: high consumption levels, the low savings volume and ineffective supervision of the banking system. As a result, the United States is gradually falling out of the role of the "global policeman". This means that it is already necessary for the EU member states to increase their responsibility for security in their direct strategic surroundings (operations in Libya in 2011 and in Mali in 2013).

However, one ought to bear in mind that the USA is still a highly innovative country characterized by a high level of entrepreneurship as well as dynamic and technical development. As the country that issues the currency in which the vast majority of financial reserves is held, the USA has a very flexible budget.

Just a few years ago, the European Union, as a whole, was perceived as the second global power. The crises verified this assessment. At the end of the previous decade the EU entered a phase of turbulences and attempts to structurally adjust to new challenges. the common currency was endangered, and as a result the very existence of the Union in its current institutional shape was in question.

The probability that in the coming decades the position of the EU among other strategic players will be weakened is relatively high. Currently, approximately 20 per cent of global GDP is generated in Europe. In 2030, this share will, however, probably amount to ca. 10-15 per cent, while in 2050, this share may fall to 5-10 per cent.

It ought to be underlined that the EU has become a stability factor in international relations at the global level and a significant normative force (international legislation). This situation should be considered an auspicious opportunity for the future.

Emerging powers. The increasing pluralism of the global correlation of forces stems mainly from the rapid growth of new powerful states whose significance exceeds regional status. As a result, for a few decades the focus of the global balance of powers has been shifting from the Euro-Atlantic area to the Pacific and Asia, which is a challenge for Europe. The change in the global configuration of powers is being brought about particularly by China, and – to a lesser extent – Brazil, India and Russia[11] (the so-called BRIC group). The total economic potential of the latter three states is notably weaker than that of the Chinese economy measured by purchasing power parity (PPP). The declared

---

[11] The Russian Federation will be discussed in greater detail in the part dedicated to the regional dimension.

strategic partnership of Russia and China did not entail establishing a defence alliance; the "emerging superpowers" also failed to form lasting coalitions. At this stage, shifts in the balance of powers do not give rise to armed conflicts, albeit clashes cannot be excluded in the future. In this aspect, what attracts attention is the growing activity of China in the Far East, which Beijing considers to be the Chinese zone of influence. This position of China might be exacerbated if the influence of the military and nationalist groups increases in the Chinese authorities. The possible aggravation of the economic situation, including social attitudes, might lead to the adoption of a nationalist direction in foreign policy by the Chinese authorities. This would probably increase the frequency of clashes between China and its neighbours, e.g. concerning the seas surrounding China. The relations between China and Taiwan, which are already very strong, are being tightened. Reintegration with Taiwan would notably strengthen the geopolitical position of China (control of sea routes) as well as their innovation, research and economic potential. This means, among other things, that one cannot exclude the possibility of an escalation of the conflict concerning Taiwan between Beijing and Washington, which is the guarantor of Taiwan's security.

Owing to the focus on economic aspects, the role of the military factor in the growth of the Chinese superpower is not decisive at the moment. In the course of time, however, the constantly rising Chinese military spending may have a significant impact on the global correlation of forces.

Brazil is quickly climbing the ranking of states that count on the international arena. Specialists of the International Monetary Fund estimate that it will take fifth position in terms of GDP already in 2015. In contrast to the remaining members of the BRIC group, Brazil devotes equal attention to the development of the economy and political power, including the so-called soft power.

According to the World Bank's GDP ranking, India takes the tenth place. In the opinion of many economists, in the next twenty years India will become a leader of the global race for the title of the largest world economy. Apart from economic expansion, India focuses on the development of its military potential (owing to the conflict with Pakistan). Significant purchases of military equipment are accompanied by acquisitions of licensed technological lines for military equipment assembly.

Increased significance of regional powers. The changes in the international balance of powers also cover a group of medium-sized states that has emerged and aspires to the role of regional powers. Important non-European representatives of this group are as follows: Iran, Indonesia, Pakistan, South Africa, Turkey and Nigeria. In the context of emerging medium-sized powers, Turkey (which is a NATO member and candidate for full EU membership) is of particular significance for the interests of Poland, as is, to a lesser extent, Iran.

Turkey holds the key strategic geographical place between Asia and Europe, and lies close to North Africa. Economic outlooks of western research centres indicate that in the next 25 years, GDP of Turkey, measured by PPP (which currently exceeds a trillion of US dollars), in the next quarter of a century will rise faster than GDP of Russia, and much faster than GDP of the EU. As a result, in 2050, the Turkish economy will be only slightly less powerful than that of Russia or Germany. In the coming decades, Turkey will have the opportunity to join the group of highest-developed states in the world.

In the coming years, it is predicted that Turkey's significance will increase in the Middle East and in North Africa, as well as in the post-Soviet area, especially in the Black Sea basin and in the

South Caucasus and Central Asia. In the face of the increase in Muslim population in the former Soviet space, this country will gain greater influence in the region.

Iran is an Islamic state with a notable and rising demographic potential accompanied by increasing political ambitions. Its future is of importance for the process of shaping regional and global security (the so-called Greater Middle East). In the Euro-Asian network of energy-related interests, this state is important, as it holds immense oil resources (third place in the world, more than 10 per cent of the market) and gas (second place in the world, approximately 15 per cent of the market), whose sales and transit to Europe would have great impact on global energy relations. The second reason for Iran's significance is of military character: acquisition of nuclear weapons by this state and a possible armed conflict resulting from this fact would have very serious consequences for the configuration of powers in the Greater Middle East, also on the global scale. If Iran gains the capacity to produce a nuclear device and obtains appropriate means for its delivery, one might assume that the USA and Israel would not accept such a situation. It cannot be ruled out that Israel would carry out armed operations (on its own or in cooperation with the USA) targeting Iranian nuclear installations.

Failed states. Threats to international security are increasingly generated by the internal affairs of states. This concerns especially the so-called failed states that are incapable of ensuring control of their territory or guaranteeing the protection and security of their borders. As a result, they become a haven for fundamentalist terrorist organizations and organized crime. In times of globalization and IT spread, the political message of these organizations and the actual tangible effects of their activity can reach recipients anywhere across the globe immediately. Until 2001, Afghanistan was an exemplary failed state. It was ruled by the Taliban regime that provided protection to training camps of international terrorist organizations. Currently, there is growing concern that the Afghan scenario might repeat itself in Mali and other Sahel states. In the perspective of the coming 20 years, the phenomenon of so-called failed states will remain the most important concern of international communities.

Erosion of international agreements and organizations and the proliferation of weapons of mass destruction. The changes in the global correlation of forces are accompanied by the erosion of most important international agreements. This process is becoming more and more apparent, especially in the case of those accords that concern disarmament regimes based on the Treaty on the Non-Proliferation of Nuclear Weapons (NPT), as well as disarmament treaties on: Conventional Armed Forces in Europe (CFE) and the Elimination of Intermediate-Range and Shorter-Range Missiles (INF). Additionally, the international community has yet to ratify the Comprehensive Nuclear-Test-Ban Treaty (CTBT) and the Fissile Material Cut-off Treaty (FMCT). More and more often, the problems connected with proliferation and armaments are discussed at informal meetings and produce informal arrangements, which is beneficial in the short run, but does not eliminate the impermanence and uncertainty related with these areas.

The growing proliferation of weapons of mass destruction can give rise to three "black scenarios": "nuclear anarchy" resulting from a breakdown of the global non-proliferation regime based on the NPT; the destabilization of a state that holds nuclear weapons; or the threat or use of nuclear means by terrorists.

The actions of Iran expose the weaknesses of the non-proliferation regime and the NPT itself. It turns out that states might obtain threshold capacities in the area of nuclear weapons and at the same time formally comply with the limitations imposed by treaties. The policy of Iran poses the risk of a chain reaction in the region, where states one after another would display interest in acquiring nuclear know-how and technology. North Korean nuclear tests also have negative regional and global effects: on the one hand, they elicit the concern of neighbouring states and worsen regional security. On the other hand, they challenge the NPT and undermine the perspective of ratifying the treaty on the global and comprehensive ban on nuclear testing. The case of Iran shows that North Korea and Pakistan might also be suppliers of technology and materials to other states interested in acquiring nuclear weapons and means of their delivery contrary to the valid international agreements.

There is also the danger that a country that possesses nuclear weapons and means of their delivery would be destabilised. Pakistan is a good example here, as it has dozens of nuclear warheads (probably not installed and stored at various locations) and ballistic missiles capable of their delivery. Uncertainty concerning the permanence of the ruling authorities and the loyalty towards the power apparatus, special services as well as the army, combined with religious and political fundamentalism, the proximity of Afghanistan and Central Asia – all that raises concerns regarding the security of the Pakistani arsenal.

One cannot also exclude the possibility of use or the threat to use (and blackmail is almost equally dangerous as fulfilment of the threat) nuclear weapons by terrorists, e.g. in a large urban centre in the West. Such weapons can be either stolen or self-assembled; today, it is already technically possible to use a conventional explosive to disperse radioactive materials (so-called dirty bomb). Even if the number of victims is low and material losses negligent, the political, social and psychological effects of such an attack would be immense. It is also worth noting that terrorists might use biological weapons, e.g. to poison drinking water.

The regime of controlling conventional arms is gradually eroding. It has been significantly weakened, among other things, due to Russia's non-fulfilment of the commitments taken at the 1999 Istanbul summit, and because it afterwards suspended the implementation of the CFE treaty. In the perspective of the coming years, there is nothing indicative of Russia resuming the implementation of treaty provisions. The breach of the culture of dialogue and cooperation in the area of arms control is another issue.

What is particularly destabilising here is the proliferation of various missile systems. The rapid development of missiles is characteristic mainly of unstable regions tormented by long-term military and political crises. In the Middle East, Iran and Syria have developed systems capable of targeting places located in Israel and American bases across the region. Combined with the nuclear ambitions of Iran, this might elicit pre-emptive reactions by Israel and the United States.

The rivalry between India and Pakistan might have dangerous consequences, as both these states possess nuclear weapons. In this nuclear arms race, India has initiated a new phase of confrontation by starting the development and construction of air- and sea-launched cruise missiles.

Poland pays special attention to the development of the missile systems of the Russian Federation. The situation is complicated by the non-transparent policy of Russia and the repeated

Charter of the United Nations signed on 26 June 1945 in San Francisco

Article 39
The Security Council shall determine the existence of any threat to the peace, breach of the peace, or act of aggression and shall make recommendations, or decide what measures shall be taken in accordance with Articles 41 and 42, to maintain or restore international peace and security.

Article 41
The Security Council may decide what measures not involving the use of armed force are to be employed to give effect to its decisions, and it may call upon the Members of the United Nations to apply such measures. These may include complete or partial interruption of economic relations and of rail, sea, air, postal, telegraphic, radio, and other means of communication, and the severance of diplomatic relations.

Article 42
Should the Security Council consider that measures provided for in Article 41 would be inadequate or have proved to be inadequate, it may take such action by air, sea, or land forces as may be necessary to maintain or restore international peace and security.
Such action may include demonstrations, blockade, and other operations by air, sea, or land forces of Members of the United Nations.

threats of developing offensive missile systems close to Poland's borders (Kaliningrad *oblast*) in response to the construction of an allied (NATO) anti-missile defence system. The situation would rapidly deteriorate if Russia withdrew from the INF treaty. The postulates of some NATO members concerning the withdrawal of US tactical nuclear weapons from Europe do not make the situation any simpler. Such a withdrawal would be a US strategic manoeuvre, while a similar decision taken by Russia (pullout of tactical nuclear weapons to the Asian part of Russia) would only be a tactical step. However, owing to the strategic interests of the USA, it is hardly likely that the Americans would withdraw their tactical nuclear weapons in the foresee – able future.

International organizations that are concerned with security and had until recently monitored compliance with these agreements are now changing their roles and functions. It is becoming more and more apparent that they do not adapt sufficiently to the dynamic changes in the international environment.

The political and military functions (peace missions) of the United Nations have dwindled. The UN Security Council has yet to be reformed, and the postulated changes would better reflect today's configuration of powers. This is significant, because the Security Council formally remains the ultimate decision-making platform that legitimizes the use of force (although force is more and more often used without its mandate).

The functions of the UN, however, have increased in the area of development and social issues. This very type of activity seems to delineate the most probable direction of growth that common international organizations will adopt in the coming years.

Global challenges and transnational and asymmetric threats.

Security is constantly shaped anew while new challenges and threats appear. They concern not only particular political actors on the political scene, but also entire regions, continents and civilization circles. These phenomena will become more intense in the future. Although they are not of military nature, they pose a threat to many sectors of public life and might disrupt the functioning of states and organizations. Threats of this sort, referred to as transnational and asymmetric, are difficult to uproot, as – being of supranational, even global, nature – they are mainly not connected with the existence of a specific state-perpetrator and specific territory. As a result, these negative phenomena acquire a new dimension: the criminal activity that had been known for years escalates as supranational organized crime, local terrorism becomes global terrorism that functions across borders, and economic crises in one part of the world have a negative impact on the economy of other, also far-off, regions.

Globalization and the information revolution impact the security environment by shaping its new quality. On the one hand, it is characterized by growing interdependence and integration at the level of states, nations and societies, and on the other hand, by increasing unpredictability and uncertain further development. Though globalization and the information revolution yield great, tangible advantages for the economy, communication and education, thanks to which these are perceived as desired instruments and engines of change, still, they are accompanied by unfavoura-ble phenomena that have a negative impact on safety and security. In the "globinfo" environment, transformations connected with the appearance of new asymmetric threats, as well as the shifts in the nature of the already existing ones, occur. The most important threats here are terrorism, cyber--threats and international organized crime. Governments have to face the additional challenge of rising up to the phenomenon of cyber-protests, which are becoming an increasingly popular form of expressing public disapproval.

Terrorism. Although for the last few years the number of attacks has been falling, terrorism remains one of the main asymmetric and transnational threats to international and national secu-rity. It poses a risk to the lives of citizens, the stability of democratic institutions, infrastructure of the state and other elements of its correct functioning. It is the tool for conducting radical political or ideological warfare. Irrespective of the initial motivation of the perpetrators, and despite the en-hancement of national counteracting mechanisms and systems and international initiatives aimed at its combating, it will remain one of the main threats to the international community (fig. 30).

Terrorism motivated by radical Islamic ideology is a particularly dangerous threat. In re-cent years, this type of terrorism has evolved from the activity of small regional organizations with a hierarchical structure to the global jihad network (Al-Qaeda). This network is composed mainly of autonomous cells functioning in various regions of the world, inspired by extremist ideology, with the common strategic goal of destroying the western world and eradicating its non-material symptoms. The expansion of global jihad will probably continue, and it will be characterized by the application of increasingly refined methods and tactics that exploit the loopholes in the security systems of states.

Fig. 30. Number of terrorist attacks and arrested persons suspected of terrorism in Europe in years 2007-2011

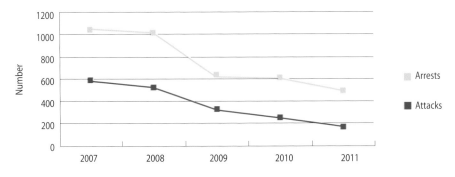

Source: TE-SAT 2012. EU Terrorism Situation and Trend Report.

What is characteristic of the current and future terrorism of this type is the attempt to shift the focus of its activity to the western world by intensifying the phenomenon of home-grown terrorism (radicalization and performance of attacks by followers of Islam who are the second or further generation of migrants born in western states or converts to Islam), as well as the call for so-called individual jihad, expressed by ideologists and organization leaders.

Terrorists will still mainly aim at shocking a given society by conducting spectacular attacks that will cause as many victims as possible. However, smaller attacks might also be performed at a larger scale, e.g. in the European countries, to destabilise order and keep up the feeling of insecurity in societies.

Extremist terrorism, which has been reawakening recently, is a type of terrorism that differs from the above-mentioned in terms of its basis and ideological motives, yet it brings about similar effects. One can distinguish: extremely leftist, far-rightist, nationalist and separatist terrorism. It constitutes a threat also for the European countries, and it stems from, *inter alia*, xenophobia, aversion towards immigrants, the economic crisis and the dissatisfaction of the society with the remedies adopted by the governments. Most attacks of such groups are aimed at business and government targets. One should expect that the number of such acts of terror will keep increasing in the future.

Previously marginalized far-rightist or nationalist movements will probably become an increasing threat to the stability of democratic states. Approaches negating the liberal concepts of multiculturalism and openness are becoming more and more popular. This leads to the formation of a dangerous new trend that employs terrorism as its method of conducting combat and manifesting radical anti-immigrant and conservative views. This phenomenon applies not only to organizations, but also to individuals (the "lone wolf" terrorists).

Susceptibility to cyber-threats. The susceptibility of states to cyber-threats, including terrorism-related cyber-risks, is growing. This is an upward trend, and it will systematically increase in the future.

The functioning of a modern economically-developed state is inextricably bound with ensuring permanent and correctly functioning systems for data collection and transmission, as well as monitoring and control systems. Cyber-aggression might also be employed by the authorities or services of hostile states that are ready to engage in an information war, as well as big concerns, non-governmental or supranational organizations, including criminal organizations, as well as groups of activists, informal Internet users groups, and even individual users. As the experience of recent years has shown, cyber-attacks might also have an ideological, political, religious and business background. One cannot rule out that in the near future cyber-attacks, targeted mainly at critical infrastructure, will become the tool for blackmailing by organized crime organizations. The fact that it is extremely difficult to prove the perpetration of such an attack is conducive to the performance of such acts. Technological development with its incredible dynamics will lead to the creation and promotion of new attack techniques and methods, and the threats classified as conventional will be reflected by new types of crime in the virtual world, e.g. as cyber-protests or cyber-demonstrations. The threats that appear in virtual space will be more and more often classified as situations that jeopardize national safety and stability. In the future, cyber-attacks will probably be treated just like any act of breaching the sovereignty of the state and its citizens. In the next two decades, such events and the responses to them will be classed as conventional activity in the area of cyber-warfare and cyber-conflict. Challenges may emerge regarding the necessity to take a political decision on whether to consider hostile activity an attack against the state. Such a decision may shift the conflict to a dimension other than cyberspace.

Terrorist organizations are also active in virtual space. Until now, cyber-space was used to perform large-scale propaganda, training and recruitment activities, however one can now observe a new type of threats and the trend to move purely terrorist activities to cyber-space (attacks aimed at information and communications technology networks and technological systems that are of strategic importance for states). In the coming years, the significance of the information environment and the security of cyber-space will undoubtedly rise and become one of the top priorities in adjusting mechanisms ensuring international security.

In this situation, it is a great challenge for governments to attempt to draw the line between personal freedom and the protection of individuals' rights in the virtual world, and the means applied to ensure security.

The scale in which cyber-space, and especially online blogs and social portals, might impact the security of states, was exemplified during the "Arab Spring" that commenced in 2011: participants of the street events and protests, when they were shut off from conventional mass media, effectively organized their activity via social networks such as Facebook and Twitter. This is most certainly an upward trend that will become more apparent in the future, parallel to the dissemination of modern technologies among users.

Source: Fotolia.

International organized crime and corruption. The globalization process also covers organized crime and corruption. Illegal trading in drugs, high-gain goods and raw materials (gold, precious stones, works of art, weapons and cigarettes), people (immigrants and "slave trade") and their organs, illegal cash flows (including money laundering), cyber-space (computer-aided fraud and forgery, extortion of information, theft and destruction of data and information, economic intelligence, breach of copyrights, child pornography, gambling, etc.) are becoming the domain of supranational groups. Some of them have at their disposal funds exceeding GDP of medium-sized states. Factors conducive to their activity include the existence of migration diasporas and weak state structures, including especially those of so-called failed states. These symptoms of crime are often linked to corruption. At the international scale, it weakens, *inter alia*, transparency and stabilization, and contributes to the appearance of crisis activities.

There is a concern (which is highly likely to come true) that these phenomena will become more intense in the coming years and will evolve in directions that are increasingly difficult to combat by national and international police services, as the funds generated by criminal activity in one state are located in legal enterprises registered in another country.

One may expect that in the perspective of next few years, criminal organizations, including the terrorist ones, will increasingly frequently opt for opportunities offered by the development of modern technologies and globalization. The fields of criminal activity will not change noticeably; however, technology will play a more and more important role in this regard. The combination of globalization processes and the development of modern technologies in criminal activity will also expand opportunities for cooperation between various criminal groups, regardless of ethnic or cultural differences. The functioning of unstable states and the existence of places and regions that constitute "hot spots" with incapable administrative and ineffective security bodies will also have impact on the international criminal groups gaining in power.

In the global environment, for the most time security-related threats and challenges other than conventional (military) ones are going to intensify in the coming decades. One of the most important challenges are **economic crisis phenomena**. They generate more and more problems connected with state security. In terms of structural economic problems, the world and Europe are in a worse position than during the first decade of the current century. Numerous risks and destabilization factors have accumulated, especially in the context of the shift in the global balance of powers: China and other states with high economic growth are simultaneously the main creditors of the USA and Europe. The deepening deregulation of financial markets has led to a massive escalation of financial speculation, where a small group piles up gains, while wide social strata are pauperised.

The main destabilization factors involve:
- The general slowdown of the economic growth rate, except for China, Brazil, India and several other states;
- the difficult debt write-off process;
- fears regarding the possibility of the US fiscal deficit slipping out of control;
- disruptions of financial systems (indebtedness) and turbulence in the real estate sector;
- the growing unemployment, difficult access to loans;
- the inflation and drop in profits from investments;
- rising prices of raw materials owing, among other things, to the multidimensional geostrategic uncertainty in the Middle East;

- the activities of some large banks and rating agencies that destabilize the monetary systems of some states;
- concerns about the financial standing of some euro zone states (especially the Greek crisis).

These problems lead, among other things, to the trust crisis among investors, and are conducive to recession.

Demographic changes. The geography of demographic changes across the globe gives rise to concerns. It is forecast that Earth's population will reach 9 billion by 2050. Population growth will almost entirely be generated by developing countries, the majority of which are incapable of providing their residents with food, housing, jobs, medical care, education and other basic living conditions. This entails the risk of uncontrolled migration to wealthier states, especially those in Europe and North America. This risk grows during conflicts, which is troublesome for, among others, the European Union, as became evident, e.g. during the crisis in the Arab world and the civil war in Libya in 2011.

On the other hand, the developed countries have to cope with the ageing of their societies. Despite insufficient labour force, these countries display xenophobic attitudes and reluctance towards immigrants, who are considered to be a threat to national identity, and have exacerbated the crisis of multiculturalism. Demographic changes, combined with other negative global developments, e.g. economic and financial crises and climate changes, carry many potential risks, especially because existing international structures are incapable of counteracting them.

Climate changes. Challenges resulting from climate changes might result in disastrous consequences that we are not fully capable of specifying yet. They also have growing influence on the security of states, including Poland. Global warming is the remarkable change with long-term consequences. According to the data provided by the most representative group of specialists in this area, the Intergovernmental Panel on Climate Change, climate warming is undoubtedly taking place and is reflected by the increase in average air temperatures, water temperatures of seas and oceans, the melting of glaciers and the raising average sea and ocean levels. This change results from the emission, generated mainly by economic activity, and concentration of greenhouse gasses (GHG) in the atmosphere. Although scientists have yet to reach full agreement here, carbon dioxide plays a special role in this process. One ought to underline that it is likely that the changes in climate "parameters", such as temperature, precipitation, geographical range of climate zones, will modify the security conditions of social systems, as they will yield both direct threats, e.g. conflicts over water, and indirect risks, e.g. migration and epidemics.

Long-term climate changes may entail epidemics – infections of people, animals and plants that have previously not occurred in the given region or have seldom taken place. The instant spread of epidemics may also be enabled by various effects of globalization such as global transportation (especially airborne) and world trade networks, the easiness of travelling, as well as temporary or permanent migration. Such threats have until now been incidental, however, the phenomenon and related trends require constant monitoring. The examples of "swine" and "bird" flu show that such scenarios are all the more possible.

Climate change is also opening up new opportunities which will become more and more possible in the future, e.g. development of the polar regionas in connection with natural resources and transportation routes (new naval opportunities), especially in the Arctic. However, this will require the development of a new formula for cooperation between the states bordering on this area and other players willing to sustain activity in this region, e.g. China. Owing to the frequently contrary interests of these states, this will not be an easy process.

Once relatively inexpensive and accessible methods of extracting the raw materials that are covered with the ice sheet are developed, it will become possible to temporarily solve the issues related to the fact that humanity will reach the limit of further growth as forecast by scientists, which will be the result of exploiting raw materials.

Access to rare earth materials. Access to raw and energy materials that are especially rare in nature constitutes an important and constantly growing conflict-generating factor in international relations. Rare earth metals currently used, among other things, to produce, among other things, a wide range of modern industrial goods and so-called green technologies, are of special importance. The short- and medium-term rivalry for ensuring raw material security, and mainly energy security, might intensify every now and then, and the struggle may involve a threat or use of force.

Across the globe, many states depend on deliveries of raw materials, while other states have almost monopolized[12] the extraction of certain fossil fuels. However, one may assume that in the long run, the significance of access to raw materials will decline parallel to the application of new technologies and technical progress. In the area of state security policy, what is gaining in importance is such issues as diversification of deliveries, alternative energy sources, protection of transmission lines, transparency and stable functioning of the market and common energy system.

Military conflicts and crises

Apart from new non-military threats, one should also take into account the conventional risks, i.e. internal and external military conflicts and crises. One may assume that in the foreseeable future, the possibility of an eruption of a conventional conflict on a global scale, with an epicentre in Europe, is highly unlikely. However, due to globalization the potential challenges and threats to Poland's security are determined not only by tensions on the European continent, but also by the appearance of various conflict centres beyond Europe.

Political and societal changes in the Arab world. At the beginning of the second decade of this century, the political and societal turmoil in the Arab world, often referred to as "Arab Spring" became a challenge for global security. The changes occurring in that part of the world took on the character of either peaceful transformations (as in Tunisia and, to a lesser degree, Egypt), or open conflicts. The military conflict in Libya (where NATO launched operation "Unified Protector" to protect civilians) and the long-lasting conflict in Syria have had a particularly dramatic course. The latter proved to be a difficult test of the effectiveness of the international community, especially in terms of responsibility for civilians. It also has had a critical impact on the balance of regional powers, especially on the influences of Russia and Iran.

Tensions in the Arab world bear the features of a long-term process, mainly complicated by the difficult economic situation. The ties between that region and Europe are obvious: the continent is inhabited by more than ten million Muslims from the Mediterranean Basin, and their population will

---

[12] For instance, OPEC member countries produce about 40 per cent of the world's crude oil, Russia provides 12 per cent, and the USA – 10 per cent. In reference to rare earth elements, 95 per cent of their extraction is controlled by China, whose territory holds approximately 35 per cent of global resources.

increase in the next decades. The indeterminacy of the political, social and economic changes in the Arab world itself undermines the stability of Europe and Poland. It influences the position of many Western European governments on the events taking place in this region.

For more than six decades, the Israeli-Palestinian conflict has monopolised Europe's attention, with brief pauses for the recurring crisis in Lebanon fuelled by Syria and Iran, Egypt is suffering from the crisis following the fall of the regime of Hosni Mubarak, religion-based tensions between Christians and Muslims, and Muslims and Jews are recurring, there are also clashes within the Islamic community: between Shias and Sunnis. The Middle East region is also destabilised by the world power and nuclear ambitions of Iran, terrorist attacks and proliferation of weapons of mass destruction.

The Iran problem is a particularly important challenge that may bring about most serious consequences for global security. The international community have introduced economic sanctions to stop Iran from obtaining nuclear weapons. Iran's going nuclear would entail the spread of nuclear weapons across the whole Middle East, as the neighbouring Arab states will also want to have nuclear weapons of their own. If the world does not stop Iran, it will not be able to stop other countries of the region. The Middle East, today's global "powder keg", would turn into a global "nuke". If that happened, the most critical challenge would be to find a way out in the conditions of a nuclearized Middle East. It would be the most serious global strategic dilemma of the following decades.

Conflicts in South Asia. South Asia is a particular area, closely observed by the international community. After the closure of the ISAF mission in 2014, Afghanistan will, for years to come, certainly remain the state that generates serious problems in terms of regional security. The achievements of the international community in stabilizing Afghanistan are fragile, and it is not certain whether they will be sustainable after 2014 without further international support.

The nuclear standstill between India and Pakistan limits the risk of a large-scale war, but the conflict in Kashmir may turn into a clash with global implications. In the worst-case scenario, the outbreak of a war between India and Pakistan and exacerbation of the confrontation might entail a conflict between China and India, as Beijing disputes some sections of their common border.

The Korean Peninsula. The Korean Peninsula is a similar hot spot in terms of the scale of potential threats (the menace of nuclear weapons use). The totalitarian regime of North Korea (DPRK) has for many years been provoking armed incidents with South Korea. The immense risk grows as the DPRK continues its acute and confrontation-seeking line of action, which may intensify these incidents and turn them into a larger military conflict that would involve not only South Korea, but also the United States and Japan. A decisive role in reducing the risks connected with North Korea's policy may be played by China.

∗　∗　∗

The global political scene is changing dynamically. As a result of the progressing globalization, the regulatory functions of states have been weakened with non-state actors, taking advantage of these developmends. This process will intensify, and will bear consequences especially in non-military security dimensions.

As new powers rise, the states that previously unquestionably dominated decline slowly and relatively. One might expect that especially China's rise will have the most spectacular global impact. Alongside the level of global security is falling with the weakening of the most important international organizations and disarmament regimes. This negative trend will probably continue in the future.

The global situation might be termed "co-dependent instability", as crises are being shifted from one region to another (sometimes very distant). In the globalized world, this trend will gain momentum.

2.2. The regional dimension

The territory of Europe, and especially its geopolitical and economic centre (the European Union), is and will be the zone of internal stability towards which other states gravitate. However, military conflicts of limited range may arise on the peripheries of the EU (such as the 2008 Georgia-Russia armed conflict), which may alter the political situation and affect the security of the Republic of Poland. Both areas (the centre and the peripheries) are characterized by security asymmetry. While central states (including Poland) are linked by a vast network of international cooperation based mainly on NATO and the EU (fig. 31), peripheral states remain in the "grey security zone".

Fig. 31. Poland's membership in international organizations and institutions – as of 1 January 2013.

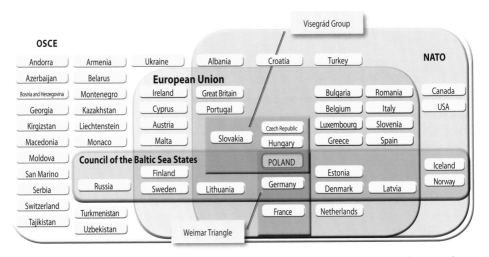

Source: authors' own compilation.

Factors influencing Europe's security environment

Currently, European security rests on a few, constantly evolving, co-related, albeit heterogeneous, components. The **North Atlantic Alliance** is undoubtedly the most important element here, as it is capable of using "hard" force to guarantee the protection of its members. Importantly, NATO strengthens the geopolitical ties between the USA and Europe and warrants American presence on the European continent.

After the end of the cold war confrontation, the Alliance successfully adapted itself to the altered international reality. This was possible because the Alliance undertook to perform new tasks (out-of-area missions), admitted new members and established and developed intense cooperation with partners.

NATO is, and probably will remain, the most powerful and effective political and military alliance capable of successful deterrence and defence. This organization has redefined its tasks in the post-cold war international situation by adding two new objectives to its core mission: crisis management (crisis response) and cooperative security. These core tasks constitute part of NATO's Strategic Concept adopted at the summit held in Lisbon in November 2010.

Though the North Atlantic Alliance remains the most powerful political and military organization, in recent years certain weaknesses have become apparent in its coping with contemporary challenges and threats. Differences in opinions within the Alliance appeared, especially in the area of risk assessment, necessary military capabilities, involvement in out-of-area operations and the pace and scale of developing relations with the former adversary – Russia. The role of NATO may also be weakened by the tendency to transform the Alliance into a *de facto* collective or "cooperative" security organization that may impair the classical functions of a defence alliance. The trends that may arouse concerns are the intensification of the "*ad hoc* coalition" practice and the perception of the Alliance as a "tool box".

Currently, the main challenge that faces NATO is the redefinition of its role in the post-Afghan period. It is hard to say whether the Alliance, after two decades of post-cold war enlargement, will move on to a new phase of consolidation focused on the basic function of ensuring direct security of its members, or whether it will continue the operational and institutional management of its increasingly global role. What seems more useful is the consolidation of NATO around its underlying defensive function following from Article 5 of the 1949 Washington Treaty, and the performance of feasible activity

The North Atlantic Treaty signed in Washington on 4 April 1949.

Article 5. The Parties agree that an armed attack against one or more of them in Europe or North America shall be considered an attack against them all and consequently they agree that, if such an armed attack occurs, each of them, in exercise of the right of individual or collective self-defence recognised by Article 51 of the Charter of the United Nations, will assist the Party or Parties so attacked by taking forthwith, individually and in concert with the other Parties, such action as it deems necessary, including the use of armed force, to restore and maintain the security of the North Atlantic area.

Any such armed attack and all measures taken as a result thereof shall immediately be reported to the Security Council. Such measures shall be terminated when the Security Council has taken the measures necessary to restore and maintain international peace and security.

that boosts the deterrence capacity of the Alliance. Such actions should consist in making appropriate investments by member states amounting to approximately 2 per cent of GDP, ensuring a balanced development of the NATO infrastructure in its member states, the consistent construction of the NATO missile defence system, conducting joint military training, including training in scenarios of collective defence, as well as regular preparation and updating of NATO contingency plans. Such activities will enable buttressing the feeling of security in all NATO member states, including especially frontline states, and contribute to increasing readiness to engage in out-of-area operations.

The **European Union** and its Common Security and Defence Policy (CSDP) constitute another fundamental element of European security. The CSDP has high value and potential for Poland. However, the usefulness of the EU security policy for Poland depends on the progress in EU internal integration and the intensification of cooperation with NATO, as well as an EU coherent policy towards Russia. Unfortunately, these very issues elicit various opinions in the EU, and these differences weaken the Union's role in the field of security.

The Treaty on European Union

Article 42 para. 7. If a Member State is the victim of armed aggression on its territory, the other Member States shall have towards it an obligation of aid and assistance by all the means in their power, in accordance with Article 51 of the United Nations Charter. This shall not prejudice the specific character of the security and defence policy of certain Member States.
Commitments and cooperation in this area shall be consistent with commitments under the North Atlantic Treaty Organisation, which, for those States which are members of it, remains the foundation of their collective defence and the forum for its implementation.

At the beginning of the current decade, the European Union was hit by the crisis and economic downturn. In spite of the unfavourable circumstances, it makes attempts to adjust to the new threats, the most challenging of which are the sovereign-debt crisis, as well as such challenges as the development of the Common Security and Defence Policy. The fact that Europe is not self-reliant in the area of raw materials is a serious challenge for the continent.

The most serious challenges for the economic security of the European Union concern finance. Assuming that the EU Member States are willing and able to adhere to the corrective measures, and the Eurozone macroeconomic policy will be reformed (mainly with the aim of expanding the Union fiscal policy), Europe should succeed in overcoming the crisis.

Despite the sovereign-debt crisis and economic standstill, divergent living conditions, income levels and access to goods and services, the intensifying demographic crisis, as well as the existence of trouble points that might evolve into conflicts in unfavourable conditions, Europe is still generally considered a continent of well-being and peace.

The activity taken by individual Eurozone members, as well as EU institutions (e.g. the European Central Bank, ECB), helped increase the trust in the economies of EU member states. In these circumstances, while at the beginning of 2012 a breakdown of the Eurozone seemed quite likely, this issue now appears to be outdated, which is significant in the context of Poland's possible introduction of the common currency.

From Poland's perspective, deepening European integration in the security zone is desired as an element that boosts the European capacity to act in emergency situations.

One of the significant problems in the area of EU security is the 2003 European Security Strategy, which is to a large extent outdated. Its revision is necessary to strengthen EU security tools and mechanisms.

The further strengthening of the CSDP will be dependent on both the political will of EU member states and the development of institutions, building capabilities and active operational involvement of the EU in its neighbourhood. The development of European military capabilities may be enhanced mainly by the pooling-and-sharing initiative, the adaptation of the EU battle groups to actual operational needs by increasing the possibilities of their use, establishing a permanent EU planning and command structure at the operational level, deepening relations with the Eastern Partnership states in the area of security policy and developing the practical dimension of cooperation between the EU and NATO.

The **strategic presence of the USA** is important for European security on the continent, both politico-military and economic. This is of great significance especially for Poland and other Central European states.

The new American policy, including the move of its strategic interest towards the region of Asia and the Pacific, gives rise to a wide range of variables in the area of European security.

In the public debate, what is especially important for Poland is the question whether the USA will limit its presence in Europe, including the military dimension. Such a reduction may be warranted by increased American interest in the area of Asia and the Pacific, India and Brazil (also in the economic sense) and Africa, and the US perception of Europe as a stable and secure region that should increase the contribution to its own security on its own. What speaks against such a reduction is, among other things, the strategic significance attributed by the USA to NATO as a reliable collective defence structure of the West, the need to have military bases for the purpose of conducting operations in the Middle East, in Africa and Central Asia and strong economic relations (the USA and Europe mutually consider each other most important trade partners, and economic relations would be further strengthened by the establishment of a free trade zone between the EU and the USA[13]). In sum, military withdrawal of the USA from Europe in the nearest future seems rather unlikely, although the US forces in Europe will continue to be reduced in quantitaty and quality.

> **Declaration on Strategic Cooperation between the United States of America and the Republic of Poland of 20 August 2008**
>
> Within the context of, and consistent with, both the North Atlantic Treaty and the U.S.-Poland strategic partnership, the United States is committed to the security of Poland and of any U.S. facilities located on the territory of the Republic of Poland. The United States and Poland will work together to counter emerging military or non-military threats posed by third parties or to minimize the effects of such threats. The increased strategic cooperation described herein would enhance the security of the United States and Poland.

---

[13] Of USD 2.3 trillion of foreign investments in the USA, as much as USD 1.6 trillion are constituted by European investments, while of USD 3.2 trillion of American investments, as much as USD 1.8 trillion was allocated to Europe.

Any radical reduction in of American interest in Europe could have particularly dramatic effects if Europe itself disintegrated at the same time. A Europe of internal divisions, a Europe of free struggle of competing interests of particular superpowers, is the real source of most dangerous conflicts. The history of the 19th century, and especially of the 20th century – the century of two world wars, is indicative of this. In both cases, it was not until the USA intervened that the hostilities were brought to an end. Without the USA, the divided Europe could not function. That is why today, in the face of the objective reduction of the strategic presence of the USA in Europe in favour of its presence in the Asia–Pacific region, the safe future of Europe depends on the pace and depth of integration in the Old World. If, for example, the United States of Europe were established, the risk of conflicts resembling the wars of the 20th century could be completely eliminated. However, if Europe fails to integrate, this risk will most certainly increase. Nowadays, it is hard to predict which tendency will prevail.

Currently, **Russia** is incapable of regaining the position it held in the Soviet era, neither in Europe nor on the global scale. The basic ambition of Russia is to play the role of one of the main and crucial global centres, including the European continent, as the US presence declines.

The Russian economic system is evaluated by experts as ineffective and uncompetitive, with raw materials dominating over modern technology (the economy is principally based on raw material exports). Additionally, the demographic structure of the Russian society is unfavourable.

The Russian Federation has significant potential of natural resources; Russia is also the sixth economy in the world (GDP measured by PPP), with the outlook to advance in the coming years by one or two ranks. Russia is also a permanent member of the UN Security Council. In military terms, owing to its notable nuclear capacity, it remains a global superpower. It then will continue to impact global and regional strategic relations.

The future of Russia is difficult to foresee. It is dependent on the approach of its authorities to the problems of modernising the economy, adapting state structures and the society to the new reality. This indeterminacy is and will long remain the main source of uncertainty among its direct neighbours. Especially that Russia, by availing itself of the good economic situation on the energy resources, is continuing the large-scale programme of modernizing its armed forces that was launched in 2008. This process, however, is not fully transparent, owing to the fact that Russia suspended the implementation of the CFE treaty provisions at the end of 2007.

Perspectives for the extraction of shale gas by some European states may weaken the hegemonic position of Russia in the area of natural gas. However, irrespective of unfavourable conditions, Russia has significant development potential, which – on condition that appropriate mobilization is ensured – may yield positive results.

The security of Poland to a large extent depends on the development of relations between Russia and the West. Today, it is difficult to foresee clearly how they will develop in the future. Will Russia maintain its policy aimed at strengthening its position as a superpower, without taking into consideration others, especially neighbouring states, or will seek to develop at their expense? Or will it switch to cooperating on collective security? Nowadays, unfortunately the former scenario seems more probable, and this scenario is unfavourable for Poland. This is also the reason why Russia is carefully examined by NATO states which are, on the one hand, open to cooperation, and, on the other hand, cautious, as Russian strategic documents still stipulate that NATO is Russia's potential enemy.

The influence of Russia in the post-Soviet area has relatively weakened. However, in recent years one may speak of Russia's increasing influence in some countries, especially those that adjoin Poland (Belarus, and to a certain extent – Ukraine). Indicative of this trend is that Ukraine's attempts to draw its foreign and security policy closer to the West have become feebler. It is quite likely that in the next few decades Ukraine will remain in the buffer zone between the EU and Russia, seeking to steer a middle course between the two centres of power.

The above-mentioned elements of European security remain cooperatively intertwined with various intensity and help maintain a relatively stable order by mitigating crises and conflicts and preserving democratic standards in Europe internally and externally.

When discussing the European security system, one cannot disregard the **Organization for Security and Co-operation in Europe** (OSCE). The OSCE focuses its activity on the territory of Europe, in the broad sense, and especially on the territory of the former Soviet Union. The OSCE's capacity has severely been limited in the past few years. This is mainly the outcome of the policy pursued by Russia. The OSCE is experiencing difficulties when engaging in activity in post-Soviet states, especially relative to the so-called frozen conflicts. Also other states, discerning the marginalization of the OSCE, limit their involvement in this organization's activity.

Nevertheless, the OSCE still has an important role to play in the strengthening of security in Europe, especially in the context of the common goal specified in 2010 at the OSCE summit in Astana. The OSCE adopted a common vision of a Euro-Atlantic and Eurasian security community rooted in agreed principles, shared commitments and common goals. Treaty-based arms control systems and military confidence- and security-building measures, including "open skies", activity in the area of the "third basket" (the human dimension), as well as the work of the Conflict Prevention Centre are also of importance. Moreover, its Central European and Central Asian activity range provide the opportunity for democratization and strengthening security in the OSCE area.

Hotbeds of tensions and conflicts in Europe

In security terms, Poland's position is unfavourable, as it is located in the vicinity of the most important European centres of potential and actual conflicts. In the region of the Black Sea and the Caspian Sea there are four frozen conflicts (Abkhazia, South Ossetia, Nagorno-Karabakh and Transnistria). Sometimes these conflicts get "defrosted" and enter a vehement phase, as in the case of the 2008 Georgian-Russian war. Another factor is the separatist trends and ethnic and religion-related tensions in Eastern Europe (the North Caucasus), as well as in Western Europe (Spain and Northern Ireland).

Poland also shares a border with the Kaliningrad oblast – the most heavily militarised area in Europe – and with Belarus, which is ruled by an authoritarian regime.

The Balkan region, after a series of wars and conflicts, is slowly and gradually restoring stability. The best prepared states of the region joined NATO and the EU. However, owing to the persisting sources of tensions in Bosnia and Herzegovina and Kosovo, it is necessary to retain international (also military) forces there to support the stabilization and post-conflict reconstruction process.

Direct military threats to Poland

Considering the whole spectrum of strategic security conditions, Poland must take into account the necessity to stand up to military threats. These might be of twofold nature: threats related to political and military crises, and war threats. The former involve international entities employing the military factor to exert strategic pressure as part of their current, day-to-day policy without crossing the threshold of a war. The latter is formed by the occurrence of an actual armed conflict.

Strategic military pressure may assume the form of:
- developing military capacity in sudden leaps that disrupt the existing balance of forces;
- demonstrating power in the form of military exercises;
- blackmailing *via* a threat of an armed conflict.

An actual armed conflict may be the consequence of an uncontrolled escalation of a crisis situation. In the foreseeable future, two types of such conflicts can be discerned:
- First, conflicts that can most generally be referred to as *aterritorial* (where the adversary does not intend to occupy the attacked territory), i.e. targeted strikes of purposefully moderate scale and range (including covert strikes with "alleged responsibility"), aimed at forcing the attacked state to take political action in the circumstances of isolation from a larger international security system, e.g. without setting in motion a NATO operation in consensus-challenging situations;
- Second, conflicts connected with a situation that is less likely nowadays, but at the same time most dangerous, i.e. a large-scale war. However, such a war could occur after a previous radicalization of the current course of international politics. It would be preceded by a rather long-standing process involving unfavourable political and strategic changes across the globe that would lead to an escalating acute crisis situation. As a result, there would be enough time to prepare a response, as well as a collective reaction of the entire Alliance, of which Poland is the member.

∗ ∗ ∗

Europe remains the area the centre of which (the European Union and the European NATO member states) is characterized by a high level of stability that results from the embedded integration ties embracing all possible areas. Overcoming of the economic and financial crisis in the EU (which seems a foregone conclusion) will confirm the role and significance of the EU also in the future. The peripheral areas of Europe, however, are rather prone to crises which are mostly "frozen" conflicts, but sometimes evolve into open clashes.

2.3. The national dimension

Conditions of security in the areas of defence and protection

Internal (national) arms-related challenges. While assessing and forecasting the national security conditions, one should, to start with, exclude with regard to the military dimension the existence of an internal military threat (rebellion, coup). However, there is a risk that organized armed crime will escalate, especially when it comes to transnational crime (crimes committed with the use of weapons on a larger scale). Also, it cannot be totally excluded that paramilitary or domestic terrorist groups will emerge, thus enforcing adoption of protection measures.

Article 228 para. 1 of the Constitution of the Republic of Poland stipulates that in situations of particular danger, when ordinary constitutional measures are insufficient, any of the following appropriate extraordinary measures may be introduced: martial law, a state of emergency or a state of natural disaster. It makes it possible to involve armed forces into various activities in order to support internal security and provide help to the society. In turn, the Act on the General Obligation to Defend the Republic of Poland imposes the obligation of participation of the armed forces in combating threats which in certain circumstances may become internal military threats (anti-terrorist activities, disposal of explosive and hazardous materials of military origin and their elimination).

> **The Constitution of the Republic of Poland of 2 April 1997.**
>
> **Article 228 para. 1.** In situations of particular danger, if ordinary constitutional measures are inadequate, any of the following appropriate extraordinary measures may be introduced: martial law, a state of emergency or a state of natural disaster.

Therefore, one of the most imminent challenges connected with the necessity of the Polish Armed Forces' involvement seems to lay in traditional support for state structures in liquidation of the effects of natural and technical disasters or in helping state agencies to counteract uncontrolled, mass migration into the territory of the Republic of Poland.

Espionage. The information resource is one of the most significant assets a modern state has at its disposal. It has direct influence not only on the political (including politico-military) condition of a state, but also on the manner it operates in the socio-economic field. The traditionally understood intelligence activities is a process of obtaining, processing, analysing, and distributing information to help policy-makers in taking key decisions. Any breach of national security by foreign special services both when a foreign country obtains specific data as the integrity of information systems, including ICT systems, is breached, may result in serious dangers.

Along with the growing significance of information in the context of the state's functioning, security threats in this field shall get bigger, too. In traditional terms, such threats are generated by states that conduct strategic intelligence activities. One should also take into account information diversion, or activities of foreign special services with an aim of influencing individual behaviour (of policy-makers in critical posts) and also civil behaviour, conducted both in the virtual and real world. E.g., there are hypotheses that interpret the particular force and range of demonstrated opposition against extraction of shale gas, which would put in danger producers who use energy sources hitherto available, as the result of such activities. This issue also involves disinformation activity, often aimed at provoking desired social and political reactions.

A threat that is particularly important when it comes to the actions of Poland in international organizations, may be activity aimed at obtaining access to negotiation positions (negotiation instructions) for Polish representatives during the debates.

However, states are not the sole entities that conduct intelligence (espionage). Terrorist organizations, for instance, also efficiently use various methods of gathering information in order to create a danger to the state. Therefore, threats connected with espionage by non-state entities will constitute an accruing category of threats.

It should be also stressed that simultaneously with the growing significance of non-state entities, espionage has also encroached the private sector. Such notions emerged as economic intelligence or industrial espionage which relate to gathering knowledge of business competition and production operations. Such dangers, which are connected with the growing significance of the private sector not only in the field of economy, but also in relation to the progressing "privatization of security", will constitute a serious challenge in the years to come.

Technological progress and computerization era, in turn, also enabled intelligence activities to penetrate the cyberspace. Cyber-espionage, as well as diversion and sabotage activities in the cyberspace may in the years to come turn out to be a serious threat generated by foreign special services. Technological progress of audio-visual monitoring tools, including the far-ranging ones, causes that in response to challenges in the context of protection of state interests the following intelligence approaches will be employed:

- *Measurements and Signatures Intelligence*, MASINT, i.e. intelligence information of scientific and technical nature obtained through qualitative and quantitative data analyses (metrical, angular, spatial, wave-length, time dependence, modulation, hydromagnetic) on the basis of data originating from advanced technical sensors;
- *Signals Intelligence*, SIGINT, i.e. information originating from communication, electronic or radio intelligence, singularly or in combination;
- *Imagery Intelligence*, IMINT, i.e. information coming from the use of photography, infrared sensors, lasers, electro-optics and radars, where images of facilities are optically or electronically reproduced in a film, electronic imaging devices and other media.

Crime and other threats to public security. Stabilization and security in Poland depend to a large extent on the crime rate, and organized crime in particular, as the latter is interlinked in a corruptive manner, internally and externally. Owing to globalization processes, these threats acquired cross-border dimensions. It may be predicted that evolving organized groups that engage in economic crime on a large scale and launder funds coming from their activity, will constitute one of the biggest non-military threats to the functioning of a democratic country.

After the period of the mid-90s of the past century and the beginning of the current century when large criminal groups characterized by high levels of organization and hierarchy dominated in Poland, numerous smaller groups have recently come into being, often loosely connected among themselves and collaborating. Such a decentralized structure makes it significantly more difficult to liquidate whole organizations. In recent years, the involvement of persons originating from circles of sports pseudo-fans in activities of organized criminal groups has been noted. Also, a phenomenon of international criminal groups acting in Poland is noticeable. It seems that such a trend will go on in the next years.

Smaller, mobile criminal groups involved in a broad spectrum of illegal activities, undertaking short-term cooperation with other such organizations, domestically and internationally, will constitute a source of varied threats to Poland's security.

Organized crime in Poland is weaker than in many other European countries due to the efficiency of the Polish police, which cooperate more and more closely with police structures of other Union countries. Nevertheless, open borders within the Schengen Area and a long external border of the EU makes it likely that threats to Poland's security caused by organized crime will continue also in the foreseeable future.

In the field of drug crimes, Poland – as a result of its geographical situation – is both a transit country as well as a target market. At the same time, it is necessary to take into account that Polish criminal structures participate in the illegal practice of large-scale production of synthetic narcotics. The production is directed both to the internal market and smuggled to European countries. In this context, it is necessary to draw attention to the phenomenon of illegal cultivation of cannabis, whereby the perpetrators often use specialist equipment in closed cultivation systems. As far as of drug threats, are concerned, one should expect in the years to come a further growth in production of synthetics; nevertheless there still be a substantial danger connected with smuggling of cocaine from South America, and heroine from Asia, and consequently, the risk that smuggling channels from these locations to Europe will remain active.

On the basis of statistical data of the law enforcement authorities, it is possible to indicate a certain trend in criminal group activities in last years. Indeed, there was a shift from the activity in the field of criminal offences towards economic crimes, and those to the detriment of the State Treasury, in particular. In this scope, one may assume that organized groups will get involved in defrauding funds coming from grants and subsidies as well as support and structural funds from the EU. Also, one can assume that criminal organizations operating in Poland, just like international criminal structures, will use state-of-the-art technologies for the purposes of their activity, and, along with technological advancement, this tendency will accrue.

With regard to organized economic crime, the most common offences are defraudment or unlawful reductions in the scope of VAT and excise tax (smuggling, illegal production and turnover of alcohol, tobacco products and fuels). Illegally obtained funds are then subject to the process of so-called laundering and deposited both at home as well as abroad. They are used, among other things, for the purposes of purchase of real estates, securities, luxury commodities, works of art; they are also invested in legal economic undertakings. A growth in criminal activity on the capital market is being witnessed. Also criminals gain profits from production, smuggling, and trading in goods protected by copyrights or patents. It is estimated that in the globalizing world, economic crime will show intensifying tendency.

Criminal offences, including also so-called common crimes, includes first of all: homicides, scrimmages, beatings, causing detriment to health, rapes, robberies, thefts, burglaries and damages to property. One should bear in mind that many of those crimes are committed in connection with organized crime activity. With regard to criminal practice, owing to changing trends in activities of perpetrators and their increasing focus primarily on the economic sphere, one may assume a drop in crime rates for such types of crimes. The effects of economic downturn, economic instability or high unemployment may temporarily negatively influence trends in the considered realm (it is confirmed by a slight increase in the number of offences, observed since 2009, after a period of several years of a distinct downward tendency).

What is worth stressing in this context is the increasing general crime detection rate. Restoration of decreasing tendency in the number of offences and maintaining the growth of the detection rate is conditioned by efficient cooperation of individual entities responsible for combating crime with the society, and also active implementation of preventative measures, including those instituted by non-governmental agencies. Of considerable significance is also education for security.

An important element of general security is road traffic security. Main reasons for traffic dangers in Poland are irresponsible behaviours of traffic participants and the low quality of the road infrastructure, resulting in large numbers of casualties. Road traffic security depends mostly on efficient systems of monitoring behaviours of traffic participants, on social awareness and discipline, general education in the road security realm, the road infrastructure condition, technical condition of vehicles, and the condition and quality of road traffic control and supervision. It should be assumed that effective actions in the aforesaid fields, primarily inclusive of the planned build-up of modern road infrastructure in the next years, will help decrease the number of traffic accidents and road casualties.

Another test of law and order is the number of collective disruptions thereof, which has been decreasing in recent years, especially during organized mass events. However, what is worth noting is the phenomenon of slow increase, in recent years, in the collective law abuses in the course of public assemblies, public protests, strikes, and blockages. As in the case of criminal offences, the number of such events may be influenced by economic factors, high unemployment or public discontent.

Natural disasters. An inseparable element that shapes the internal security of Poland will be challenges related to disasters caused by the man or natural catastrophes. Human activity, which remains high and even grows systematically in many fields of activity – often burdened with high risks – (e.g. power engineering, extracting industry, environmental interferences), will obviously increase the risk of occurrence of events with disastrous effects for property, health and life of people.

Similar is the case for disasters caused by natural factors, such as heavy rainfalls or violent windstorms, hurricanes and whirlwinds. Climatic conditions and changes will result in ever more frequent violent weather phenomena in the climatic area, in which Poland is located. One of the most serious challenges to the internal security of the country will be extensive floods. Their frequency may grow in a ten- to five-year cycle, which – given deficiencies of the protection infrastructure – would cause the losses of the state and its citizens even more severe.

Social conditions of security

National identity and cultural heritage. National heritage is an important element of life and activity of nations and the society as well as individual citizens. It is a result of a multi-century process and consists of tangible as well as intangible accomplishments of the past generations. At the same time it determines the identity of the contemporary nations that, as the community linked with ethnical and cultural and civilization bonds, are characterized by a sense of separate identity and the capability of transmitting it to next generations.

The globalization processes which are now making their way, inclusive of the integration of European Union states, lead to the tightening of relations between individual countries in economic, legal, social and political terms. Such situation creates conditions for diffusion and unification of cultures.

Therefore, a challenge for the identity of nations and their cultural heritage, also in Poland, may be the expansion of a uniformed mass culture which is an element of the globalization process.

8 July 1997,
Flood in Kłodzko
Photo: Adam Hawalej/PAP

26 May 2010,
Flooded villages near
Płock.
Photo: Paweł Brzeziński/PAP

17 July 2012,
Tuchola Forest.
Damages after tornado.
Photo: Tytus Żmijewski/PAP

Diffusion and mixing of various nationalities and cultures lead naturally to underrating of the significance of tradition and to reassessing of values, ideals or principles observed so far in a given society. In the long run it may lead to disintegration processes.

Social conditions. Economic condition of a country translates directly into its social conditions, structure of the society, and living conditions of the population. A natural consequence of the economic cycle when it deteriorates is a growing unemployment and limitation of opportunities to realise one's own initiatives and professional development. In a longer run, such situation may cause growing despondency and impoverishment of the society, build-up of the group of those excluded, intensification of radical and extreme views, and, as a result, social discontent and unrest. People who lack sufficient means to satisfy their basic needs are automatically subject to marginalization, and children that are brought up in such conditions have poor chances to change their situation. Therefore, an important thing in social support is to place an emphasis on helping the family, as it is first of all an investment in the young generation, which – instead of being a possible threat – may constitute future human capital and support national economy.

Demography. All scenarios forecast an unavoidable decrease in the population count and an accelerating process of ageing of the Polish society. An Eurostat demographic forecast indicates that in 2060, every third Pole will be retired, and Poland will be on the first position in Europe in terms of the percentage of people above 65 years of age. It is also estimated that Poland's population shall drop from 38 million to 31 million (fig. 32)[14]. The estimate was prepared only on the basis of results related to the number of births and deaths, without taking into account the so-called after-accession outflow of Poles, namely their economic emigration to EU countries.

Also disturbing are demographic forecasts prepared by the Chief Statistical Office. They indicate that Poland's population will decrease systematically; the first years will bring about a slight decrease (by approximately 10 thousand per year); however, after 2015, the demographic decline in Poland will accelerate, and the Polish population in 2020 will be fewer by nearly 200 thousand than in 2015.

The Polish demographic structure will deteriorate; first of all the process of ageing of the society will gather momentum. In 2035, the number of people in post-working age will amount to approximately 9.6 million and will constitute 26.7 per cent of Poland's population in general[15]. The shortage of people of working age will amount in 2035 to as many as 3.8 million people. The number of people aged under 18 will be lower by 2035 by ca. 2 million, so they will account for only 15.6 per cent of general population. Therefore, the demographic dependency ratio for people of post--working age in relation to people of working age will go up from 55 in 2007 to 74 in 2035.[16] (fig. 33).

---

[14] Europe in Figures, Eurostat yearbook 2010. http://epp.eurostat.ec.europa.eu/cache/ITY_OFFPUB/KS-CD-10-220/EN/KSCD-10-220-EN.PDF

[15] Demographic forecast for 2008–2035, Main Statistical Office, Warszawa 2009.

[16] The demographic dependency ratio is determined by the number of people of non-working age per 100 people of working age.

Figure 32. Population and demographic forecasts for selected EU states in years 1990 – 2060 (in millions)

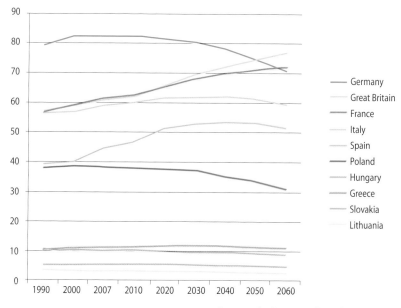

Source: authors' own compilation based on Eurostat data.

Figure 33. Population forecast for years 2010-2035 (in millions)

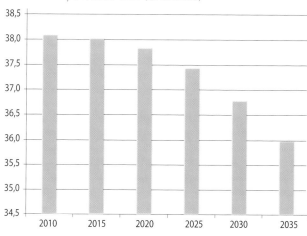

Source: authors' own compilation based on Central Statistical Office data.

The demographic decline and the ageing of the population will have an adverse effect on the labour market and the pension system. This may call into question Poland's ability to continue civilizational development at a fast rate. To put it in other words: weakening of the demographic safety of a country will also negatively affect its internal and external security.

The most painful effect of the difficult demographic situation of Poland may be a crisis of the pension system and of the state finance system. Studies indicate that in countries of the Organization of Economic Cooperation and Development, approximately half of the public debt is generated by the pension system. Therefore, it requires an adequate and effectively implemented reform.

The declining and ageing society will increase the demand for labour force from other countries, although it may be alleviated by the increase in labour efficiency by technical progress, by extending the employment period and by increasing the fertility rate. In the years to come, social and cultural factors connected with the inflow of large groups of immigrants would be of importance for possible changes in the security environment. As the most favourable solution, Poland would remain a coherent society in which new citizens would be integrated with the rest. Otherwise, an ominous phenomenon of immigrant ghettos on the one hand, and the intensification of xenophobic attitudes and antipathy to the newcomers on the other, would occur.

Social capital. The period of the systemic transformation, which took place in Poland after 1989, caused numerous changes in the social structure. New social groups emerged, such as the middle class, entrepreneurs and persons permanently unemployed or with extremely low income. At the same time, the diversification of income levels in the society significantly deepened. The degree of concentration of incomes is systematically rising: the gap between salaries of the wealthiest 10 per cent and the poorest 10 per cent of people is widening, indicating the strong intensification of social stratification. The correlation between the level of education and the professional position is getting lower; in result of expansive development of higher education and a growing number of high school graduates, the market value of education is decreasing. These are phenomena which – should no activities aimed at elimination thereof be adopted – shall cause material social perturbations in the future.

Surveys of public opinion point, *inter alia*, to the lack of trust in state institutions. The latter are still sometimes perceived as a hostile bureaucracy and not structures serving the society. A significant role in the unfavourable perception of state institutions, and the consequential perception of corruption, is played by the historical and cultural factor. The aversion to cooperation with state bodies is rooted in the society in the same way as the fear connected with revealing crime perpetrators, the shame associated with snitching, and even sometimes the conviction that to cheat "them" (i.e. authorities understood as alien to society) is something of merit. Such attitudes are not only a factor that determines social connivance to corruptive behaviours, but also to antisocial, hooligan and criminal activities (in particular towards property). They bring negative influence to bear on the economy and its functioning.

The issue of attitude to the state should be raised in a broader context of the low level of trust in interpersonal relationships in the Polish society. In the case of Poland, this indicator is among the lowest in Europe. It has a negative influence on the development of social bonds and weakens the thinking in categories of the common good. Among Poles, owing, *inter alia,* to the high unemployment rate among the youngest and the oldest citizens' groups of working age, the phenomenon of economic stratification and the accompanying sense of frustration, social injustice, rejection, lack of fulfilment of expectations and ambitions and the incapability of achieving one's aims, grow systematically. Such feelings may be sometimes accompanied by aggressive and destructive behaviours that disavow the social order. What should be considered particularly dangerous is the intensification of individual attitudes and civil movements of distinctly extremist character. It may lead to an erosion of the public order, the legal system and the system of values. Such situations call for adopting of adequate measures on the part of the authorities, because the incorrectly managed, negative social energy may be utilised by forces unfriendly or even hostile to the state. Directing – for example from the outside – the emotions of frustrated and excluded strata of the society may pose a material danger for economic stabilization, and thus for the state security.

The catalogue of negative social phenomena, which should be addressed in an interventional manner, is long: emigration of the young generation; lack of effective pro-family policy; the sense of helplessness in confrontation with the bureaucratic machine; inequalities stemming from the gender, age, location (region) of residence, and access to education.

Intellectual and technological potential. The intellectual and technological potential is a factor of fundamental importance for national security; the basis for working it out is constituted by a modern, adequate education system at each level. True, the Polish education system at the primary and secondary level may be considered to be in line with the requirements of the future[17], however, one should also take into account that successes in the secondary school do not always translate into achievements in high education – the standing of Polish universities in international rankings is rather poor; in the group of the best universities there is not even one Polish higher education school. Particularly low results of Polish universities are visible in technological and bioengineering sciences. This weakness of intellectual and technological potential, combined with low and often inadequate expenditures on research and development, translates into low innovation levels of the whole Polish economy, which is moving from the stage in which efficiency is the most important factor of growth to a stage in which what counts most is innovation. Differences in levels of innovativeness of Poland and select countries of the European Union and world are shown in fig. 34. This situation should be consider a significant challenge, to be managed in the coming period of time.

Figure 34. Degree of innovativeness of selected countries – as of 2012 (on a 0-100 point scale)

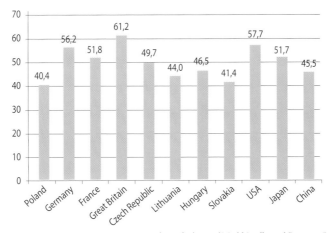

Source: own study on the basis of World Intellectual Property Organization data.

---

[17] In rankings coordinated by OECD (PISA 2009 – The Programme for International Student Assessment), assessing educational capabilities, Polish students of secondary schools achieve very high results; almost in all assessed categories of school skills Poland is in the first ten of EU countries.

Polish sciences face many problems, among which the most serious ones are: the weakness of pro-innovative attitudes, lack of full connection between research and practice, the bureaucratic manner of operation and financing in decision-making circles of the economy, and the brain-drain. These factors, along with the insufficient financing of higher education and culture, are among main reasons for insufficient level of Poland's development. However, the phenomenon may also have a positive impact, as it is often connected with the transfers of income and *know-how* onto the Polish market. Employees staying abroad gain experience hardly possible to obtain at home, and many a time they bring certain solutions onto Polish turf. Poland should be expected that, taking care of its own interests, it will pursue policies aiming at taking full advantage of all possible benefits which may stem from the migration of specialists. The most favourable solution would be connected with an immediate work on the Polish policy towards brain-drain and using this policy as a means to increase local scientific and technological potential.

The IT dimension of functioning of the state and citizens. The globalization of economic processes creates a network of interlinks between supranational corporations operating on various continents, which may result – similarly as in the case of critical infrastructure – in the risk of the "domino effect" with consequences that are difficult to predict.

In order to fully utilise the possibilities brought about by digital revolution and development of the cyberspace, Internet users must be convinced that it is secure: sensitive information is protected, trade online will not be interfered, and the network infrastructure is immune to infiltration. Nevertheless, reality in this scope is far away from the perfect state. Losses resulting from criminal activities in the cyberspace are estimated globally in hundreds billion dollars per year[18].

Another type of threats stemming from the cyberspace is also threats to the so-called information society, connected with the uncontrolled flow of unidentified data and information which may arise in public circulation in consequence of disinformation activities. Modern societies witness today the process of gradual extension of the scope of information media (TV, radio and Internet) that more and more often operate on international and even global scale. The influence of the media on shaping social attitudes or views is significant, which creates a risk of manipulation and a possibility of eliciting public reactions undermining internal security of the state.

The role of mass media as a factor shaping social attitudes, behaviours and expectations will grow together with expanding technological possibilities, while at the same time limiting to some extent the significance of other forms of social participation. To put it differently, electronic media will slowly replace traditional social bonds (peer, collegial, environmental, and maybe also family ones).

The "third sector" and the national security system. At present, the "third sector" is a commonly used term to denote the area of public life which is separate from the private sector (the domain of profit-oriented enterprises) and the public sector (the domain of state institutions), in which citizens mobilise, associate and establish entities (NGOs) in order to satisfy public needs, solve social problems and articulate and represent collective interests (e.g. of certain communities or groups).

It should be expected that as civic society structures solidify, both the number as well as the attractiveness of non-government organizations constituting an inseparable part of the global stream of public diplomacy will grow. Non-governmental organizations may also be a subject of the national

---

[18] Based on the "Norton Cybercrime Report 2011", it was 388 billion dollars in 2010.

security policy in a negative sense – as a possible source of risk or threat. The risk of NGOs being used by criminal groups to hide illegal property, launder money and avoid taxes cannot be excluded. Besides, there may be risks connected with terrorist organizations which use e.g. charity mechanisms (grants, subsidies, donations, etc.) or NGOs (mainly charities that lend material development support) without the informed participation of the latter as a platform to launder illegal profits or to transfer property and in-kind support to terrorists.

Economic conditions of security

Poland and international economic relations. In times of growing indebtedness of many countries and persisting global economic slowdown, Poland is a country that stands out in a positive manner, which is evidenced by the gradually improving position of Polish economy in competitiveness rankings. An important determinant of such state of affairs is the inflow of foreign direct investments to the country, which in 2011 amounted to nearly EUR 11 billion. In this regard, Poland is the leader among 10 new EU members and in the years to come it shall probably retain its standing. The role of Poland on economic markets is also evidenced by the growing importance of the Warsaw Stock Exchange which is perceived by markets as the financial centre of Central and Eastern Europe.

Despite these positive phenomena, it should be borne in mind that the Polish economy is not regarded as a highly competitive one. Among its vulnerabilities one should point to the still too low innovativeness and effectiveness of the labour market, the poorly developed infrastructure, and numerous barriers such as unfavourable conditions for start-ups, long time of collection of receivables under agreements, complex tax procedures and too long and overly formalised process of obtaining construction permits.

One of the most important challenges for the Polish economy, which should enable it to improve its competitiveness, will be the growth of innovativeness. It requires above all a change of approach to education, which must be treated as an investment in the economy.

A dominant share in the commodity turn-over of Poland is attributed to European countries, and particularly states of the European Union. After the deep recession in 2008-2009, most of them witnessed a slight recovery in 2010. However, negative effects of the financial crisis are still palpable. They manifest themselves, *inter alia,* in the profound indebtedness of certain EU economies or in a serious deterioration of ratings of many an EU country, which in turn jeopardises the prospects for their constant development. The consequences of such a situation for Poland include a declining share of commodity exchanges in this direction and its growth vis-à-vis non-European countries, such as China, Brazil or India. It is significant in the light of development forecasts for those powers in the coming decade or more years, and at the same time in the perspective of ever-growing readiness of Polish companies to expand on foreign markets, stepping up investments there and trade in technologically advanced commodities.

In recent years, Poland's position in international economic relations has been systematically strengthening and within next two decades one may expect continuation of this trend (the premises for such situation already exist). Nevertheless it should be pointed out that Poland will not be only a recipient of foreign capitals and a location for foreign companies, but it will also become an origin of the expansion of domestic companies onto foreign markets. It is reflected in the fact that in 2011, the value of Polish foreign direct investments reached EUR 5 billion (fig. 35). One should also bear in mind that competitive edges in foreign trade will also change, resulting in further strengthening of Poland's position in trade in more advanced goods.

Figure 35. Polish direct investments abroad in years 2002-2011 (in millions EUR)

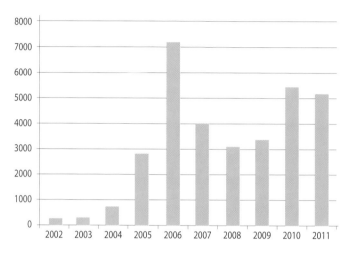

Source: authors' own chart on the basis of NBP data.

Risks in the financial area. Numerous destabilization factors which may adversely affect the level of security of Poland are concentrated around finance, above all at the internal level. However, the effects of the situation in the region and in the world are also clearly noticeable. It should be stressed that the significance of the international influence of Polish financial security will become even more apparent along with the progress of globalization processes. Financial risks concern (and will concern in the future), among other things, the following:

- The negative influence of financial crises in the EU countries on the economic growth and public finance stability, as well as the stability of the sector of financial institutions in other countries of the European Union, including Poland;
- The lack of guarantees given by relevant Polish financial institutions for deposits accumulated in branches of foreign lending institutions;
- The negative influence of exchange rates on the market of internal currency loans;
- Deregulation of markets and the need of their renewed regulation.

From the external surroundings engulfed by the crisis, inflationary phenomena will penetrate the Polish economy. Stopping the inflation caused by factors originating from crises abroad and to develop defensive mechanisms which will alleviate the negative influence from the outside in the future, is a great challenge for the Polish economic policy. The problem concerns first and foremost the character of monetary policy, all the more so that fighting the soaring inflation should not lead to arresting the growth of Polish GDP. Widespread crisis phenomena and Polish economy relations with the global financial system constrain the wiggle room for the government in economic and social policy, including the room for manoeuvre within the taxation and pension system, healthcare and transport infrastructure. What is more, they limit the general control over globalization phenomena in the fields of finance and technologies. Divisions and divergences among euro zone countries may also put Poland at risk of being pushed out of the main circle of European economic and political integration.

The European crisis also illustrated that foreign market groups may rapidly limit demand for Polish securities. This may cause a sale of Polish bonds by foreign investors as well as a majority of banks operating in Poland. Therefore, it is necessary to increase in Poland the share of banks controlled and managed at the national level. Poland's security is connected with ability to flexibly adapt to changes and to guarantee itself the participation in steering (or influence on) the economic processes in the EU and inside the country, and of ensuring a relevant pace of economic growth and modernization.

Business activity online. It is worth noting the importance of Internet business activity, which is not only becoming a showcase of Polish innovativeness, but is also an opportunity and a driving force of the economy. Online economy, if accounted as a separate sector (e-economy), constitutes 2.7 of Polish GDP. Today its estimated volume amounts to PLN 35.7 billion, which accounts for a higher share in Polish GDP than the share of the mining industry which for many years had been the pillar of the Polish economy. It is estimated that in 2015 the value of e-economy will total nearly PLN 77 billion, or 4.1 per cent of GDP. The Internet will have then a higher share in GDP than the finance, energy or healthcare sector, and will grow twice as fast as GDP itself.

The energy sector. Poland enjoys energy independence based on coal, but it largely depends on supplies of oil and gas. What is more, the problem of lack of adequate investments in the energy infrastructure is coming to a head – energy companies are more and more ineffective, thus increasing energy costs. Moreover, coal has ceased to be attractive and exploiting it raises the costs of energy independence.

In the coming years, the most critical threats in the field of energy safety affecting the security policy will be connected with:
- The transmission grids from Russia to Western Europe, bypassing Poland and Central and Eastern Europe, which causes the cut-off of the country from the West in the field of transit and distribution of oil and gas; all this is connected with Russia's manner of treating energy supplies as means of political pressure;
- The dependence of the reliability of supplies on relations with producers and exporters of energy carriers (Russia) and transit countries (Ukraine, Belarus), and also the danger of destabilization in these countries;
- physical stoppages in supply of energy resources;
- the depreciation of the generation infrastructure, and transmission and distribution grids (it is the case with nearly 70 per cent of the infrastructure).

So far, Poland has been procuring gas and crude oil from producers located in the east, as its transmission infrastructure had been built earlier in this region. After 1989, the infrastructure has not been significantly modernized, and major investments made in the mid-90s (Yamal pipeline) did not change the supplier dominant on the Polish market. The construction of new gas and oil pipelines for transmission of resources from farther regions of Russia to the European Union, without using the existing routes running through the territory of Poland, poses challenges for energy safety of the country. Diversification of supply sources and transportation routes will enable to minimise possible dangers stemming from disruptions of or limitations on fuel supplies. Security may be strengthened with the use of tools provided by the European Union legislation. These legal instruments stimulate the development of the free market of energy transmission and are focused on the sector of natural gas and electricity. Implementation of the principles of the community law will reduce the potential of monopolistic practices applied by the suppliers of energy carriers.

In the coming 10-20 years Poland is likely to witness a better diversification of supplies and a sustainable energy balance. However, the scale and character of this diversification remain open. The bigger it will be the more stable will be grounds for Poland's development, and also its internal security. Poland has at its disposal several options as regards diversification of the balance and supplies. In the case of gas supplies, short-term diversification will be ensured by an LNG port which will be constructed in Świnoujście, and the construction of the so-called interconnectors (connecting pipelines) with the Czech Republic and Germany.

Good hopes for a significant strengthening of energy safety of the country lie with developing industrial extraction of shale gas. If estimates relating to the volumes of this resource are confirmed during exploration work, and its extraction turns out to be technically feasible and justified in economic terms, the national energy sector will undergo a significant restructuring. Launching of shale gas extraction will lead to an increased share of gas in the so-called energy mix, which will cause a reduction of demand for other, less competitive energy carriers. One cannot exclude that the development of the gas energy sector will limit development plans of such branches as coal and nuclear energy industries. According to preliminary estimates, shale gas will guarantee 30-year coverage of the present energy demand of Poland. Should the estimates be confirmed, Poland would emerge as an important exporter of the resource and ensure the diversification of shale gas supply in the region. However, should no significant changes in the energy balance occur, Poland would remain to a certain extent susceptible to the negative influence of possible gas conflicts or energy blackmail.

The crucial factor that puts the national security at risk is the systematic loss of control over Polish deposits of energy resources. Many concessions for natural gas and unconventional gas have been taken over by foreign companies. Such situation may result in delays in exploration and exploitation of the resource and, in the worst scenario, a "concession freeze". Also, Poland lacks an adequate geological service which would exercise supervision over Poland's natural resources. The powers of the Polish Geological Institute are limited and focused mainly on geological surveys and risk monitoring. The postulated geological service would be a new body to take over hitherto tasks of PGI and also take on additional tasks, connected, *inter alia*, with rational management of geological structures, including fossil resources and protection thereof, as well as underground water and environment management and protection.

New prospects would brighten for Poland also by progress in the field of technology aimed at carbon capture and storage (CCS), which generates the so-called clean carbon. The European Union adopted a directive with an aim of creating a favourable regulatory framework for implementation of CCS technology in the EU countries. Moreover, Brussels took a decision on ensuring financial support for the first demonstration projects in a couple of member states, including Poland (two CCS demonstration projects).

The policy of reducing greenhouse gas emissions is accompanied by the so-called carbon leakage problem, namely the outflow of emission to a cheaper country or countries with lower standards that do not undertake activities aimed at its reduction. European restrictions with regard to emission and emission amounts of greenhouse gases, adopted accorded to individual countries, encourages the industry that emits particularly high volumes of pollution to transferring them to other countries which failed to sign international treaties on climate protection. The scale of this phenomenon is estimated at a dozen or so per cent of the primary energy-intensive and high-emission reduction, but some estimates indicate even several dozens per cent of outflow of emission abroad. In consequence of relocation (transfer) of industrial activity to countries where restrictions connected with reduction of the greenhouse gas emission are not as severe as in the European Union, neither does the expected decrease in gas concentration occur, nor is the so-called ozone hole reduced in this way. The greenhouse effect that affects the whole globe does not decrease, while countries from which the emission "escaped" lose not only the production, transferred (in most cases) to China, but also jobs. One cannot rule out a total exclusion of Polish energy industry based on coal, while the "escape" of chemical, paper, and cement industry abroad has not yet occurred solely due to the weakness of investments in these branches. The EU policy related to emission quotas for carbon dioxide, provided it remains unchanged, may therefore lead not only to escape, but also liquidation of a substantial part of Polish heavy industry, while not bringing about the expected benefits in limiting the greenhouse effect.

An opportunity for diversification of the Polish energy balance is provided by the decision on the construction of a nuclear power station, and the slowly growing share of renewable energy. Irrespective of changes in the energy balance, the problem of dependence on external factors will remain actual in the long-term perspective. It is impossible to ensure energy the safety based on shale gas or clean coal technology without coming to terms with necessary substantial concessions to be granted to big concerns. In turn, relying on clean energy requires taking into account the use of rare metal elements, necessary to exploit virtually all renewable energies, but available solely on the territory of several countries. Purchases of fuel for nuclear plants are also connected with the necessity to import it, while the possibilities to diversify the suppliers are very limited. Polish natural resources offer a hypothetical possibility of obtaining domestic fuel for nuclear plants, but it would call for an extremely expensive investment process.

In addition, Poland needs a grand programme of modernization of energy infrastructure. 37 per cent of electric energy generated in Poland is produced by power plants which are 20 to 30 years old, and 43 per cent of power plants have been operating for more than thirty years. As little as 8 per cent are relatively new facilities (5-10 years). Despite expectations, after 1989 the process of an intensive build-up of the country's energy infrastructure and its modernization has not been started. On the contrary: the absence of necessary investments (so-called replacement investments) has resulted in a significant technical degradation. In order to reverse this tendency, measures and actions are necessary.

Infrastructure, including critical infrastructure (CI). The gradual process of making the modern society contingent on services and goods used in every-day live leads to the growing significance of the country's critical infrastructure.

In Poland, there are today nearly one thousand elements of this type of infrastructure, and their number will grow. The scale of effects related to its operation is also on the increase. This situation requires diagnosing possible consequences of critical infrastructure dysfunction, developing methods of CI protection against such dysfunction, and elaborating of a model providing the population and business entities with the conditions necessary for survival in the event of destruction or a failure of one, few, or a larger number of CI elements. A significant portion of critical infrastructure elements is managed by business entities which are not connected with public administration. It raises a possibi-

26 November 2012,
The biggest highway
junction in Poland – A1
(north-south) an A2
(east-west) junction near
Stryków.
Photo: Grzegorz
Michałowski/PAP

lity of using business (e.g. legal purchase of shares in an enterprise) to obtain a means of influence on the level of internal security by possible CI exclusion.

The Polish infrastructure is quite obsolete. For instance, only 8 per cent of Polish rail tracks are adapted for trains travelling with a velocity of more than 150 km/h, and an average railway car in Poland has been used for nearly 30 years.

In Poland, one of the lowest rates of the highway length per area was noted. The nearest decade will be of critical importance for Polish infrastructure: either it will be possible to stop the „strategic devastation" trend through new investments, or already in 2020 the country will face a total depreciation of possessions. In order to meet the needs, infrastructural investments are necessary, which amount to approximately EUR 16 billion a year. This amount is significantly higher than the lending capability of banks operating in Poland. A factor which enables planning further investments is, however, means from the European funds. Still, it is necessary to find additional direct financing methods from the state budget and private companies in favour of increasing the rate of investments, even at the expense of limiting the growth of the consumption rate. A constant growth of consumption without a modernization of the infrastructure is bound to become impossible soon.

* * *

Conclusions drawn from the assessment of domestic security conditions are a kind of warning signals. Should they not be addressed soon and adequately, they may become threats. Especially serious are demographic and energy challenges, as well as those connected with rapidly developing activities in the cyberspace.

2.4. Strategic scenarios of the development of security conditions

Analyzing the possible development of security conditions in Poland, and assuming dynamic changes of the international environment as well as excluding static behaviour of international and domestic actors, one may consider the following possible scenarios (variants) of unfolding of the security conditions of the Republic of Poland for the next 20 years:

1. An integration scenario, which assumes a possible prevalence of positive and desirable phenomena and tendencies in shaping of the future security conditions, and especially integration and rapid economic development of the EU, including Poland;

2. A disintegration scenario, which can materialise if unfavourable and dangerous external and internal phenomena prevail, including a breakdown of the European integration and the rate of civilization development of the country;

3. An evolutionary scenario, as a continuation of the present trends, with a relative balance of negative and positive phenomena from the viewpoint of Poland's security.

While analyzing the above-mentioned scenarios one should bear in mind, however, that they are viewed in a long, twenty-year perspective. For that reason, they may change, evolve and turn into another in consequence of unpredictable changes in the international and domestic security environment.

An integration scenario

An integration scenario (very favourable, optimistic one) proceeds from the assumption of intensification of trends in the global, European, and domestic security environment, which are favourable to Poland, and especially: durable returning of Europe to the path of economic growth; overcoming the euro zone crisis as well as the crisis of the European Union itself, and a deeper European integration; maintaining the vitality, coherence, and reliability of NATO; continuation of political and military presence of the USA on European soil (including full implementation, in accordance with the adopted schedule, of the anti-missile defence system, the American part of the European Phased Adaptive Approach (EPAA); counteracting effectively terrorism and the proliferation of ballistic and mass weapons as well as adequate respect for international law.

In this scenario, EU countries would arrive at a common solution to the euro zone crisis, strengthen the structure of the monetary union and implement an efficient budgetary and fiscal discipline. A Europe which is strong in economic terms would mean a competitive economy that accounts for ca. 10 per cent of global GDP, with stable trade balance and balance of payments and a strong currency, a guaranteed food and raw material safety (including energy), capable of further growth at a rate enabling its significant position in the world to be retained. Strong Europe would keep up with other countries of North America, South America and the Far East in terms of innovativeness. This scenario is – for obvious reasons – the most favourable one for Europe's security in all areas, including the military one.

In the reformed Europe, Polish exports would enjoy a constant growth. By modernising the structure of its economy thanks to the increase of the innovativeness and competitiveness and lowering the demographic pressure (by way of relevant social politics and controlled migration), Poland would make another civilization leap forward.

A positive effect on the development of the country would also be evident through a successful diversification of energy carrier supplies. In the optimistic scenario it should be assumed that earlier estimates related to the deposits of shale gas would be positively verified during exploratory works, the extraction would turn out to be easier and cheaper (as a result of technological progress) than forecast, and Poland would not only satisfy its own energy needs, but also become a significant exporter of the natural material to the countries in the region. Having substantial and own resources of shale gas would practically mean elimination of the threat of stoppages of energy resources delivery from outside, resources which are necessary for stable economic growth.

Such situation would allow Poland to continue stable economic development, and also make it possible to maintain a relatively rapid increase in direct investments and export of services to EU countries. It would boost chances for the growth of prosperity of the society, faster strengthening of defence capabilities as a contribution to the security of NATO and the EU and for consolidation of the role and position of Poland in the European and North Atlantic structures.

Convincing other countries that Poland is a stable country would result in the positive feedback, i.e. it would improve ranking assessments of Poland made by international financing institutions and translate into a possible increase in foreign direct investments and Poland's access to foreign capital. Then, one could assume Poland's accession to the common currency, Euro, in the second half on the current decade. This in turn would positively influence further civilization development of Poland and, in this regard, catching up with countries of western and northern Europe within 15 to 20 years. Possibly, it would also be a beginning of creation of a national brand to promote Poland as a significant country of the EU. An ambitions but achievable goal would be to strenghten Poland's position on the market of food export and high-quality industrial consumables. Export of services to EU countries would witness a substantial increase, which means that Polish enterprises would take over bigger and bigger part of the added value in the European economy.

In the optimistic scenario, it would not be necessary for Poland to verify the main assumptions of its security policy, but only make sure of entering decision-making bodies and effectively achieve the detailed objectives adopted at operational and tactical level, and also help promote the positive processes referred to above. In such situation, Poland would have influence on directions of the development of European integration, inclusive of influence on increasing the effectiveness of the Common Security and Defence Policy of the EU. It would also become a more and more important member state of an efficient and effective NATO, thus leading to ultimate liquidation of the division into "old and new" members of the Alliance, increasing the number of Poles in international structures of the Alliance, and possibly bringing to effect the deployment of further elements of NATO's infrastructure on the Polish territory.

Of positive significance for strengthening Poland's position would be partner-like relations with Russia, an maybe even a breakthrough in mutual relations, on the assumption that Russia would depart from the imperial policy towards its neighbours and embark on a path to increased democracy.

A favourable international environment would create an opportunity for Poland to continue calmly its process of modernization of the armed forces and to eliminate the existing shortcomings in the field of defence capabilities. It would also make it possible to more extensively address selected, specialist elements of the defence system, such as development of special forces or streamlining capabilities in combating cybernetic threats. Such capabilities would possibly become a showcase and an asset of Poland on the international scene. Stable and predictable direct surroundings of the country would enable to have more active involvement in international security abroad. The growing economic strength and military potential would allow Poland to achieve the status of a regional power, able to co-create European and global security, as well as widen its strategic horizons by way of developing relations with new partners.

A disintegration scenario

A disintegration scenario (highly unfavourable, pessimistic one) would comprise several parallel and mutually enhancing trends that are inauspicious for Poland. One of the most significant among them would be a lasting, and even deteriorating, political, financial and economic crisis in Europe, expressing itself and resulting in social disorders, stemming from the evolution of the so-called "occupy" movement and eurosceptic circles seizing power (in the wake of elections).

A manifestation of such tendency would be first of all deepening discrepancies in the interests of the EU countries and the accompanying centrifugal tendencies in the European Union and in the eurozone, the growing popularity of nationalist and populist groups that undermine common values, thus leading to a weakening of the cohesion of this organization and limiting the scope of the so-called community (integration) method. It would mean also a considerable renationalization of the security policy and a decline of respect for international and EU law. (Alternatively, it may be the emerging of a "two-speed union", i.e. a permanent division of the EU countries into: the "hard core" *versus* the remaining countries, with Poland possibly falling outside the group of countries taking strategic decisions.) In an extreme variant one cannot rule out a possible collapse of the euro and disintegration of the European Union itself, which would be unavoidably accompanied by a weakened NATO and other multilateral institutions, internal and interstate conflicts, and even a return to the power politics pressures.

A determinant of the social and economic crisis on a European scale would be: economic stagnation or recession; an inefficient pension and social security system in conditions of ageing societies in the European Union as a whole; exacerbation of internal stemming from incompetent integration of immigrants and an increasing dependence of Western European countries on supplies of energy resources from outside.

The disintegration scenario would also mean a gradual decline of the European Union's share in world GDP, with further downward trend and weakening position of the competitive economy. It would be bound up with a permanent balance of payment deficit, large budget deficits and a weak currency (or even weaker national currencies).

When it comes to Poland, it would probably face a slower pace of the economic growth, limited financial means for social goals and state security as well as the occurrence of crisis-related social tensions. Poland would then be perceived as an economically backward region of the weakening West. The biggest social and economic burden of the EU and Poland would be expenditures on social goals, including the pension system. In case of any disintegration of the EU (from a "two-speed Europe" to its overall collapse), Poland would risk finding itself in the area that is weakest in economic terms. The weakening economy would result in marginalising of the political position of the EU, and also Poland, on the international arena.

Should such unfavourable circumstances really occur, a chance for Poland, which would partly neutralise negative trends, could turn out a continuing cooperation and good relations with partners in the Weimar Triangle and the Visegrád Group, as well as with the Baltic and Scandinavian countries.

Negative consequences of the changed correlation of forces on the continental and global scale would also be related to a progressing decrease in the scope of presence of the USA in Europe politically (no interest in maintaining strong transatlantic bonds), militarily (withdrawal of a majority of the stationed armed forces, abandoning plans related to the construction of the American part of the allied ballistic missile defence system), as well as to somewhat smaller degree – economically. It would also mean a deep crisis in the field of security on the continental scale. In the extreme case, Poland would witness a weakening of guarantees for its defence and a fall of importance of the NATO protection function. The eclipse of power of the USA as a stabilising factor would disturb the strategic positions of many allies (e.g. Israel or South Korea). Farther changes as regards involvement of the USA in Europe would have the maximum negative influence on Poland and other countries of Central and Eastern Europe and would contribute to a crisis, and even a collapse of the present defence system which is based on NATO, the EU and strategic relations with the United States. Probably, it would lead to strategic isolation of Poland in the context of renewed competition between the powers.

Such a process would inescapably be accompanied by intensifying assertive, neo-imperialist politics of Russia, and by attempts to partially regain its influences in the post-Soviet space. Such developments, which would render Poland and Europe much weaker, would pose the greatest challenge. Russia would repeatedly and effectively take advantage of resources owned by it, employing them as political means. Possible domestic problems of Russia would limit, however, its capability of assuming full domination in Eastern Europe. Changes in the balance of powers would also lead to a constrained stabilising role of great powers and intensified chaos in international relations. It would mean, among other things, the intensification of conflicts and threats, terrorist attacks, and the erosion of counteracting globally the proliferation of weapons of mass destruction and means of their delivery. Such development of events would result in a necessity to adopt even more costly efforts aimed at preventing such tendencies and their elimination. Also, one could not exclude then attempts to limit civil liberties in the light of intensifying strategic threats.

Should Iran (and possibly other countries too) acquire nuclear weapons, it might lead to an arms race in this field. Quite likely would be the lowering of the so-called threshold of use of these weapons in case of crisis. This situation would pose a threat to the existing world stability, including also Poland in the vicinity of which large amounts of atomic weapons are located. The cost of Poland's participation in stabilizing and protection ventures would probably exceed the possibilities offered by the Polish economy.

In the pessimistic variant, one should also consider an exhaustion of possibilities in regard to Poland's economic growth, caused by arrested inflow of EU funds, which would result in a halt of the modernization processes in the country. The pace of growth of Polish economy would significantly decrease. Western investments would outflow from Poland to other European countries offering lower production costs (Romania, Bulgaria, Ukraine, and countries of the former Yugoslavia), and to non-European countries. The Polish banking system, in which most banks are subsidiaries of foreign banks, makes it easy to transfer crisis-related financial phenomena from outside, that is the limitation of accessibility of lending, disposal of foreign banks' branches, obstacles in financing Polish debt, maintaining a reasonable exchange rate of the Polish zloty, etc.

The worst version of this scenario would mean the persistence of PLN for indefinite time and no possibility of entering the euro zone (should the latter survive) due to a weak condition of the Polish economy.

The scenario which assumes an inhibition of the Polish economy would mean, for the Polish exports, a probable growth of share of agricultural, low-processed products, and, at the most, a slight growth in industrial products, and also an increased dependence on other markets. It means that the economy would be so much uncompetitive that the trade balance would grow strongly negative.

Aggregation of unfavourable circumstances in the Polish energy sector (in internal and external terms) would create threats to development and stability of the Polish economy, and thus - to the general security condition of the state. Pessimistically, it may be assumed that extraction of shale gas would turn out unprofitable or its future production would be minor and remain poorly significant to play a role in satisfying the national demand for this resource.

Lack of necessary replacement investments in energy sector might also lead to radical technical degradation. If Russia took over control of the gas transit routes (provided the hitherto share of imported gas in the Polish energy balance would be kept), it might increase the pressure potential of the eastern neighbour.

Economic problems would also lead to an impoverishment of the society and such situation would translate into a radicalised civil mood. Extreme groups would stand to gain public support.

Another problem for Poland would be its inability to implement EU directives in the fields of climate protection as well as the limitations connected with carbon dioxide emissions and environment protection. Owing to EU restrictions, especially related to energy production based on coal, the competitiveness of Polish industry would fall.

The possible accumulation of unfavourable phenomena in the internal development of Poland would mean:
- in the political area – deepened divisions, intensified political struggles (along with their radicalization) and a paralysis of the state;
- in the economic area – failure of modernization strategies, stagnation and recession, and a growing dependence on import of energy resources;
- in the social area – intensifying claim attitudes, problems stemming from the demographic decline and immigration problems.

Such combination would cause a dramatic deterioration of the international position of Poland. Therefore, Poland would be forced to fundamentally redefine its security policy, including its rationalization and focusing on costly efforts aimed at building up its own defence and deterrence capabilities. Also, seeking immediate bilateral alliances in Europe would be necessary, sometimes obtained with substantial concessions. Poland would also have to limit its international activity, and resign from aspirations to play a defined role in international security operations.

In strategic terms, such developments would mean a radical limitation of Poland's freedom of action, a loss or dramatic limitation of its subjectivity. In such a variant it would be difficult to indicate the best direction for the security policy apart from the one that prescribes damage limitation.

An evolutionary scenario

An evolutionary scenario (realistic, most probable one) is a scenario which would envisage a continuation of the relative balance of positive and negative tendencies in the development of security environment in the context of Polish interests and their realization. It assumes that no radical (revolutionary) changes will occur – neither overly negative, nor excessively positive ones.

In this scenario, integration processes in Europe would continue (but their pace would be fairly less dynamic), and despite crises, basic elements of cohesion of the European Union would be preserved, inclusive of its ability (albeit limited) to operate on the international arena, also with Poland's participation and contribution. It is very probable that the EU will gradually manage crisis-related phenomena and head towards a deepening of cooperation, in particular by implementing integration elements in the field of fiscal policy. In this scenario, given the above-mentioned general cohesion of the European Union, numerous initiatives aimed at creation of the so-called 'hard core' may occur. The German-French leadership would be quietly accepted provided that it would not be in contradiction with the basic national interests of the member states.

There are many reasons to assume that the debt crisis in the euro zone will be tamed, and the mechanism of joint decision-making processes will be adjusted. If so, discipline would be strengthened and divergences reduced in the countries of the Union. A recovery from the crisis in the euro zone would have a relevant influence on the level of valuation of the Polish debts and the exchange rate of the Polish currency. At the same time, first steps would be taken towards a greater takeover of the burden of defence expenditures by the European allies within NATO.

The option of continuation of the present economic tendencies and decision-making mechanisms in the EU seems to be the most likely one, on the assumption of economic crises of low or average intensity. This embraces the problem of differentiation of the European Union's development rate, that is, not to allow an existence in an institutionalized form of two integration areas. This process would most probably be accompanied by a gradual weakening of the global economic position of the Union states, including Poland, as well as a decline in their competitive capability on internal and global markets.

In the scenario under consideration, a certain limitation of the United States' presence in Europe would happen, and some cooperation plans would be modified, however with maintaining the Americans' engagement within NATO. The probable scenario assumes that the North Atlantic Alliance would survive the crisis perturbations, and basic components that make NATO a defensive alliance would be preserved, while at the same time new missions of the Alliance would be developed.

It may be assumed that the whole western world will also gradually restrain its domination, including military one, on the international arena. Beneficiaries of such situation would be first of all the so-called emerging powers gaining more influence on the world affairs.

Also, it may be assumed that all the aforesaid threats and challenges as well as hotbeds will remain, however without any distinct escalation signs, especially in the military domain.

As far as Russia is concerned, it is likely that no radical changes in its internal and foreign policy would occur. In effect Russia would strive for maintaining the *status quo* by way of intensification of an efficient political and economic subjection of the former Soviet Union republics (with the exception of Baltic countries) as well as by continuous use of the energy carrier supplies for political aims. However, effects of such a policy would be diverse in relation to individual countries, but would not bring about any breakthrough in the form of a strong political structure steered from Moscow as a counterweight to the united West. Relations with the latter would constitute a dynamic combination of cooperation and rivalry as well non-military confrontations from time to time.

It should be also assumed that over the next twenty years there would be sporadic, individual terrorist attacks in the USA and Europe, but without any dramatic influence on the international policy, as it was the case with similar events at the beginning of the 21st century. Also, the regime of prevention of nuclear weapons and missile proliferation would not collapse, even though probably further countries would come into possession of or steer towards obtaining such a capacity. This general trend would certainly stall disarmament efforts.

Materialization of the realistic scenario would mean an economic growth of Poland at an average pace of 2-4 per cent yearly, which would enable retaining the present role in the regional context, but make it difficult to function within the "big six" of the EU. The influence of Poland on the EU foreign policy would remain at a similar level as today, but globally it would probably decrease.

Poland would primarily become a place of manufacturing mass products, the import of which from other continents would be unprofitable. This variant would also mean a slight growth in agriculture and services, both in quantitative and qualitative terms, as well as a growth in exports. An increase in direct investments in Poland might be assumed, however at a lower level than in the optimistic scenario. At an opportune time, Poland would decide on introduction of the euro.

Poland would remain an average-developed economy in technological terms, which in connection with changes in non-European countries would mean a deterioration of its competitive edge on the global scale. It would mean that in 2020, the Polish economy would have less favourable competitiveness perspectives for next decades (2020-2050). Faster than in Europe and Poland growth of other centres of dynamic economy would pose a danger of marginalization in the long run, that is until 2050. Disruptions of Poland's internal development could hamper active actions on the international arena, in some areas of the European security policy.

The evolutionary scenario also assumes a gradual putting in order of the internal crisis management system as well as a more extensive and effective consideration of demographic, social, cultural, and other issues in developing a more effective Polish security policy.

The continuation of the present energy security policy would enable increasing the long-term safety of Poland in this regard, however without a radical lessening of related threats. It would comprise construction of a nuclear plant, and completion of the liquefied petroleum gas port. However, a certain dependence on gas supplies would continue, as would do the still excessive share of coal in the energy balance (the importance of renewable energy in the resources balance, despite a gradual growth, will remain slim). The situation would possibly change should the profitability of extraction of the shale gas in Poland be confirmed and the industrial rate of its extraction be achieved to a degree entirely satisfying the domestic demand. It ought to be assumed that at European Union level no legal regulations will be introduced, which would cause a significant growth of costs of shale gas extraction.

Objective external difficulties and the insufficient sense of one's own strength would enforce "self-containment" adjustments in setting goals and implementing the Polish security policy. Even though both NATO and the EU would remain a reference point for Poland's security, the main stress would be put on extension of the country's own defensive capabilities, however to a fairly lesser degree than in the case of a pessimistic scenario. The Polish authorities would also have to seek additional safety guarantees through bilateral agreements (e.g. with the USA), or agreements with several select on countries (closer cooperation within the "big six" of the EU at the expense of developing the CSDP).

Uncertainty and lack of stability in the global context would call Poland to get involved to a greater degree in the strengthening of institutions and international law, and above all in extension and development of detailed norms and principles of conduct in relations between countries.

In this scenario, there would be a possibility of maintaining the state of internal and external security at a level close to the present one. And even if it were slightly limited (however not in the internal context), it would nevertheless be compensated by the gradual civilization progress and economic development of Poland.

* * *

Strategic conditions of Poland's security have a increasingly complex and quickly-changing character in qualitative terms. The contemporary world carries a lot of challenges and threats that call for consolidation and solidarity both at international cooperation level and in the internal policy. At the same time, the present opens opportunities unknown before.

Two decades that have passed since regaining by Poland of its sovereignty mark a period of a civilization leap. It is reasonably forecast that in the next two decades this advancement will continue.

Each modern state must be prepared to respond to any scenarios, including situations which are difficult to predict. In order to seek for an answer to questions related to future security conditions, it is not enough to articulate warnings against the threats that should be staved off, but also to recognize opportunities which should not be squandered. Of equal importance is to correctly identify challenges to be taken up, as well as to assess and reduce the risks stemming from the country's own activity.

Chapter 3

CONCEPT OF STRATEGIC ACTIVITIES (OPERATIONAL STRATEGY)

The diagnosis of Poland's security and the forecast of development of its conditions provide the foundation for formulating a concept of strategic activities (operational strategy). The concept is understood as a division (area) of national security (state security) strategy encompassing the rules and methods of attaining strategic objectives (implementation of operational strategic tasks in the field of national security) in the predicted security conditions (environment) as well as the determination of operational requirements with regard to the national security system.

Warsaw,
14 November 2011.
3rd plenary conference
of the National Security
Strategic Review debate
on the principal theses
elaborated by the Strategic
Activities Concept Team.
Photo: Łukasz Kamiński/
prezydent.pl

3.1. Foundation and guiding principle of the operational strategy

Current challenges for Poland's national security system are scattered and more numerous than ever before in the contemporary history. It is a qualitatively new situation which requires a modification of the state's approach towards security issues. In this context, the possible scenarios of shaping Poland's future security conditions – integration, disintegration and evolution – imply three **operational strategy options**:

1. An option of **maximum internationalization of Poland's security**, related at the same time to a shift of priorities towards non-military actions – corresponding to the integration scenario;
2. An option of **strategic autarky** (self-reliance and self-sufficiency), assuming a decisive strengthening of self-reliance as far as the state's activity in the field of security is concerned, in the context of a crisis of the collective defence policy in Europe and in the transatlantic community – corresponding to the disintegration scenario; and
3. An option of **sustainable internationalization and autonomy of Poland's security**, assuming the strengthening of allied bonds and bilateral relations with the most important partners and, through this, making external pillars more credible, with the simultaneous readiness to act autonomously in

situations in which full allied credibility cannot be guaranteed – corresponding to the evolutionary scenario.

The planning of actions of the state within the framework of the operational strategy should, pursuant to the most likely scenario of the development of security conditions, be founded on the third option – of sustainable internationalization and autonomy of Poland's security. At the same time, however, one should predict and include in plans a possibility or a necessity of appropriate implementation of elements included in the options of both maximum internationalization and autarky.

Within the basic option, it is possible to distinguish three main operational priorities (main security policy guidelines):

- **Maintaining and demonstrating one's determination and readiness to act** within a full spectrum of national security domains, fields and sectors, in particular with regard to those in which allied (joint) action could be hampered.
- **Strengthening the international security community**, in particular by acting in favour of deepening of integration processes based on a community of interests and values, including especially the consolidation of the North Atlantic Alliance in relation to the function of collective defence, the development of the EU Common Security and Defence Policy, as well as strengthening of strategic partnerships (also with the USA), and within their framework – of the strategic good neighbourliness;
- **Supporting and selective participating in actions of the international community** aiming at preventing the emergence of hotbeds or the spillover of already existing crises on the basis of an explicit international mandate.

Depending on conditions and development of the situation, strategic activities may take on a form of one of three types:

- **Stabilizing security** (promoting and developing cooperation, seizing opportunities, taking up challenges, preventing risks and threats, etc.);
- **Crisis response/management** (monitoring, recognizing, informing, preventing, suppressing, eliminating effects of a crisis);
- **Defensive measures** (deterring, preventing, repelling aggression, counter-attacking).

Guided by the priorities enumerated above, as well as taking into consideration the three types of strategic activities, one can distinguish a range of significant actions (operations) in the domain of security which Poland should undertake with the aim of pursuing national interests and achieving strategic objectives. These actions should be part of an active policy of seizing opportunities and pre--emptive risk reduction in the domain of security.

The most important action, which conditions all other actions, consists in **achieving agreement (consensus) of all political forces regarding the political will to treat national security issues as a priority** of the state policy. Such a will, underpinned by consensus, should be presented in an unambigous and decisive way, both in domestic policy and – or perhaps primarily – in external policy. National security needs to be placed above all political (party) divisions. It is a foundation of the effectiveness of all other strategic operations in the domain of security. It conditions the strength of Poland in international relations, which is needed in order to both "attract and deter" – to attract allies and partners, and to deter potential adversaries. What is more, it enables to respond effectively, if necessary, to any possible pressures, political and military blackmail, as well as other forms of information warfare in international relations, which may intensify in the years to come. A good place to forge political agreement in relation to security issues above party divisions is the National Security Council, which operates with the participation of persons constitutionally responsible for the security of the state. For the past three years, it is also possible for leaders of all political forces represented in the parliament to join the work of the Council.

Political will and consensus among the most important political forces are especially needed in elaborating a new National Security Strategy of the Republic of Poland, a document defining the national interests and strategic objectives in the field of security, describing a prospective development of the international environment, and defining operational and preparatory actions connected with the integrated system of national security.

In addition to shaping and presenting a consistent and uniform political position in terms of matters which are key as far as security is concerned, the second strategic activity within domestic policy consists in **responding in a professional (adequate and effective) manner to all current internal threats**, which are detrimental to state institutions and safety of citizens. It refers not only to routine operations of the national authorities, but also to responses to crisis situations and to the implementation of tasks in situations of particular dangers in which the Constitution of the Republic of Poland foresees introduction of a state of emergency. It also refers to active policy in terms of new and important areas of security, such as cyber security, energy security, and financial and social security.

A wide complex of strategic activities in the field of security is related to the **strengthening of the international security community**. In this regard, Poland should concentrate on three fundamental tasks: consolidating NATO in its defence function; engaging in the deepening of the integration processes in the European Union in the domain of the CSDP; and developing strategic partnerships (also with the USA) and good neighbourly relations (including the strengthening of the status of an entity for the East European countries).

Establishing and intensifying relations with emerging powers should constitute an additional objective.

The main external pillar of Poland's security is NATO. This is why the key activity in the framework of NATO should be the strengthening of the Alliance's credibility and, in particular, the **consolidation of its defence function**. For Poland's security, it is necessary to strongly support the fundamental principle of collective defence as reflected in Article 5 of the Washington Treaty. In this connection, it is important to strive for the effectiveness of allied mechanisms designed for the purposes of collective defence, such as: periodical revision of contingency plans, conduct of exercises with the participation of troops based on scenarios foreseeing the use of Article 5 of the North Atlantic Treaty, and an even territorial distribution of the allied infrastructure. It is also important to maintain the reliable defence planning within NATO. Its planning documents have to include the requirement to have adequate military capabilities for all, and not only the most likely contingencies, i.e. also for the most demanding collective defence missions.

Moreover, the military capabilities of the NATO member states should be strengthened, as they have been depleted due to the decrease in defence spending in the wake of the economic crisis. In this context, it may be helpful to carry out common projects within the concept of "smart defence". Poland should also constantly strive for an increase in appropriate defence expenditure of all member states. Aiming to achieve the level desired by NATO, close to 2 per cent of GDP, should be the goal. Joint threat assessment effectuated by the member states is also essential for the sake of the unity and cohesion of the Alliance.

Chicago, 21 May 2012.
2nd day of the NATO
summit.
Photo: PAP/EPA

Poland should emphasize the fact that only the effectiveness as a transatlantic defence alliance allows NATO to reliably engage in bringing crisis situations under control and settling conflicts outside the treaty area. For this purpose, political agreement will be necessary regarding these NATO operations which require the involvement of all member states, as well as those where the flexibility rule can be further developed. At the same time, it should be emphasized that the essential value of the Alliance is its unity. That is the reason why special attention should be paid to minimizing the risk of adversely undermining NATO's unity while applying the rule of flexibility.

Another necessary task to be undertaken in the framework of NATO is strengthening the transatlantic ties between Europe and the United States. The North Atlantic Alliance should remain the principal forum of this cooperation.

An important task of reinforcing the security of NATO's treaty area is the construction of an allied anti-missile defence system. Poland advocates its finalization on time, including the deployment on Polish soil of elements of the allied system delivered by the United States within the framework of the *European Phased Adaptive Approach* (EPAA).

An important role in NATO's policy is also played by the allied partnership policy. It refers, *inter alia*, to Poland's steady support for the "open door policy", as well as to the Alliance's cooperation with Ukraine and Georgia within the NATO–Ukraine Commission and the NATO–Georgia Commission. The allied partnership policy is currently focused on NATO's southern neighbourhood in particular. Nevertheless, Poland should strive for its geographical (and, consequently, also financial) balance, especially in the Eastern Europe.

Poland is also interested in the development of NATO-Russia cooperation, particularly in such areas as combating terrorism, non-proliferation of weapons of mass destruction and their means of delivery, and exchanges of data relating to airspace traffic (*Cooperative Airspace Initiative*). The condition for the effectiveness of this cooperation is the rule of reciprocity and transparency.

The **development of the European Union**, is the second external pillar of Polish security policy. The EU countries will remain the main economic partner having by far the largest share in the

Polish trade balance and in cumulative foreign investments. Therefore, the Polish economy will remain highly correlated with the economic condition of the EU.

For Poland's security, its engagement in the deepening of security integration processes in Europe is very important. It is fundamentally critical in the context of the EU's ability to play the role of a significant actor in this field. The character of the European integration is functional. The prospects of integration depend on whether it will adequately respond to the needs and interests of the member states. At the moment, it is at a turning point. For the integration, the crisis in the euro zone is an existential challenge, which calls into question the potential of mutual trust between the member states.

Poland should ensure that it will be able to participate in all Union decision-making processes. A guarantee of being rooted in the EU mainstream would be the joining the euro zone at the most favourable moment for Poland. From the Polish perspective, the preparation for joining the euro zone would be connected with a firm striving to balance the public debt and the budget deficit. Entry into the euro zone will also have to respond to significant challenges. The requirement to maintain a moderate budget deficit under control and to carefully monitor the functioning of the banking system is of special meaning in this context.

Poland's ambition should be to join the avant-garde of the EU countries, which would allow to ensure better development conditions, as well as a greater impact on decision-making processes and the future shape of the EU.

Poland should also aim at building a strong position of the EU in the world, building its maximum defence against the existing crisis and maintaining the ability to influence global processes more efficiently. The creation of CSDP structures and procedures, in particular the European External Action Service (EEAS), needs to be accelerated. In this context, Poland should try to increase the number of its diplomats working in the EEAS.

Strengthening of the CSDP would have a positive impact on the strengthened global position of the Union.

Poland should support further enlargement of the EU not only because of the stabilizing influence of that process on the direct neighbourhood of Poland, but also because of the additional effect supporting the image of the EU as a strategic actor involved in shaping the global balance of power.

The dynamic process of changes in the neighbourhood of the EU (Eastern Europe, North Africa, the Middle East, potentially the Arctic), the evolving global balance of powers which is influenced by emerging powers and the global economic crisis, all have forced the Union to face the challenge of redefining its interests and the objectives of its security policy. The strategic foundation of the EU – the 2003 European Security Strategy – has become less and less adequate to the contemporary security environment. This observation is supported by the fact that at the same time the EU itself is changing because of its own widening and deepening (Treaty of Lisbon).

Of late, the member states are increasingly interested in the debate regarding strategic problems related to the functioning of the Union, both at the regional and global level. The need to elaborate a new EU strategic document in the domain of security has been noticed. In 2012, actions were undertaken to develop a European Global Strategy. Their results will hopefully constitute an important point of reference in the debate regarding a new EU security strategy.

Warsaw, 1 July 2011. From the left: President of the European Commission, Jose Manuel Barroso; President of the European Parliament, Jerzy Buzek; President of the Republic of Poland, Bronisław Komorowski; Prime Minister of Poland, Donald Tusk; President of the European Council, Herman Van Rompuy; and Prime Minister of Hungary, Viktor Orban; before the premiere of the opera entitled "King Roger", presented on the occasion of the inauguration of the Polish Presidency in the Council of the European Union. Photo: Pawel Supernak/PAP

A new security strategy should comprehensively diagnose the European Union as a security actor in order to determine its mission in this domain more precisely than before. It will also be indispensable to review and agree upon a catalogue of common interests and strategic objectives of the member states. Moreover, it is desirable to determine, by way of the assessment and forecast of the development of the close and distant security environment of the Union, the most probable scenarios of its evolution. The new security strategy should outline, in accordance with these scenarios, a concept of framework actions. They would aim at the achievement of agreed objectives (operational strategy), as well as at preparing the necessary ways and means and keeping them ready (preparatory strategy).

From the Polish point of view, the most important common interests of the EU countries include the following:
1. The Union should have at its disposal an appropriately strong, commensurate with threats, security potential, including the defence one.
2. The capacity to ensure individual (citizens) and collective (population) protection against random and deliberate threats to their lives and health;
3. The guarantee of safe conditions for the development of societal and economic potential of all member states, as well as optimal use of this potential in the support of security operations.

Strategic objectives of the member states derive directly from their common interests. The Union should conduct an active policy of using opportunities and reducing risks pre-emptively, which implies the need to conduct international military and civilian security operations. In this context, a particular role is played by the ability of the EU to stabilize its neighbourhood. Moreover, the Union should maintain its political decision-making, planning and training readiness to effectively respond to threats faced by the EU countries. This will imply a necessity to elaborate mechanisms for co-operation between the Union and NATO, as well as a reform of the EU operational planning and command system.

In addition to the elaboration of the above-mentioned strategy, it is important to join specific practical projects reinforcing the CSDP. For Poland it means a continuing commitment to the reform of the EU battle groups concept, aiming at their actual consolidation and use as a real, practical tool of the EU Common Security and Defence Policy, strengthening of the EU-NATO cooperation, particularly between the European Defence Agency and NATO's Allied Command Transformation, as well as creation of a permanent EU command for the purposes of military operations. Poland should also back the strengthening of the European military potential by developing, within the framework of multinational projects, capabilities to be at the disposal of individual countries (pooling and sharing), as well as by cooperation in the field of development and purchase of armaments.

A possible evolution option for the CSDP may be an emergence of a European leadership ("avant-garde") in security matters, which would translate into bigger CSDP effectiveness, strengthening of civilian and military crisis response capabilities, as well as modernization and wider cooperation of defence industries of the European states. In such a situation, Poland should seek to join the avant-garde. Actions of this kind could be implemented through the provision of *permanent structured cooperation*, laid down in the Treaty on the European Union (taking account of the amendments introduced by the Treaty of Lisbon (Article 42 para. 6), for which the Weimar Triangle could constitute an initiative group. Irrespective of the current concerns about a threat to the EU cohesion, Poland should actively participate in the enhanced cooperation mechanism, which creates a chance for real reinforcement of the Common Security and Defence Policy.

Poland should also strive to effectuate the provisions of both the Treaty on the Functioning of the European Union regarding the solidarity clause (Article 222), and of the Treaty on the European Union, pertaining to the mutual defence clause (Article 42 para. 7). The first treaty establishes an obligation to cooperate and to support each other in the event of a terrorist attack or natural disasters and crises. The second one establishes a requirement for cooperation in the event of an armed attack. The entry into force of the Treaty of Lisbon notwithstanding,

Treaty on the European Union

Article 42 para 6. Those Member States whose military capabilities fulfil higher criteria and which have made more binding commitments to one another in this area with a view to the most demanding missions shall establish permanent structured cooperation within the Union framework

Treaty on the Functioning of the European Union

Article 222 para 1. The Union and its Member States shall act jointly in a spirit of solidarity if a Member State is the object of a terrorist attack or the victim of a natural or man-made disaster. The Union shall mobilise all the instruments at its disposal, including the military resources made available by the Member States, to:

a) prevent the terrorist threat in the territory of the Member States; protect democratic institutions and the civilian population from any terrorist attack; assist a Member State in its territory, at the request of its political authorities, in the event of a terrorist attack;

b) assist a Member State in its territory, at the request of its political authorities, in the event of a natural or man-made disaster.

successful operational implementation of the two clauses is not prejudged. This creates room for active Polish diplomacy.

In order to ensure the consistency of this effort with actions undertaken by the entire EU, it is necessary to strengthen the common security threat assessment, and hence develop the strategic culture. The development of EU civilian capabilities in the realm of crisis response is important as well.

Strategic cooperation between NATO and the EU, including reinforcement of its political cohesion and an increase in the effectiveness of their actions, will also be very significant for Poland's security. The initial stage of Poland's membership of NATO and the European Union ran in parallel with profound transformations of both organizations. From the moment of its accession, Poland has consequently been in favour of deeper integration within the framework of both the North Atlantic Alliance and the European Union, assuming that the very existence of the two organizations is an effective guarantee of its own security. At present – in the face of structural strains which affect both NATO and the EU – Poland has to move to another stage of its membership of the two organizations by promoting solutions which would enhance their strength for the benefit of Poland.

It is particularly important to strive for enhancing NATO–EU cooperation, which would pursue the goal of creating a Euro-Atlantic security tandem able to effectively head off an entire spectrum of contemporary threats. It is in Poland's interest that the two organizations complement each other within the framework of strategic partnership and, thanks to the resulting synergy, obtain better results of joint actions. In this respect, it is important to ensure a better coordination of initiatives regarding the development of defence capabilities both within NATO, in the framework of the smart defence initiative, and within the EU, with regard to the pooling and sharing concept. Direct cooperation between the two organizations in international security operations conducted in the same places is needed too.

Strategic partnerships and good-neighbourliness. It is in the interest of Poland to develop a close strategic cooperation with the USA, with other strategic partners and with the neighbouring states.

The United States is currently reducing its military presence in Europe. This process should not be played down by the European members of NATO. Poland should advocate a decreased scale of withdrawal of the US military potential and help define the new foundations of American presence by linking it closely with the readiness to respond to threats to Euro-Atlantic security. Simultaneously, Poland should aim at a real increase in European military capabilities within the CSDP.

Poland should develop its cooperation with the United States, as this collaboration serves to consolidate transatlantic ties and allows both sides to achieve measurable benefits. It should, among other things, concern enhancing the ability to undertake joint actions and joint military operations.

The success of Polish-American cooperation in the domain of security will in the coming years be determined primarily by the effectiveness of implementation of specific military cooperation programmes (training, in particular, of special forces, permanent presence of the US Air Force component in Poland and consistent implementation of plans to build the American part of the allied anti-missile defence system, to be deployed in the Polish territory in the third phase of EPAA), which are perceived to be advantageous for both sides.

It is in Poland's interest to have the American arsenal of tactical nuclear weapons (TNW) kept in Europe and to oppose various proposals for its unilateral withdrawal. Alternatively, reductions of

TNW should be taken into consideration solely in accordance with the rule of transparency and reciprocity in relations with Russia.

The multidimensionality of Polish-American relations, consisting in expanding the scope of cooperation to a greater number of fields and areas (energy, science and research, etc.), and thus deepening the sphere of joint Polish–American interests, should become a new paradigm.

Poland should work in favour of consolidating the status of an entity for the **East European states**. This refers, in particular, to countries covered by the Eastern Partnership initiative of the EU. The Eastern dimension of the Union's policy has to be continued and deepened by Poland as the advocate and promoter of this region. Consequently, it is especially important to share the transformation experience, to constantly support the pro-western vector in Ukraine's security policy, and to gradually include Ukraine in the mechanisms of European integration. The quality of cooperation between the EU and Poland, on one hand, and Ukraine, on the other, will considerably determine the evolution of developments across Eastern Europe. The development of relations with Moldova and the South Caucasus states – in addition to the support for their modernization and their European choice (in particular, in the cases of Georgia and Moldova) – promotes stabilization in unsettled conflict zones. Poland should strongly defend the principle of territorial integrity of states in the region, as well as their right to freely choose alliances. Outside Eastern Europe, beneficial prospects for Poland are also offered by closer relations with the Central Asian states by way of, *inter alia*, the possibility to import natural resources and the geopolitical position of the sub-region. A more extensive cooperation should be developed with Belarus, as soon as it starts meeting the basic criteria for democratization.

The foregoing actions ought to be accompanied by a development of cooperation with Russia based on the rule of reciprocity. The appropriate way to proceed in this regard is, however, to free relations with this partner from the logic of spheres of influence. Russia still considers Eastern Europe a territory in which a zero-sum game is played. Proceeding from this assumption, Russia seeks to consolidate a quasi-monopolistic influence across the former Soviet Union space. It is in the Polish interest to demonstrate that the Europeanization of Eastern Partnership states is also advantageous for Russia, since it is tantamount to implanting the principles of democracy, building the predictability at the socio-political level and the stable economic development. All this contributes to an increased stabilization of the region, thus serving the common interests of the European Union (including Poland) and Russia. The first step towards establishing of a common foundation of norms and similar rules of conduct in the triangle of the EU–Eastern Europe–Russia may consist in extending the WTO norms to all states of the region (note that Belarus and Azerbaijan, as well as Kazakhstan, remain outside the organization).

Cooperation with neighbours is also important for the security of Poland. It takes place both in formal (Weimar's Triangle, Visegrád Group) and *ad hoc* formats (the Baltic states). The Nordic countries are also important partners, as they are interested not only in the security in the Baltic Sea, but also in political cooperation at regional and global levels (*e.g.* the common Polish-Norwegian initiative regarding tactical nuclear weapons).

Afghanistan, patrol in Ghazni province.

Developing strategic good-neighbourly relations with Ukraine is of special importance for Poland. Independent, stable, and open for cooperation Ukraine is a key element of stability in Central and Eastern Europe.

Taking a glance on the neighbourhood issues from a broader perspective, in the era of decreasing defence expenditure in Europe, which is especially notable in Poland's closest vicinity, states that are trying to maintain their military ambitions at levels adequate to the challenges are gaining in importance. In this context it is worthwhile to mention Romania and Turkey as potential partners in politico-military cooperation.

Relations between Poland and **emerging powers** in terms of economy constitute an opportunity for development. As an EU member, Poland will become an increasingly attractive investment market for enterprises from the BRIC countries which will want to access the European common market. Moreover, by means of cooperation with these countries, Poland will open new avenues of exportation for its domestic products.

As far as the military dimension is concerned, it is important, however, to pay attention to military expenditure of these countries. A significant, abrupt augmentation of their spending would pose a serious challenge for NATO, the EU – so would for Poland.

Participation in activities of the international community aimed at nipping dangers in the bud is an important operational priority. A revitalization of other than NATO and EU organizations, institutions and international security regimes would be a factor enhancing this course of action.

Globally, it is advisable to increase the activity and emphasize the importance of Poland in the United Nations. A catalogue of actions should comprise more active involvement in the debate undertaken by the UN on the effectiveness of peace operations. Furthermore, Poland should take into consideration the renewal of its participation in select peace missions carried out by the UN, and

Photo: Waldemar Młynarczyk/The Team of Reporters Combat Camera DOSZ

increasing its engagement in disarmament efforts (in particular, to implement the Chemical Weapons Convention and the Treaty on the Non-Proliferation of Nuclear Weapons).

Regionally, there is a need to restore the importance of the Organization for Security and Co-operation in Europe. However, the process requires a constructive approach on the part of all participating states to cooperation within the OSCE.

It is also necessary to review the norms of international law, which would increase its effectiveness in countering new threats, especially those related to the proliferation of weapons of mass destruction, terrorism and organized crime, as well as to the destabilizing influence of failed countries. It also concerns the enhancing of the effectiveness of regimes and regulations in the domain of arms control and disarmament, as well as confidence- and security-building measures. In many cases, in particular in the field of terrorism and cybernetic threats, given the network nature of the phenomena which have to be head off, intensive international cooperation becomes more and more important and is an indispensable condition of successful efforts.

The character of modern and future threats to security necessitates identification of their sources as early as possible and taking quick preventive actions as the main operational strategy principle. It is necessary to undertake comprehensive actions which take into account political, economic, social and military elements. Not only states and international organizations, but also NGOs should be involved in the above-mentioned actions. Poland should also take part in these actions.

Participation in operations beyond national borders is a significant tool of the Polish foreign and security policy. At the same time, it is a source of operational experience and one of the indicators of the transformation course of the Polish Armed Forces. Military actions should be concurrently reinforced by means of civilian involvement (actions aimed at achieving political stability and ensuring social rehabilitation and economic reconstruction of conflict regions), including the provision of development assistance.

It is necessary to analyze Poland's involvement in the actions of the international community taken in recent years in order to settle regional and global conflicts, crises and problems. That is the basis on which the most important criteria of such participation in the coming years should be established. Decision-making on whether Poland should participate in a given operation ought to result from its national interests, strategic objectives and capabilities of (resources possessed by) the state. The secondary criterion would refer to the entity carrying out the operation (NATO, the EU, the UN, the OSCE or a coalition of the willing ones). An important premise of taking a decision with regard to Poland joining a given operation is whether the latter has been given an explicit international mandate.

3.2. Strategic tasks of national security operational subsystems

The defence subsystem

The basic course of action of the defence subsystem is the permanent readiness to effectively respond to threats to the independence and territorial integrity of the Republic of Poland. In this respect, Poland should also encourage security organizations, of which Poland is a member, to maintain and enhance their readiness to undertake political decision-making, planning and training actions. Supplementary actions should focus on conducting active policy of using opportunities and pre-emptive risk reduction in the domain of security, e.g. by participating in international efforts to avert dangers, including international security operations.

Security activities of the foreign service. The globalization and the increasing scale of international interdependence have shed new light on the security-related tasks of the diplomatic service which has to adjust its actions to the changing milieu.

It is assumed here that Poland's alliances, as well as its current structures and international relations will continue in the long term. Therefore, Polish diplomacy should constantly participate in actions aimed at consolidating their cohesion, reliability and effectiveness.

The Polish diplomacy has to take into account the ongoing strategic change consisting in the shifting of the centre of global economy from the Atlantic area towards the Asia-Pacific region. For the diplomacy, it would imply a task of expanding partnerships with the emerging powers.

The most important tasks of the Polish diplomacy in the context of requirements related to the national security concern:

- Maintaining the importance of the fundamental NATO mission, that is the common defence, while expanding the activity of the Alliance by adding new tasks, also in the domain of crisis management and cooperative security;
- Participating in the renewing of the European project via both political initiatives and effective communication of benefits which arise for Poland thanks to the European integration;
- Intensive support for improving the EU Common Security and Defence Policy by enhancing it on a politico-strategic (amendment of the European Security Strategy), as well as institutional (permanent command) and operational (EU battle groups) levels;
- Developing cooperation with the strategic partners in the EU, including Germany and France in the framework of the Weimar Triangle, as well as building possibly durable coalitions with the countries of the Visegrád Group and of the Baltic Sea region;

- Expanding the spectrum of bilateral cooperation with the United States (energy, science and research, innovations) while intensifying politico-military cooperation;
- Developing the partnership with Russia in accordance with the principles of reciprocity, transparency and respect for the sovereignty of neighbouring countries;
- Promoting non-proliferation of weapons of mass destruction and their means of delivery as well as arms control, and disarmament;
- Strengthening the European energy policy by way of building up the transmission infrastructure and respecting the competition rules, also in relation to entities from energy-supplying countries;
- Developing relations with emerging powers, including the dialogue with regard to security.

Military activities. As was mentioned before, the key course of action of the defence subsystem is to maintain the political decision-making, planning and training readiness to effectively respond to threats to the independence and territorial integrity of Poland. Ultimately, the Polish Armed Forces have to be able to effectively perform three key missions, the scope of which will not change compared with the one currently adopted in strategic documents. These three missions are and will be: defence of the state, international engagement, and support of internal security (public and civil institutions of the state). A certain re-assessment should, however, take place in relation to the emphasis placed on each of them.

The fundamental task of the armed forces should remain the defence of their own territory. In this context, they should be ready to: act autonomously in case of a small-scale local conflict; receive allied force back-ups and retain certain points of defence until their arrival in case of a large-scale conflict; participate in an allied defence operation in the event of an attack on another state, in keeping with the principles of collective defence. The mission of defending the national territory also includes the function of military deterrence by demonstration of the readiness to defence with the use of forces kept in peacetime and the readiness to mobilize them in the event of a large-scale war.

The Polish Armed Forces should be ready to carry out counter-surprise operations and to independently operate in the most effective possible way in consensus-challenging situations, i.e. in which it is difficult to reach a consensus (among allies), as well as in the circumstances of *aterritorial*, selective, unpredicted threats of a limited scale, caused by unclear or hidden political motives. The doctrinal premises and the guiding principle of the national defence should fully correspond with the strategy of NATO as a whole, but, above all, they should take into account the Polish national interests and conditions for their implementation.

Within the second mission, the Polish Armed Forces should stay in readiness for engaging in various types of international security operations conducted both at regional and global levels in an increasingly complex environment. Such engagement should be considered a significant tool of the Polish foreign and security policy (support for the diplomacy), ensuring the influence on shaping the international environment. At the same time, it is a source of operational experience and one of indicators of the directions of transforming the Polish Armed Forces.

The level of future involvement in the activities pursued in the international arena is contingent on the capabilities of the state determined by financial, human, material and organizational resources. The decision concerning the participation of the armed forces should result from the national interests and capabilities of the state, as well as international obligations towards allied partners and organizations. While making a decision regarding any participation in future missions, it is necessary to take into consideration primarily the convergence of aims of these missions with the Polish interests and strategic objectives.

The third mission of the Polish Armed Forces is to support national security and to render help to the society. Fulfilling this function they should: monitor and protect the airspace; support the protection of the land borders and territorial waters; conduct reconnaissance and intelligence activities; monitor radioactive, chemical and biological contaminations in the territory of the country; clean off the territory from explosive remnants and dangerous military objects; conduct search-and-rescue operations; and aid the state authorities, public administration and the population in crisis situations and in the event of natural disasters.

As far as the security of the state is concerned, apart from the above-mentioned basic missions of the armed forces, the following additional operational tasks should be performed:

- Pursuing the expansion of military cooperation between NATO and the EU, based on the rule of complementariness;
- Developing the capability to receive allied back-up forces in the territory of Poland and to conduct exercises preparing to joint operations;
- Contributing to the development of EU military capabilities related to crisis response;
- Building confidence in relations with Russia (on the reciprocity principle) by expanding the military cooperation within the existing possibilities resulting from the membership of NATO;
- Participating in the verification of compliance with agreements on arms control, disarmament and confidence- and security-building measures, including, in particular, avoiding unfavourable changes in the balance of military forces in the region;
- Cooperating in the field of modernization and reconstruction of Poland's industrial defence capacity, in line with the national needs; and
- Assisting in the evacuation of Polish citizens from abroad in a situation in which their lives would be at risk.

The armed forces are responsible primarily for executing defence tasks. However, changes in Poland's security environment constantly result in accumulating new tasks. The increasingly ambitious strategic objectives of Poland in the domain of security, along with the globalization, force changes in some of the tasks and have impact on the sustainability of engagement of the forces. They also call for undertaking action in a difficult operationally environment and cooperating with numerous, both military and civilian, participants in order to achieve common goals. The limits of military action are determined by an ever-increasing range of legal regulations. The tasks executed by the armed forces are and will be watched and assessed with a growing interest by the media and the society. The situation calls for adjustment, i.e. constant transformation of the armed forces in order to enable them to effectively and timely perform tasks which are laid before them by the state.

Intelligence activities. The intelligence services should: recognize and inform about the existing and potential threats to Poland, its interests and citizens; identify and monitor opportunities for and risks to the national security; support the forces participating in operations outside the country; track the international trade in arms and the proliferation of weapons of mass destruction and their means of delivery; monitor actions related to energy and raw materials policy; expand their own capabilities by cooperating with allies and coalition partners. The mission of the intelligence should also be to effectively identify intentions of third countries that are detrimental to the Polish interests.

Apart from operational activities conducted by the intelligence services, an important role, as far as security is concerned, is played by open-source intelligence. Tasks performed in this field are focused on analyzing and processing information from publicly available sources (mainly from the mass media, including open electronic communication means, registries, personal sources) concerning, in particular, events, places and persons having potential impact on the internal and external security of the state. The "verified open-source intelligence", which comprises data collected from open sources and databases, including confidential information, is equally important. Open-source intelligence constitutes one of the priorities of analytical and information activities performed by the services and is an integral part of all activities conducted within the framework of precise intelligence (operational) tasks described above.

Counterintelligence activities in support of the Polish Armed Forces and defence industry. An extremely important aspect of the military counterintelligence activities consists in preventing actions which could threaten the security or combat capability of the Polish Armed Forces. In this context, important are activities aimed at protecting the security of military units and personnel of the armed forces. Among the specific tasks, one should mention activities aimed to counter espionage, to prevent attempts at military units and defence facilities and installations, corruption in the area of threats to national defence, as well as violations of classified information security, including the aspect of information combat in cyberspace. Another significant task within this area is to protect the security of research and development ordered by the armed forces and other units of the Ministry of National Defence, as well as to secure the production and turnover of military goods, technologies and services.

Defence production. In the coming years, the Polish industrial defence potential should be engaged, to the maximum extent, in the processes of technical modernization of the Polish Armed Forces. Analysis of the problem indicates that the Polish defence industry entities are capable of producing, within a relatively short period of time (2–3 years), elements of armaments and military equipment demanded by the Polish army.

Support for Polish arms companies and enterprises and their involvement in the implementation of the prioritized modernization programmes of the Ministry of National Defence are therefore legitimate. The most important of them, specified in the Main Directions for the Development of the Polish Armed Forces as well as their preparation for defence of the state in the period 2013-2022, are: air defence (including anti-missile defence), IT systems, and mobility of the land forces (helicopters).

Long-term plans regarding purchases for and modernization of the Polish Armed Forces should be elaborated on the basis of a complex diagnosis, in close cooperation with representatives of science and industry. These consultations, supported by real financial investments, e.g. from the National Centre for Research and Development, will make it possible to harmonize and systematize defence expenditure for the coming years. Such activities should result in modern products utilized and exploited by the Polish army both at home and in international security operations.

The protection subsystems

The main tasks within protection subsystems include the securing of conditions for maintaining the constitutional order, internal stability and public safety. These tasks concern, in particular, the protection of state institutions, citizens, common and individual tangible and intangible assets against non-military threats. Such dangers result from both human activities and natural forces. In the first case, they do not always need to take a form of violation of the provisions of applicable law. According to the operational strategy rules, tasks in this respect have to be executed both within the national security system and within the network of international ties, in particular, in the framework of NATO, the EU and through bilateral cooperation.

Strategic tasks performed within the protection subsystems concern, in particular, the domains of public safety, combating terrorism and political extremism, as well as threats resulting from cyber crime, including civil protection.

A complementary objective of activities undertaken within the Polish protection subsystems should be the participation in promoting internationally and fostering domestically the rules and awareness of duly enjoying the rights and freedoms of man and citizen.

The judiciary. The main function of the judiciary is to settle in a binding disputes between defined entities. The supreme objective of Poland as a democratic state governed by the rule of law is to eradicate dangers to the liberty of exercising the rights and freedoms, as well as consistent prosecution and punishment of offenders against the above-mentioned liberty. In this regard, the state should ensure that courts and public prosecutor's offices function efficiently, proceedings are carried and cases are resolved in a timely manner, and decisions are enforced effectively.

Another extremely important task of the judiciary is to ensure the security of trade, which is possible when there are simplified and flexible legal procedures offered to business entities.

The judiciary has to ensure that the constitutional guarantees of rights and freedoms are implemented. This is possible when there is a broad access to judicial institutions which function fast and in a citizen-friendly manner. Indeed, everyone has the right to a fair and open hearing without undue delay (i.e. smooth and timely) conducted by an appropriate, independent and impartial court.

A the same time, however, the judiciary has to function in a way which makes citizens realize that punishment for a committed offence is inevitable, as well as justified and proportionate to the scale of the public violation. Adjudication of fines for minor offences, rather than imprisonment, is advisable. The catalogue of punishments, also those for economic crimes, has to be reviewed in order to avoid the impression that the Polish justice condemns minor offences too severely, and that it is too lenient for the perpetrators of serious crimes. Moreover, the judiciary should support actions aimed at promoting and strengthening human rights, the rule of law and democracy.

An important challenge is to strengthen the image of Poland as a well-functioning state governed by the rule of law, supporting and protecting its citizens both at home and abroad. Therefore, it is necessary to promote the commitment to human rights and civil liberties; to combat all forms of discrimination (including the discrimination of Polish citizens abroad), since such activities will consolidate a positive image of Poland abroad; have prejudices and negative stereotypes humiliating Poland and Poles eliminated; and to prevent manipulations of history (such as the expression "Polish concentration camps").

Counterintelligence shield. The strategic task of counterintelligence services is to protect the constitutional order and the democratic system of the state against violations of the state's stability and to operationally identify threats to Poland's security resulting from the activities of foreign secret services. The latter take, *inter alia*, steps aimed at gathering information in the areas of business, political, scientific and technical intelligence, which may constitute a threat to the security of the state. As far as the counterintelligence protection of the country is concerned, of utmost importance is also to safeguard the key strategic information resources, which ensure the proper functioning of the state.

The main tasks of the counterintelligence service should therefore include: effective reconnoitring of potential and real threats and preventing them by means of available operational and procedural methods; continuous monitoring and analysis of identified threats to the security of the state; taking preventive actions, in particular in the field of protection of secret information; coordination of activities and cooperation with other components of Poland's national security system, as well as with foreign and international (transnational) entities, in conformity with allied obligations.

Combating terrorism and political extremism. Threats related to terrorism in Europe are connected with the activeness of both the global network of Al-Qaeda and groups of extreme left (the renaissance of which can be seen in connection with the financial crisis) or extreme right (resulting, among other things, from the rise of xenophobia and anti-immigrant attitudes) nature. The activity of this type of extremist groups may constitute a threat to the political stability of the state, regardless of whether they are able to undertake purely terrorist activities or not.

Strategic tasks of entities responsible for combating terrorism and political extremism may be catalogued in the following way: reconnoitring terrorist threats to Poland, both at home and abroad; continuous monitoring of threats and working out forecasts of likely attempts on the basis of risk analysis; neutralizing terrorist threats, including physical fight against terrorism; eliminating sources of financing terrorism; prosecuting perpetrators of terrorist threats and acts, in accordance with the norms of international law applicable in Poland; reconnoitring symptoms of radicalized behaviour and preventing it; cooperating internationally on political, operational, analytical and legal levels in the fight against terrorism; information struggle aimed at reducing the impact of views promulgated by extremist and terrorist organizations on the Polish society; anti-terrorism prevention, including shaping the public awareness of the significance of terrorist threats and forming the appropriate behaviour to increase the security of citizens; constant reinforcement of the state's and population's resistance to terrorist attacks, focused on minimizing material (direct) losses and psychological traumas (indirect losses), as well as on maintaining the continuity of the state's functioning critical infrastructure.

Protection of information. The protection of information is one of the most important areas of the national security system. In the era of the growing significance of information security, including the vital importance of information collection, processing and distribution processes within certified information technology systems, the role of cybernetic information security is also increasing. A specific domain of information security is the protection of information, i.e. information of which unauthorized disclosure causes or may cause harm to Poland or would be unfavourable from the point of view of its interests.

Strategic tasks within the information protection system include the securing of information security of the state and an effective exercise of those of its functions which require processing and distribution of information via preventing unauthorised access to information and its disclosure, providing personnel, technical and physical security of information, accrediting information technology systems which serve to store and process information, and exercising tasks related to the national security authority in order to make possible the international exchange of information.

Cybersecurity. Cyber threats concern the interests of citizens, of the state and of business entities alike. Therefore, the cyberspace is an arena on which the information struggle is taking place. The most serious threats are related to data theft, obtaining bank accounts access data, the takeover of control over computers, and DDoS[19] attacks. There have been cases of acquisition of control over the computer system steering the operation of an industrial facility (e.g. attack on nuclear installations in Iran).

Strategic tasks in the field of cybersecurity are the follows: prevention of threats in the cyber space; protection of information systems of the state; development of cooperation and coordination of protective activities with the private sector – above all the banking sector – entities, regarding, in particular, access to information about the attacks carried out and their types; conducting actions of preventive and prophylactic character with regard to the protection of citizens against threats from the cyberspace; identification of offences committed in cyberspace and preventing them, as well as prosecution of their perpetrators; conducting offensive and defensive information struggle in cyberspace, as well as coordination of activities with other entities of Poland's national security system.

Cybernetic threats are underestimated by the majority of the society. Counteracting them requires large groups of specialists equipped with appropriate equipment and financial means to collaborate, and safeguards against the reduction of possibility or failure to use digital data transmission. This cooperation should be closely integrated with the state defence system.

Law and order. Existence of threats to the public safety and order calls for the identification and neutralization of negative phenomena, and if they occur – the reduction of their extent and impact, including effective prosecution of their perpetrators. In the context of real and potential threats, the fight against organized crime has to be considered a priority. Although organized crime was traditionally related to criminality and drugs, nowadays it more and more often takes the form of broadly--conceived economic crime. Another priority is protection of the public order, also during mass events and gatherings.

Basic objectives of the state, as far as the infringement of law and order is concerned, consist in achieving a high effectiveness in:
- the identification of offences and public safety breaches;
- the inevitability of punishment of their perpetrators;
- recovery of lost property and reducing of losses of the state treasury.

These activities have to take into account the need to conform to human and civil rights standards as well as to the democratic rule of law. In this respect, the tasks include:
- Constant monitoring of criminality with the aim of elaborating and implementing solutions regarding its combating in various dimensions, including a current threat analysis;
- Conducting current and long-term analyses with the aim of detecting changing trends and tendencies related to threats;
- Increasing the effectiveness of the prosecution of persons responsible for violating public safety and order, in particular as far as organized crime is concerned;

---

[19] DDoS (Distributed Denial of Service) – attack on a computer system or network service, which aims to prevent it from functioning by making it overloaded with connections; launched from many computers.

- Organizing and coordinating activities with the aim of fighting against the most serious crimes, in particular those against life and health, as well as extortions and offences with the use of weapons or other dangerous devices;
- Undertaking actions aimed at recognizing and combating drug-related crime; preventing crimes of economic nature, in particular those related to the trade in goods subject to excise duty and VAT frauds, as well as countering money laundering;
- Intensifying activities aimed at identifying and fighting against hooliganism, including the activities of groups of so-called pseudo-fans;
- Performing tasks concerning combating child pornography and paedophilia;
- Ensuring the road traffic safety by pursuing control activities and analyses of circumstances in which collisions and road accidents take place; and
- Undertaking effective activities of preventive nature by means of appropriate organization and co-ordination of tasks; conducting widespread prophylactic activities.

It is important to identify and monitor sources of threats, to neutralize and eliminate them by introducing changes to the law, as well as, where necessary and possible, carrying out direct intervention by the authorities responsible for law and order (this primarily refers to a radical restriction of legal means, discretion within the administrative procedures limiting the possibility of corruption).

Coordination of activities and cooperation with other components of the Polish national security system, including private entities operating in the security sector (e.g. SUFO), as well as with foreign and international (transnational) partners, is of utmost importance. In particular, one can point to: police cooperation within the framework of the Union Area of Freedom, Security and Justice, as well as cooperation with entrepreneurs, government entities, local authorities and other public institutions; improvement of the public security system; streamlining of legal mechanisms and effectiveness of the judiciary in combating crime, in particular, organized and economic crime; protection of the independence of the judiciary and absolute protection of the judiciary against political pressure; education for security and engaging the people in the process of forming the national security foundations; preventing unlawful infringement of intellectual property rights of the state and of its citizens, as well as supporting activities aimed at fostering and strengthening human rights, the rule of law and democracy.

Civil protection in crisis situations. The primary purpose of the state as far as crisis response is concerned is to remain in high readiness and to be prepared at planning, training and operational levels to promptly react in the event of a crisis menace (individual to citizens and collective to the population and their property). In most cases, effective neutralization and minimizing of the results of disasters require cooperation and coordination of many entities. Enhancing of the state's capacity to react in this regard has to concentrate on preventive activities and efficient operation in case of a disaster.

Concepts elaborated in relation to this domain should emphasize the need to create a universal model of cooperation of bodies, services and other entities performing tasks connected with civil protection, improving the coordination of the rendered humanitarian assistance and promoting appropriate behaviours of the society in case of threats. Such comprehensive approach is proposed within the framework of the National Fire Fighting and Rescue System as an integral element of the state security system.

The strategic tasks in this area include:

- Current risk analysis and identification of sources of threats to the safety of the population;
- Elaborating emergency plans including the threat analysis, embracing particularly rules for the use of forces and means, means of communication, coordination and rules for cooperation of entities during the emergency response;
- Protecting life, health, property or environment by dealing with natural or man-made disasters, as well as eliminating other local dangers;

Szczekociny,
3 March 2012.
Rescue operation after
a collision of two trains.
Photos: Andrzej Grygiel/PAP

- Organizing and conducting rescue operations, in particular, in the field of technical, chemical and environmental rescues as well as emergency medical service;
- Monitoring, informing, warning and alarming people and institutions, services and other entities performing tasks related to civil protection about threats;
- Preventive, scientific and educational activities in the area of civil protection;
- Organizing rescue exercises;
- Cooperating with emergency formations and services from other countries as well as with international organizations, and utilizing international cooperation mechanisms related to civil protection.

Protection of the state border. Safeguarding the integrity of borders is a significant indicator of sovereignty of every country. Therefore, protecting the state borders is one of key strategic tasks within the national security system of Poland. In order to perform this task, the designated authorities undertake a range of protection activities aimed at preserving the inviolability of borders and the control of border traffic.

The specific character of duties of the ***Border Guard*** which executes tasks in this domain has significantly changed in recent years in connection with the Polish accession to the EU and the joining of the Schengen area. These changes were primarily connected with the cessation of physical protection at border crossings on those parts of the Polish border which became the EU's internal borders, and with the enhancement of controls in those sectors which became the EU's external borders.

In connection with the requirement of a full implementation of the above-mentioned obligations, a series of concept papers, legislative and organizational changes were elaborated and implemented in order to transform the Border Guard into a modern border-and-immigration service responsible for carrying out border clearances and protecting the EU external border, and at the same time performing control tasks in the territory of the country.

Photos: the Border Guard

Modifications relating to the European integration notwithstanding, the range of strategic tasks of this formation has not changed much and includes: protection of the state border in such a way as to ensure the protection of the territory of the Republic of Poland against illegal flows of goods and persons, as well as to prevent hazardous substances and materials from entering the territory of Poland, which is especially important in the era of asymmetric threats, those related to terrorism in particular; organization and performance of the control of border traffic in such a way as to ensure that it is smooth and, thus, that it has a positive impact on the development of cross--border economic relations; the fight against cross-border crime and crime involving foreigners. Furthermore, as far as security of the state and of citizens is concerned, the Border Guard fulfils the task of backing up the objectives of Polish migration policy. The scope of this task is apparently going to expand. Rescue operations conducted on the Polish sea border are also turning into a more and more important task performed by the BG.

In accordance with the Act on the State Border Protection, the body responsible for the protection of the airspace of the Republic of Poland is the Minister of National Defence. His duties in this respect are fulfilled by the Operational Commander of the Polish Armed Forces with the help of the air defence command authority. In order to perform this task, the Polish Armed Forces maintain appropriate forces and resources within a system of standing duty shifts, keeping them in appropriate readiness for use.

What is more, the Polish Armed Forces are responsible for taking preventive measures if a foreign aircraft crosses the Polish border unauthorized, under the so-called RENEGADE procedures. In an extreme situation, such as a terrorist attack, these procedures provide for possible destroying of an aircraft, whether it is a military aircraft or a civilian aircraft on board of which there are no people or there are only persons who launch the terrorist attack.

The broadly conceived state border protection subsystem comprises also the **Customs Service** which does duties related to the protection and safety of the EU's customs territory, including the legality of goods import and export. By fulfilling its obligations, this formation has to meet the expectations of entrepreneurs regarding the assurance of a smooth flow of goods, on the one hand and, on the other, to ensure effective control which protects the economic interest of both Poland and the EU with regard to: performing of activities related to the assignment of goods to the customs destination; preventing violations of provisions regarding importation to and exportation from the Polish territory of goods subject to trade restrictions or bans with due respect for public safety and order or international security, and the fight against fiscal offences.

The system of the state border protection also imposes certain obligations on **province heads**. They are particularly obliged to permanently keep road, rail, air, sea and river border crossings in conditions making it possible to carry out efficient and effective security, borders, customs, sanitary, veterinary, phytosanitary, chemical and radiometric control, as well as to supervise the trade quality of agricultural and food products.

The state border protection subsystem is also connected with the migration system. The **Head of the Office for Foreigners** plays an important role as far as the regulation of issues related to the stay of foreigners in the country is concerned. It is a task which will be more and more important due to the demographic decline and forecast increase in the dynamics of immigration processes within the framework of an watchful, clearly defined migration policy allowing for an increase in the population potential of the Republic of Poland.

Protection of the supreme authorities and public administration bodies. In Poland, tasks in this area are performed by the Government Protection Bureau, the principal strategic objective of which is the "protection of persons and objects important for the good and interest of the state". This basic task is fulfilled both within and outside the borders of the country – in direct relation to persons and objects. Among the most important actions undertaken by the service, one can mention: planning of the safety of persons, objects and facilities; identification and analysis of potential threats and prevention of their coming into being; coordination of the protection activities implementation; direct protection; securing objects and facilities, as well as training and improving working methods of the service.

Fulfilling these tasks requires a permanent access to resources of credible information which can constitute a point of reference for planning and implementing protectio actions. It implies a need for close cooperation with both civil and military (depending on the theatre of the conducted protection operations) classified services. One of the essential conditions for the effective performance of tasks by the Government Protection Bureau is the most optimal introduction of mechanisms making it possible to use information furnished by the Police, the Internal Security Agency, the Intelligence Agency, the Border Guard, the Military Counterintelligence Service, the Military Intelligence Service and the Military Gendarmerie.

Ensuring the maximum protection of Polish diplomatic missions, consular posts and representations with international organizations in places of high social tensions or regions highly threatened by terrorism is becoming a priority. It results from the Poland's engagement in activities of the international community, which determines the presence of its representations and representatives in particularly dangerous regions. This requires that the Government Protection Bureau improve its cooperation with other institutions involved in protection. Actions undertaken by officers in the war-risk zones and ensuring of safety to persons subject to protection who visit countries such as Afghanistan constitute an additional challenge, since in such situations non-standard procedures are used, which require elaborate systemic coordination solutions taking into account political and diplomatic, as well as civilian and military actions undertaken by other services in this field.

An important category of activities related to the protection of the very important persons of the state is also the planning and implementing of security procedures (not only at the level of tactical protection provided by the Government Protection Bureau, but also of standing procedures) concerning locations (co-location) of VIPs, especially in the event of an introduction of the state of emergency, in time of war and during transportation, by means of air transport in particular.

Combating corruption. Corruption is a serious threat to the correct functioning of a state. Therefore, combating this phenomenon constitutes one of the main priorities of activities aimed at ensuring the protection of citizens' rights and effective management of the country's development. An effective anti-corruption system and an efficient functioning of services responsible for law and order constitute guarantors public life integrity. As far as law enforcement agencies are concerned, the Central Anti-Corruption Bureau, the Police, the Internal Security Agency and the Military Counterintelligence Service are responsible for preventing and combating corruption.

At the level of public administration, the system comprises the Ministry of the Interior, as well as controlling authorities, i.e. the Supreme Audit Office, fiscal audit and units of internal audit in public administration offices.

The main strategic objective is to curb corruption and corruption-generating phenomena. It should be first of all realized by means of educational activities conducted at many different levels (media, school, administration). Strategic tasks of the state with regard to combating corruption are specified in the document elaborated in 2011 by the Ministry of the Interior and Administration – in cooperation with other central institutions – entitled the Government Anti-Corruption Programme for the years 2012-2016, and include[20]: elaboration and implementation of a coordinated national anti-corruption policy; strengthening anti-corruption mechanisms in the public administration (including the enhancement of cooperation and coordination of activities undertaken by law enforcement agencies and the judiciary, as well as the streamlining of legal solutions); increased participation of the society, including non-governmental organizations, in the process of preventing and combating corruption; strengthening cooperation with the public administration and forming anti-corruption attitudes in the society, as well as fulfilling Poland's international obligations related to anti-corruption prevention and education.

In 2008, a concept of an "anti-corruption shield" was elaborated. Actions within its scope are undertaken by the Internal Security Agency, the Military Counterintelligence Service and the Central Anti-Corruption Bureau in cooperation with relevant government departments and their subordinate organizational units. The coordinating institution is the Chancellery of the Prime Minister. Strategic operational activities include the creation of preventive mechanisms aimed to fend off the corruption dangers and counter irregularities in two major areas: privatization of key enterprises and the assets of the Treasury, as well as public contracts worth in excess of PLN 20 million.

Other protection subsystems. In addition to the aforesaid basic protection subsystems, the strategic operational tasks in the field of select activities aimed at maintaining public order, both on central and local levels, are performed in the following areas:

- **Civil protection** – actions are focused primarily on protecting health against the impact of harmful and burdensome factors, and preventing infectious and occupational diseases in particular, performing veterinary checks in trade exchanges and veterinary border control aimed at protecting public health (e.g. General Veterinary Inspectorate, State Sanitary Inspection);
- **Rescue** – as far as selected activities related to rescue are concerned, an important role is played by volunteer fire departments which struggle with fires, natural disasters and other local threats. Specific tasks in this area include: activities aimed at preventing fires and cooperation with the State Fire Service, local authorities and other entities in this respect; participation in rescue operations conducted during fires, environmental risks associated with environmental protection as well as other disasters and incidents; informing the population about existing fire and environmental hazards, and about ways of protecting against them; conducting educational activities addressed to local communities;

---

[20] In 2009, the implementation of the 2nd stage of the "Anti-Corruption Programme – Anti-Corruption Strategy" was completed. On 23 April 2010, the Council of Ministers adopted the "Final report on the implementation of the Anti-Corruption Programme – Anti-Corruption Strategy – 2nd phase of 2005-2009 implementation," in which one of the recommendations was to establish a body responsible for the preparation of a subsequent draft government programme with regard to preventing and combating corruption by the Minister of the Interior and Administration.
http://cba.gov.pl/portal/pl/48/1531/rzadowy_program_przeciwdzialania_korupcji_na_lata_20122016.html.

- **Protection of areas, objects or facilities important for the defence, economic interest of the state, public safety or other significant interests of the state** – they are realized by specialized armed security formations (most of the services they offer are provided in the private sector); spheres subject to obligatory protection are areas indicated by ministers, heads of central offices and province heads, and detailed lists of such areas, objects and facilities are drawn up by: the President of the National Bank of Poland, the National Broadcasting Council, ministers, heads of central offices and province heads in relation to subordinate, dependent or supervised organizational units;
- **Road safety and transport protection** – particularly control of the compliance with existing regulations regarding the road transport and transportation of passengers and goods aimed to eliminate all negative phenomena related to road transport, and tasks related to the compliance with order regulations, protection of life and health of people and of property in the railway area (e.g. Road Transport Inspection, Railroad Guard);
- **Local safety cooperation and coordination of actions** – particularly preservation of law and order in public places, cooperation with relevant entities as far as saving lives and health of citizens is concerned (commune and municipal police, volunteer fire departments).

3.3. Strategic tasks of national security support subsystems

The societal subsystems

The fundamental strategic objectives in the field of societal safety sectors ought to be identified as follows: creating conditions for the civilization and economic development which determine the purview of national and state action; creating safe conditions for a decent life of citizens and the development of the nation as a whole, in material and spiritual dimensions, and the protection of spiritual and material national heritage (natural resources, property of individual citizens and the collective national wealth), including the opportunities ensuring its safe development in all the spheres of national activeness, especially the economic, social and intellectual ones.

Strategic tasks executed within the societal security subsystems concern particularly: preventing negative demographic trends, undertaking actions with the aim of protecting and strengthening the national identity, improving social safety of the citizens, improving the level of Poland's technological advancement and developing the broadly understood education for security.

National identity. One of the most important tasks of the state in the domain of societal security is to preserve national identity by developing culture and cultivating the national heritage. This problem is especially important in the light of challenges stemming from the globalization which, in many cases, prompts peoples and states as well as, to a lesser extent, social groups, to re-assess within their identity.

The emergence of new phenomena nowadays, such as global mass culture or the European integration process, force Poland to face new tasks which, in the long term, should be focused not only protecting the cultural heritage and national identity, but also on liberating their potential for development and creation of a modern state. The most important tasks in this area include: guaranteeing universal and equal access to culture; raising the profile of culture within the structure of administrative tasks, e.g. by increasing the amount of financial outlays; elaborating a policy enabling the use of the national heritage potential as an element of the state's development; supporting local associations and organizations promoting patriotic attitudes and taking care of the national heritage, as well as working out a new model of cultural patronage.

Undertaking appropriate steps in the sector related to culture will be essential in the light of the challenges faced by Poland in the context of recently emerged negative demographic trends and the influx of migrants expected in the coming years. Enhancing the national identity should constitute an integral component of the policy aimed at achieving a stronger identification of citizens with the state. Strong identification with the motherland might make them rethink their decision regarding emigration. Taking into consideration the significance of social capital, a passive acceptance of brain drain will result in the dwindling population which, in a long term, can mean Poland's waning importance on the international arena.

Education for security. Current threats to the security of the state and its citizens are more numerous and more complex than they were several decades or even a dozen or so years ago. It is a qualitatively new situation which calls on the state authorities, local governments and non-governmental organizations to modify their approach to the society's education for security. In this context, two priority courses of action (implementation of a broadly conceived education for security) can be distinguished:

- First, increasing the public awareness regarding the contemporary phenomena and processes which are the perils, as well as equipping citizens with knowledge and skills which would allow them to react to the arising threats in a conscious, purposeful, effective and rational ways. The goal of this

Swobodno (Warmińsko-Mazurskie Province), 14 January 2013. 2.500 students from the Olsztyn county took part in the demonstration entitled "Safe Ice – Safe Winter Holiday". The children had a chance to watch an operation with a hovercraft on the ice, learn how to notify emergency services about an accident, how to help a drowning person and how to defend oneself in the case of an attack of an aggressive dog. The event was organized by the County District in Olsztyn, Municipal Police Headquarters, Centre for Education and Cultural Initiatives (*Centrum Edukacji i Inicjatyw Kulturalnych*) and foresters.
Photo: Tomasz Waszczuk /PAP

activity is to build a common will and readiness of the social segments of the national security system to support and finance it by citizens;

- Second, increasing the effectiveness of activities by the public administration (state and local, acting collectively and individually) in security matters by systematically and continuously raising the level of skills in order to obtain high-level readiness and capabilities of forces, services, guards and administration to efficiently respond to occurring threats. The aim of such activities is to create professional human resources of the national security system.

Depending on the target group (students, staff of the uniformed public services as well as of forces, services and guard), the organizer (state, local government, non-governmental organizations) and implementing bodies (public, private), as well as on the problematic specificity of the national security domain, the education for security should take on the form of one of the three following types of action:

- Teaching and training on the secondary and upper-secondary levels, organized within the curricula of the public education system:

  a) teaching students about general security and behaviour in case of threats to life and health, including the acquiring of skills relating to medical rescue and behaviour in crisis situations;

  b) teaching students, parents and teachers about communications security, preventing social dangers and pathologies (peer violence, including cyber violence; drug- and alcohol-related menaces; safe behaviours near water reservoirs, in the mountains, e.g. during the holidays); and improving their knowledge regarding criminal responsibility of minors.

- Training courses within the system of vocational education (improving occupational qualifications and skills of the uniformed public services staff, employees of national and local administration, including education-for-security classes' teachers);

- Academic courses relating to the integrated national security within the higher education system, including the vocational preparation at all academic levels of the research staff and employees of the uniformed public services.

Scientific research and development work in the domain of security. The level of Poland's development stage and a balance between development and security are two issues which have to be included in the scope of scientific research and development studies.

First, the technological foundation of the state's civilization development should be consolidated. Polish science – like the society, economy and other domains – has been and, in the coming years, will be influenced by technological progress which, on the one hand, has contributed to the modernization of the state, but on the other – has created a trap of excessive imitativeness of technological, institutional and organizational innovations. Therefore the key course of the currently conducted research policy is innovativeness. This direction should remain the priority in the coming years.

Second, development should be correlated with security issues, as security and development are inextricably linked, interdependent (threats to security are simultaneously barriers to development; in turn, development stabilizes security). It concerns, *inter alia*, long-term harmonization of the energy, food and environmental security with progress, modernization and technological development of the country.

There is no doubt that science has an important role to play in this matter. Scientific research and development should be focused not only on the innovativeness and civilization progress, but also on issues related to the broadly conceived integrated security, especially with regard to social and economic security. Moreover, the share of the potential of science and research should be increased in relation to the state security and defence in activities directed towards the creation and development of systems constituting the foundation of civilization based on knowledge and of integrated economy. The above-mentioned potential not only provides modern technological know-how to the national security system, but also is a source of numerous innovations and technology transfer to other fields, including the economic and social ones.

Another important course of actions related to research and development for the state security and defence should be the augmentation of the number of inter-departmental research programmes and projects. This task is more and more important in the context of budget constraints and the increasing number of demanding requirements regarding effective public spending. Research related to the aforesaid domain should be focused on integrated national security issues and the integrated national security system which serves to fulfil tasks in this sphere. After designating an entity responsible for social and economic security, it will be necessary to include these topics into the range of scientific research and development.

Social safety. One of the most important tasks of the state, as far as the societal security sector is concerned, should be to strengthen the sense of social safety, and to prevent the social stratifying and exclusion, e.g. by providing all citizens with access to manufactured goods enabling them to satisfy at least their basic needs. It is of extreme importance to support families, also via providing children with full access to education (kindergartens, public education) and health care. Otherwise, the above-mentioned processes may lead to an increase in social discontent, escalating extreme views and intensified claims against the state which, as a consequence, will negatively influence the internal security level and weaken its international position.

In the contemporary world, the state is a guarantor of security, including social safety. Its main objectives comprise providing the citizens with conditions for having quiet existence. The role of the state in this regard is to create a development framework, e.g. by means of relevant social, demographic or education policies, which will prevent social stratification and exclusion.

It is also important to develop good relations based on mutual trust between the state and its citizens. The citizens should be certain that in a difficult situation they will not be left alone and the state will provide them with necessary aid. To strengthen the social safety, active citizenship, including participation of citizens in undertakings of the state, is necessary, which allows them to change their existing status.

Demography and security. An important element of the state security should be to decrease significantly the number of people emigrating from Poland, particularly those who are young and well-educated. The offer by the state in relation to appropriate working and living conditions should also be addressed to persons who live currently abroad and who declare their willingness to come back. Return to Poland or suspending the decision to leave Poland are likely to significantly limit the adverse demographic trends. At the same time, they will pose a serious challenge for the state, e.g. due to the increase in the number of persons looking for a job or having problems with adaptation, which will the case with some of the repatriates, and especially their children.

The immigration policy of the state is also important. Within its framework, it is necessary to intensify activities which could, at least to some extent, meet the expectations of the Polish labour market, particularly in the domains which will show a significant deficit of employees. It is important, however, to take into consideration the fact that the influx of immigrants will require, as it is the case of emigrants, a provision of appropriate working and living conditions, and may generate additional problems, particularly those of integration related to culture adaptation. Therefore, the Polish migration policy should be targeted towards certain groups of foreigners who have the potential for integration (e.g. cultural proximity) or occupational qualifications required in the labour market. People with the Polish roots should be especially preferred, including scientists and graduates from Polish universities, as well as members of the families of people who already legally reside in Poland.

In the long run, the essential objective of the state's policy should be, however, to reverse the observed unfavourable trend and to lead to a significant increase in the fertility rate, e.g. by means of an appropriate family-friendly policy and, as a result, a change in the ratio of working-age population to the post-working-age population. It would have a significant impact on the security of the state, particularly on the finance security, the stabilization of economic growth and the defence sector.

Social capital. The national security system cannot function in a social vacuum. It has to be assumed that a high-quality social capital not only increases the chances to find a good job and to avoid poverty and social exclusion, but is also important in making decisions aimed at sustainable economic growth, including the need to protect the environment. Without an increase in the quality of social capital, it will be much harder to make another leap forward in civilization terms, which would make it possible to catch up with more developed EU countries and to respond to challenges created by those countries which systematically enhance their competitiveness.

Therefore, it is indispensable to plan the development of social capital in Poland in a way which will support objectives laid down in the European Union's strategy document entitled "Europe 2020," particularly the employment growth, the increased level of citizens' competences and the decreased poverty level. The principal objective, consistent with the provisions of the Human Capital Development Strategy 2020 project[21], is its development achieved by bringing out the potential of people so they could participate in the social, political and economic life on every stage of their lives.

It implies a necessity for the Polish state authorities to concentrate on supporting the development of social and human capital in Poland by, *inter alia*, systematically overcoming social inequalities, eliminating poverty and unemployment, enhancing social cohesion and, in consequence, increasing the competitiveness of the Polish economy.

Health care within the security system. The basic operational objective of the health care system is to ensure the continuous functioning of medical entities and the provision of medical services by the latter in a crisis situation, a threat to the security of the state or war. The most important tasks in this area include:

- Creating conditions to protect the health and life of the population, including formal and legal, organizational and logistic conditions;
- Preparing and maintaining the readiness of the health care system to operate in case of threats to the state security and war;

---

[21] Draft document of February 2013. The project is available on the website of the Ministry of Labour and Social Policy (as of 15 February 2013) at http://www.mpips.gov.pl/praca/strategie-i-dokumenty-programowe/strategia-rozwoju-kapitalu-ludzkiego-srkl---projekt-z-31072012-r/.

- Mitigating and eliminating the consequences of threats and reducing the happening of mass losses;
- Supporting the health care system of the uniformed services;
- Fulfilling the obligations of the host state towards allied forces resulting from the Host Nation Support (HNS) programme.

Media in the national security system. As far as shaping social behaviours is concerned, a significant role is played by the mass media which have at their disposal numerous means to reach citizens with information about a crisis situation in a fast and effective manner. The modern media constitute the basic source describing not only the emergence of a threat, but also transmitting possible guidelines concerning steps and behaviour appropriate to face the events that have taken place. Therefore, they influence the attitudes of their recipients to a significant extent. Cooperation of the administration and the services with the media should therefore concern principally social awareness issues regarding appropriate responses to the emerging threats.

The task of the mass media in case of a crisis situation or war should be to credibly convey warnings and information about situations posing a threat and to pursue educational activities aimed at dissemination of the knowledge concerning proper identification of threats and effective reactions to such situations. Cooperation with the services responsible for security is an extremely important source of information for both the services and the societ, should a crisis situation arise. The responsibility for the performance of the aforesaid tasks should be borne especially by the public media, taking their mission role into account.

The economic subsystems

The principal strategic objectives relating to economic subsystems comprise: protection of entities with economic potential against the destructive impact of external and internal threats in peacetime, in the time of crisis and war, as well as financial, energy, infrastructure and material support and other types of support for the functioning of operational links of the national security system.

Financial security. Ensuring financial security is related to achieving the best possible internal conditions and eliminating existing external threats which can affect the economic development of the state. In the coming years, the most important action regarding this type of security for Poland will be the strengthening of its financial stabilization, understood as an increased competitiveness, and of the foundations for sustainable development, as well as a reduction of risk concerning the unfavourable impact of financial markets on the economy. What is more, the next stage of the internationalization of economy has to be started by expanding its presence in global markets. These actions should be manifested by an increase in the export of capital, as well as in the creation and expansion of domestic transnational corporations.

The most important tasks aimed to reinforce the financial security include: fiscal consolidation, or the reduction of the budget deficit and halting the accumulation of the public debt, an element of which are structural changes in spending, and a decrease in its growth dynamics; imposing of financial supervision on all institutions providing services of banking nature, which will enable to increase the stability of the fiscal system; acceleration of structural changes in the economy, which will allow to gain a new competitive edge and create sources of growth; creation of a new system for financing research, which would connect more closely scientific, research and academic institutes with the business world. This is of particular importance in the free market conditions, where small and medium enterprises dominate. These firms are unable to generate adequate means for: conducting their own R&D; increasing the economic awareness of the society by popularizing financial knowledge as well as shaping social attitudes and behaviour in case of a financial crisis.

As the basic macroeconomic parameters are concerned, it is to be assumed that in the coming years the doctrine of debt reduction and sustainable economy development will prevail. Under the pressure of financial markets, Poland will have to adhere to fiscal discipline, in accordance with the requirements applicable in the euro area.

In a medium-term perspective, the most effective protection against monetary and financial turbulences and at the same time Poland's strategic objective should be to adopt the common European currency. After the crisis in the euro zone is over, Poland should elaborate a strategy for entering the euro zone and join efforts to strengthen the financial discipline as well as coordinate macroeconomic undertakings within the euro zone. In this regard, it is also indispensable to take steps aimed at reducing the Polish debt, the most important element of which is the budget deficit and the negative balance of foreign trade. In the long perspective, the increasing debt of the state constitutes not only a barrier limiting the development of its economy, but also a way of making the country dependent on foreign and transnational financial institutions and other states. The membership of the euro zone will augment the importance of Poland among other EU countries, while at the same time ensuring full participation in the EU's decision-making processes.

Poland has to strengthen instruments of market supervision. Its Financial Supervision Authority should be able to make sure that foreign financial institutions fulfil their investment commitments in Poland. Another aim should be to restrict the outflow of capital within banking groups, which would inescapably lead to limiting the Polish enterprises' access to loans.

Energy security. The strengthening of the energy security includes a collection of internal actions aimed at creating a legal and economic system which would enforce:

- Reliability and security of supply;
- Fulfilment of requirement related to environmental protection;
- Sustainable and varied structure of energy carriers constituting the so-called fuel balance of the country;
- Optimum level of the so-called energy mix, i.e. the diversification of raw material sources consistent with EU guidelines, given the acceptable level of costs and expected demand related to the projected development of the country;
- Geographical diversification of raw materials supplies;
- Efficiency of the mining and manufacturing system, as well as of systems of transfer, distribution and transportation of fuels and energy;
- Preparation of fuel reserves specified in days and volumes (safety of the demand of end-users and industry) in the amount ensuring the continuity of supply;
- Preparation of parameter-based (consistent with the provincial and national plans), detailed plans related to electricity, heat, gas and water supplies to communes;
- Economic competitiveness of the energy sector, allowing a stable, innovative and long-term development.

Apart from internal factors, main external factors have to be taken into account, including: the energy and climate policies of the European Union; Russia's energy policy, the political situation in other countries which have significant deposits of natural resources (petroleum and natural gas), and particularly the current political changes in the countries of the Gulf, the South Caucasus and the Caspian Sea; and the rate of development of new technologies, their accessibility in particular.

Energy security of Poland is to a certain extent connected with the Baltic Sea region. In the coming years, cooperation with the Nordic and Baltic countries will gain in importance. Among them, an important role is played by Norway which, after Russia, is the second largest supplier of energy resources to the EU countries. Taking into account the universalization of the technologies of liquefaction of natural gas in Europe, it looks essential to establish closer cooperation with Norway in order to make it possible to transfer Norwegian gas to Poland via the gas terminal in Świnoujście, currently under construction. It seems equally important to continue cooperation between Polish enterprises and foreign partners with regard to the hydrocarbon resources management on the Norwegian shelf.

Cooperation with Finland should to a larger extent concern the exchange of experience and technological solutions regarding the functioning of the nuclear industry and obtaining energy from renewable resources. Likewise, the intensification of scientific and research contacts with Sweden ought to result in the development of technology regarding the exploitation of renewable energy, primarily in northern regions of Poland, as well as in further integration of electricity markets through construction of subsequent system connections.

Owing to its geographical connection, Poland can play an important role towards Lithuania, Latvia and Estonia, as well as the Visegrád Group countries, regarding the diversification of sources from which these countries can obtain energy resources. Recently, these states have explicitly indicated the diversification of energy resources supplies as their vested interest.

Transmission lines
near Lublin
Photo: Wojciech Pacewicz/
PAP

Poland should, in an effective manner, take advantage of this trend not only by developing intersystem connections related to gas and electricity transfers, but also by increasing the number of Polish investments in different sectors of the energy market in the region. As far as these activities are concerned, the opportunity to cooperate with Ukraine should not be left out.

The shale gas deposits constitute a chance for Poland. In order to seize this possibility, the Polish authorities need to closely cooperate with the countries (especially with the USA) which possess the technology necessary to extract this raw material, to oppose any possible attempts to block the exploitation of shale gas on the European arena, and to strive for having this raw material regulated by Western companies so as to make concluded contracts profitable for Poland to the largest possible extent.

Furthermore, cooperation with European countries interested in the exploitation of shale gas should be strengthened without delay. Poland's natural partners in this respect would be Slovakia, Hungary, Bulgaria, Romania, Ukraine and Turkey. Nor can cooperation with Sweden, Denmark and the United Kingdom, which do not exclude exploiting their shale gas deposits, be ignored.

As the majority of Polish domestic power units is in large measure exploited or has low quality parameters, their adequate modernization is necessary. This process should be an integral part of the implementation of the Union's energy and climate policies. Besides, investments in mining, mainly in the opening of new exploitation levels and the construction of new or the extension of currently used mineshafts, are also necessary, as they will help stop the decline of coal mining.

Polish coal mining gains a significant advantage thanks to collaboration with universities and design offices, technical resources, i.e. machinery and mining equipment factories, as well as the managerial staff and specialists working in mines. Therefore, not only the optimal use of resources already exploited is important, but also the management of new prospective deposits: Gubin–Brody and Legnica–Głogów. The yield of prospective deposits may rise to the level of 100-110 million tonnes per year.

At present, it is difficult to determine the possible scale of the shale gas extraction. This is why until 2022 Russian Gazprom will supply considerable quantities of natural gas to Poland, although its dominant position is to weaken after 2014, when the LNG marine terminal in Świnoujście will start up.

It is also planned that in the next years the construction of the first nuclear power plant in Poland will begin. The first nuclear unit is supposed to begin to generate electricity between 2020 and 2025. The entire project of construction and development of nuclear energy in Poland is assumed to account for ca. 6 per cent of total national demand for electricity, as well as to facilitate the diversification of the manufacturing base of the electricity sector and the reduction of carbon dioxide emissions.

The fulfilment of obligations towards the European Union requires the gross electricity production from renewable energy sources at the level of about 31 TWh in 2020, mainly from wind power stations and biomass.

Tasks aimed at strengthening the energy security include: stepping up necessary investments in the energy sector (including the construction of nuclear power plants), as well as conducting an appropriate policy in regard to the climate package (CO_2 aspect); creating competition conditions in the fuel and energy market; developing an infrastructure for the transmission and use of energy; effective activities of the authorities regulating and supervising companies operating in the fuel and energy market (URE), the Office of Competition and Consumer Protection (UOKiK); continuing the processes of restructuring and improving the operation of energy companies; strengthening the environmental security of the state; utilizing rationally accessible, renewable energy sources, and increasing the efficiency of energy used.

Safety of the infrastructure, including the critical infrastructure. Efficiency and smooth functioning of the country's infrastructure is fundamental to its economic development and, as a consequence, to the safety and prosperity of its citizens. The most important component of the broadly-conceived infra-

structure is the part called the critical infrastructure. It includes key elements and systems which ensure, among other things, the continuous functioning of the public administration bodies or make it possible to provide a range of essential services to citizens (e.g. water supply, medical rescue). For this reason, the protection of the critical infrastructure constitutes one of the most important objectives from the viewpoint of providing an effective operation of the modern state.

As for this field, the role of public administration bodies, according to their competences, consists in the creation of legal mechanisms aimed to protect the critical infrastructure and to enforce their application. Owners and holders of such an infrastructure, regardless of whether they are public or private entities, are obliged to ensure a total protection of facilities, devices, installations and individual elements of systems making up the critical infrastructure.

This protection consists primarily in the elaboration and implementation of protection plans, also when special threats emerge, and in the maintenance of their own back-up systems ensuring safety and sustaining the operation of the infrastructure until its complete restoration.

Also, legal protection of the critical infrastructure has to be provided in the course of organizational and ownership changes relating to entities being owners of such infrastructure. Currently, after the privatization transformations which took place over the last twenty years, a significant part of the critical infrastructure is in the hands of the private sector. Efficient and collision-free cooperation between the public and private sector is therefore needed, and within its framework transparent rules and procedures of collaboration between bodies and services of the state and the owners of critical elements of the infrastructure have to be elaborated.

Thus strategic tasks in the field of infrastructure safety include:
- Elaboration and implementation of procedures and mechanisms of cooperation between the public and private sector, with the aim of effective, multidimensional protection of the critical infrastructure;
- Elaboration of a programme aimed to protect the telecommunications critical infrastructure against disturbances of its operation caused by activities in virtual space (cyber attacks of criminal or terrorist nature or being a symptom of hostile actions by a specific state);
- Implementation of a legal mechanism which would make it possible to control, block or suspend decisions of bodies or companies relating to problems regarding, inter alia, hostile takeover, merger or the sale of certain elements of the infrastructure, particularly those considered critical.

Transport safety. One of the important tasks of the state in the coming years is to develop and modernize the transport (both road and railway) network, as well as to ensure a high quality of transport services which not only constitute an important element of the economic development of the country, but are also significant from the viewpoint of the national security system.

Preventing communications and industrial disasters by developing the transport system has to be considered not only from the economic perspective, but also in terms of the country's spatial planning, the natural environment protection and the safety of road users. Because of the scale of accidents, including fatal accidents and their social consequences, one of the key challenges will be to improve the safety of transport users.

Strategic objectives in the domain of transport safety include: development and modernization of the transport network in order to enable performing tasks in the field of the most important national interests, both in peacetime and the state of emergency or war; prevention of communications and industrial disasters by developing the transport system; enhancing the integration in the domains of security management and monitoring, rescue, information system and research.

Natural environment protection (**ecological safety**). The state's policy regarding the environmental safety should concentrate on two areas: improvement of the environment quality and preventive activities.

As for the improvement of the environment quality, the following actions are significant:
- Progressive reduction in carbon dioxide, sulphur and nitrogen, and fine dust emitted during energy generation in order to fulfil obligations under the treaty of accession and the relevant EU directives;
- Adopting solutions favouring energy saving and obtaining it from renewable energy sources as set forth in the Polish new energy policy until 2030;
- Making steps towards preparations for the implementation of technologies on capturing and storing carbon dioxide;
- Maintaining or achieving a satisfactory condition of waters by concluding the programme for the construction and expansion of the wastewater treatment plants and sewage systems for agglomerations within the framework of the EU's Operational Programme Infrastructure and Environment;
- Elaborating a water management plan for every river basin; preparing a water and environmental programme for the country;
- Reducing the contamination caused by dangerous substances from industrial sources;
- Increasing the energy recovery from municipal waste;
- Increasing up to over 50 per cent the amount of recovered waste produced in households;
- Creating an efficient system of surveillance over chemicals admitted onto the market;
- Removing the polychloride biphenyl from transformers and other devices as well as removing asbestos.

As for preventive actions, the priorities should be as follows:
- Monitoring air, water and soil contamination as well as conducting ad hoc control and measurement tests;
- Informing decision-making bodies and the population about contamination and alerting them in case of a particular danger;
- Eliminating consequences of dangers within the framework of rescue operations;
- Preventive and educational activities concerning threats related to dangerous substances and actions aimed to restore the environment to its natural state.

Maintaining strategic reserves. Strategic reserves are maintained with the intention of making them available in case of broadly conceived crisis situations. They should therefore be considered to be one of the most important elements of the system ensuring the security and protection of the state. The main objective in this field is to have the Council of Ministers elaborate and adopt the Government Programme of Strategic Reserves. Because of the role played by these reserves in the system of broadly conceived security of the state and the need to spend considerable funds on the purchase and maintenance of the reserves, the formula of a multi-annual programme was chosen. The programme will be prepared for a period of five years and it will be possible to review it every year in case of a change in the circumstances which constituted the premises for its elaboration. In addition, the adoption of the Government Programme of Strategic Reserves requires in addition that certain budgetary outlays are guaranteed in a medium-term perspective for the purposes of pursuing objectives specified in the programme.

* * *

Pursuant to the prognosticated scenarios of the security environment evolution, it was possible to distinguish three **operational strategy options for Poland**: the option of maximum internationalization of Poland's security; the option of strategic autarky (self-reliance and self-sufficiency); and the option of sustainable internationalization and autonomy of Poland's security.

According to the most probable scenario, the main (fundamental) operational option should preferably be the third one. It assumes that strategic activities for the sake of security should, on the one hand, be focused on maintaining, as a priority, the country's determination and readiness to act in the domains, fields and sectors in which allied joint operations may be difficult, and, on the other, on strengthening the international security community, by consolidating the integration processes in Europe (NATO, EU), as well as strategic relations with the USA and other partners, and, if possible, selectively participating in the international community's undertakings based on an explicit international mandate in order to head off the emergence of new threats.

These activities should be taken into account in the course of preparing a new National Security Strategy of the Republic of Poland, and afterwards described in detail in the implementing documents: the Political and Strategic Defence Directive of the Republic of Poland or the Political and Strategic National Security Directive of the Republic of Poland supplemented with non-military aspects, amended plans for the use of the Polish Armed Forces and other operational plans.

After this process is finished, it would be desirable to carry out another National Security Strategic Review.

Chapter 4

CONCEPT OF PREPARING THE NATIONAL SECURITY SYSTEM (PREPARATORY STRATEGY)

This chapter presents a desirable and feasible concept of strategic preparations to be undertaken by the Republic of Poland in the field of security, i.e. its preparatory strategy. The latter is understood as a division (area) of national security (state security) strategy encompassing the rules and methods pertaining to the preparation (maintenance and transformation) of a national security system (the implementation of preparatory strategic tasks in the field of national security) in accordance with the requirements stemming from the operational strategy.

Warsaw, 9 March, 2012
4ᵗʰ plenary conference
of the National Security
Strategic Review.
Discussion on the key
theses elaborated by the
National Security System
Team.
Photo: BBN

4.1. Foundations and leading theme of the preparatory strategy

Pursuant to the three operational strategy options presented in the previous chapter, three corresponding preparatory strategy options can be formulated:
1. An option of **internationalization of the national security system**, which corresponds to the option which involves the maximum internationalization of Poland's security;
2. An option of autonomy **of the national security system**, which corresponds to the option of strategic autorky;
3. An option of **sustainable integration of the national security system**, which corresponds to the option of sustainable internationalization and autonomy of Poland's security.

It is the third option which should be viewed as the primary choice that should guide the formulation of tasks and the development and implementation of preparatory programmes, especially those which entail substantial expenditure. At the same time, however, such programmes should (especially in their planning and training dimensions) be in readiness to move to the implementation of possible or necessary preparatory tasks which rather belong in the other two options – either the more advantageous one or the one which is not advantageous, but the application of which is necessitated by possible negative developments with regard to the strategic conditions of security.

The national security system as a whole as well as its individual subsystems and links should be prepared for taking effective action in three possible variants with regard to the functioning of the state.

The first of these variants is a normal operation where the state (or another entity) operates in accordance with its mission and assumptions and pursues routine activities to make sure that this state of affairs is maintained.

The second variant is the situation wherein the existing development process breaks down, with the given entity's functioning becoming disrupted in one or more of its fields of activity. Routine operations become insufficient, leading to an actual loss of control over the situation and the existing decision-making process is disrupted, with reactions being overtaken by events. This state of affairs can be described as a state of crisis.

Finally, the third variant describes a situation where the taken actions fail to produce the intended results, and the circumstances make the given entity cease to operate in either of the above variants – averting the crisis and returning to normal operation prove impossible. In such cases the nature of the entity is prone to change radically. The situation in question usually involves a failure, collapse or liquidation of an entity but may also result in another organizational state which involves system change. In that case we have to do with a state of emergency. In the case of a state (or a group of states) an unresolved crisis may also degenerate – in the worst-case scenario – into an open armed conflict.

Symptoms of likely external and internal threats to national security and development – both those existing today and those emerging – are diffuse, unpredictable and ill-defined as to their significance, scale, direction and the type of entity involved or source of origin. It necessitates the preparation or adaptation of the national security system so as to adequately respond to a variety of situations in the national security environment – from those which are local and limited in to those having a nationwide range. An ultimate system must therefore be prepared in advance as a fully developed, multi-faceted and multi-purpose legal and organizational system, encompassing all state structures involved in the execution of security tasks, capable of responding to a variety of threats and, at the same time, designed for quick adaptation, allowing it to take actions aimed at averting those threats which had not been foreseen earlier.

The ultimate objective is the system that must rest on a uniform legal basis, allowing it to be "adjustable" to a specific operational strategy. Such adjustment of the system may be effective solely in a medium-term and long-term perspective, as it requires both time and substantial organizational efforts. If a need were to arise for a sudden re-forming of the national security structures, it would mean that the state was caught unawares. This would only serve as testimony to the ineptitude of analytical institutions, while poorly planned moves to adjust the system would not guarantee an effective outcome.

4.2. Preparation of the national security control subsystem

National security control belongs to the most important functions of the state, intended to ensure its continued existence and development in a constantly changeable security environment.

The key function of the managing entity in the national security control process is discharged – within the scope of the applicable law – by the public authority bodies and the heads of organizational units performing national security-related tasks, including the command authorities of the Polish Armed Forces. Control functions are carried out by entities which specialize in executing individual tasks related to the attainment of security objectives, and operate at all organizational levels of the state.

Control authorities and their advisory and staff bodies

The objective of the subsystem which, thereafter referred to as the national security control system, should be first and foremost to ensure the continuity of the decision-making process and the coordination of activities aimed at maintaining and restoring national security in any possible conditions and circumstances of the functioning of the state. The structure of the national security control system should be designed in a manner consistent with the universal control model which encompasses three components: a decision-making entity, a collegial advisory body and a standing (full-time) body. The decisions developed within such structure are subsequently forwarded to the executive components for implementation (fig. 36).

Figure 36. Universal control system model

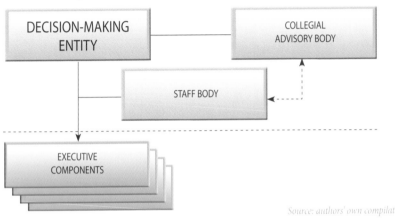

Source: authors' own compilation.

The current national security control system in Poland does not, regrettably, suit the model. According to the Constitution of the Republic of Poland, the function of the political decision-making entity is discharged jointly by the President of the Republic of Poland and the Council of Ministers – both comprise the executive branch. The President is equipped with both an advisory body (the National Security Council) and a staff body (the National Security Bureau). The Council of Ministers, on the other hand, possesses neither an advisory nor a staff body with regard to the issues of integrated national security. The Government Crisis Management Team and the Government Centre for Security come closest to performing these functions; their current scope of competence, however, remains restricted to crisis management tasks and does not extend to national security as a whole.

For the aforesaid reason, in the course of laying down the groundwork for national security control in the coming years the existing system should be gradually reshaped in order to attain the target structure presented above (fig. 37): the political decision-making entity – the functions of which, pursuant to the provisions of the Constitution, are jointly discharged by the President of the Republic of Poland and the Council of Ministers; advisory and consultative bodies supporting both decision-making entities – the National Security Council, in support of the President, and a new Council of Ministers Committee for National Security (or a Government Committee for National Security), headed by the Prime Minister; administrative bodies supporting both decision-making entities: the National Security Bureau, providing support to the President, and a Government Centre for National Security, providing support to the Council of Ministers (established by way of extending the scope of competences of the current Government Centre for Security and incorporated into the structures of the Chancellery of the Prime Minister).

Figure 37. Proposed main (central) national security control system

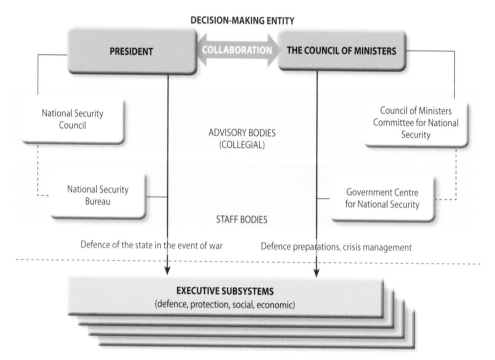

Source: authors' own compilation.

The proposed Council of Ministers Committee for National Security (KRMds.BN) should incorporate the existing collegial structures which deal with specific security-related issues (the Government Crisis Management Team, the Collegium for Secret Services); its activities should encompass the analysis and submission to the Council of Ministers of concepts for solution of national security issues having a supra-ministerial, nationwide significance.

The proposed Government Centre for National Security (RCBN) would, in turn, perform, *inter alia*, the following tasks:
- Preparing draft strategic plans, concepts and programmes in the field of national security;
- Supporting the operations of the Council of Ministers Committee for National Security (the head of the Government Centre for National Security would discharge the function of the chairman of such committee);
- Ensuring appropriate conditions for the operation of the Council of Ministers and the Council of Ministers Committee for National Security in crisis situations or during armed conflicts;
- Organizing the Central Control Post of the State Defence within the scope necessary;
- Coordinating inter-ministerial activities for ensuring security;
- Analyzing and evaluating security conditions and threats to the interests of the state;

- Coordinating tasks fulfilled by the secret services;
- Preparing draft documents (guidelines) for international agreements and legislative work pertaining to security issues.

The operation of the main control system at times of crisis should also make it possible for the state to take actions in the event of an armed conflicts for the purposes of controlling state defence. No significant organizational changes need be made at the strategic management level in the event of a crisis, except for the "contingency" mode of work of the President and the Council of Ministers.

Solutions to be adopted in the event of an armed conflict with the direct participation of the Republic of Poland take on a particular importance. In wartime, the role of the President increases; furthermore, in such situation it would also turned out necessary to work out guidelines as to the composition and nature of operations of the Council of Ministers.

During the normal operation of the state, ministers perform tasks in the field of national security within the administrative departments which they control. The situation is the same in the event of a crisis, except that in such cases the importance of those ministers who compose the Government Crisis Management Team (or the KRMds.BN – if established) is increased. The situation undergoes a substantial change when martial law is introduced. In such a case, the national security control wielded by ministers designated by the Prime Minister for this purpose, is exerted within the framework of the Central Control Post of the State Defence.

The province (*województwo*) is a peculiar feature of the Polish government system. The province governor (*wojewoda*), among many competences and tasks which he has as the representative of the Council of Ministers in the province and as the head of the combined administration, remains the individual (one-person) authority with regard to the issues entrusted to him as a coordinator of all activities which encompass the entire province and extend beyond the scope of competence and capabilities of the heads of both combined and non-combined administration. Auxiliary bodies which support the work of the governor, both in an advisory/consultative and staff (assistant) capacity, should therefore be used for the purposes of performing by the governor their duties in the field of territorial security within the province (as a part of the national security effort), without substituting the competences of individual heads of administrative authorities operating within the given province.

As in the case of the central level, where it is recommended that an integrated Council of Ministers Committee for National Security be established, the provinces and local-government bodies would also benefit from the transformation of the existing crisis management teams into broader, integrated territorial security teams (*zespoły bezpieczeństwa terytorialnego*), responsible for both defence issues and issues of crisis management – acting as advisory and consultative bodies of, respectively, the province governor, the district governor (*starosta*), the mayor, and the head of the commune (*wójt*). This also applies to their respective bodies (fig. 38).

The advisory staff body supporting the province governor, the Province Territorial Security Team (WZBT, *Wojewódzki Zespół Bezpieczeństwa Terytorialnego*), should take the form of a collegial body which, in ordinary circumstances (in the absence of any threats) does not operate on a permanent basis, only convening at regular intervals for the purposes of, *inter alia*, evaluating the security status of the province, supporting the coordination efforts with regard to planning and the organizational efforts made in this regard, examining financial issues, determining the directions of streamlining the security system in the province and undertaking other necessary actions in order to avert any possible threats. The composition of the team, apart from its permanent portion, should be determined according to the needs and the nature of the given situation. During normal operation of the province and in emergencies or during armed conflicts, this advisory entity would operate by holding sessions headed by the province governor, providing him with substantive support in the course of decision making, the coordination of the flow of information and the implementation of the adopted decisions.

Figure 38. Proposed territorial security control system (province, district, commune)

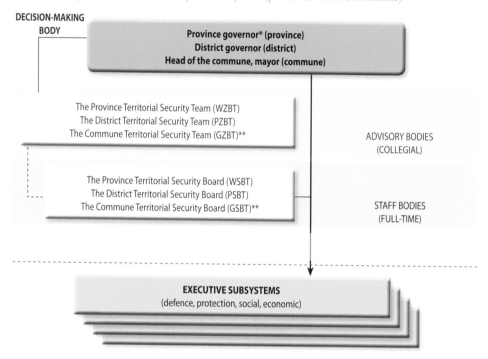

*The marshal of the province also participates in the process of territorial security control exercised by the province governor
**Established when necessary

Source: authors' own compilation.

The basic composition of the staff body operating within the province should be based on the personnel of the relevant department of the province governor's office (including the province centre for crisis management, operating on a 24-hour basis), acting as the core of the governor's board which could be expanded in a manner reflecting the given situation (also in times of crisis or armed conflict).

The tasks of the staff would include:
- Substantive management of non-military affairs which rest within the competence of the province governor;
- Analysis and evaluation of the security status of the province on the basis of data provided by other administrative leaders, including the central authorities, the neighbouring provinces, combined and non-combined administration bodies, districts and communes;
- Preparation of variants of solutions with regard to various situations; and
- Facilitation of the implementation of adopted decisions.

Heads of both combined and non-combined administrative bodies should take on the role of functional coordinators in the process of planning and organization of interdisciplinary activities, and not just of formal managers of their respective institutions. Leaders within combined and non-combined administration structures, for the purposes of coordinating the functions entrusted to them, should have at their disposal an analogous management body structure (should the need arise).

The underlying concept for national security control at district (*powiat*) level with regard to each specific variant of the operation of state structures is similar to the solutions proposed with respect to provinces.

At district level, the applicable functions should be discharged by the following entities:

- decision-making entity – the district governor (or mayor of a city having the status of a district);
- advisory body – the District Territorial Security Team (PZBT, *powiatowy zespół bezpieczeństwa terytorialnego*), comprising the heads of district-level organizational entities competent with regard to the planning, organization and performance of tasks in the field of territorial security;
- staff body – the District Territorial Security Board (PSBT, *powiatowy sztab bezpieczeństwa terytorialnego),* e.g. having the status of a department (section).

National security control activities at commune (*gmina*) level has a specific set of characteristics which are slightly different than at district level. The distinguishing feature is that there are no local government bodies the scope of activities of which would only extend to the territories of individual communes.

However, the tasks performed at commune level make it necessary for a control system to be established at this level as well, considering the capabilities of these local government structures in terms of organization, human and financial resources. The functions of the decision-making authority are discharged by the head of the commune (*wójt*) or mayor, who, depending on the needs, would be entitled to establish an advisory body (the Commune Territorial Security Team, GZBT, *gminny zespół bezpieczeństwa terytorialnego*) and a staff body (the Commune Territorial Security Board, GSBT, *gminny sztab bezpieczeństwa terytorialnego*).

Control infrastructure

The infrastructure functioning within the framework of the control apparatus encompasses control positions and centres which consist of technical facilities and devices necessary for the purposes of ensuring an efficient and secure functioning of control bodies in performing their tasks in the field of security. One of the fundamental objectives with respect to the preparation of the said infrastructure is to establish and maintain a system of control positions. This system, at every level of it (i.e. national, province, district and commune levels) encompasses primary and back-up control positions. Within the framework of primary positions it includes buildings and other structures, including special facilities; stationary and mobile communications systems, including secret communication; ICT systems, including warning and alert systems, etc., as shown on fig. 39.

The preparation of buildings and other structures, including special facilities, for the purposes of ensuring the functioning of individual authorities in case of a threat to national security as well as in wartime encompasses the designation and subsequent adaptation as well as the build-up, when specific circumstances arise, of such facilities and structures. Within the framework of planning and organization activities, these facilities are adapted for the purposes of ensuring proper conditions for discharging the functions of the given authority. Their adaptation includes, *inter alia*, the provision of the necessary communication systems, ICT systems as well as systems aimed at ensuring the security and "viability" of such facilities, e.g. in case of biological, chemical or radiological threats.

Figure 39. System of national security control positions

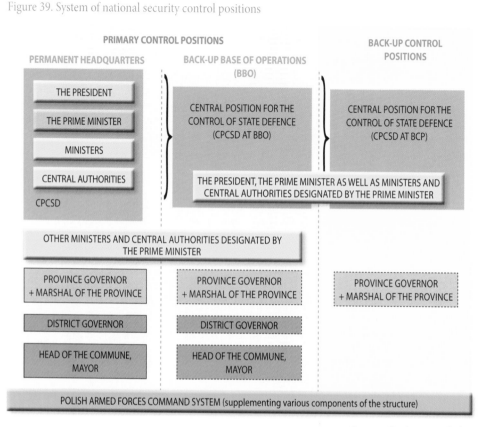

Source: authors' own compilation.

The facilities in question should fulfil a number of criteria which make it possible for the situation to be continuously monitored and enables the given authority to adopt the necessary decisions. Additionally, proper working and living conditions for the support staff need to be ensured within the aforementioned facilities.

Stationary (as well as mobile) communications, including secret communications, should enable decision-makers at every control level to gain access to the necessary information and public administration authorities which are engaged in performing security-related tasks. The preparation of these systems also concerns secret communications and connections, which calls for applying adequate cryptographic measures. In this regard, it would be advisable to attain the full national capacities both regarding the establishment of the system (design, manufacture of devices, owner's supervision over components of the system) as well as with respect to its subsequent usage. Moreover, one should take into account the needs to ensure the availability of communication channels in cases where the national/territorial security control authorities need to change their location using various means of transport (air, land and sea), to an extent which corresponds with their role within the system. Such means of transport should be able to provide the select individuals with the continuous capability of controlling national security within the administrated area. This also applies to communication services provided for the purposes of armed forces command and control (including the activities of the Commander-in-Chief of the Armed Forces).

The usage of ICT systems – including those related to warning and alert systems – utilized for the purposes of security control needs to be put in order. The integration of such systems should ensure the capacity to exercise control within a designated area (nationwide or at province, district or commune level), which necessitates the establishment of information exchange platforms and the elimination of the department (ministry)-based approach.

The issues related to the preparation of the national security control system infrastructure are addressed in the 2004 Council of Ministers regulation. The analysis of these issues indicates that a part of the provisions in question should be elevated to statutory level, which means that they should be transferred to the proposed act on national security control.

National security control procedures

Statutory regulations need to be put in force with regard to the rules pertaining to the functioning of the national security control system, possibly as an act on national security control. Such act should precisely determine the role of the authorities and state institutions within the national security system, including:
- an unambiguous definition of the tasks and competences at executive level;
- a more precise description of the competences of the President and the Council of Ministers, as conferred upon them by the Constitution;
- ensuring the efficiency in the area of control and coordination of the entire national security control system, working out the principles of cooperation of the bodies within the system in any conditions, situations and circumstances of the functioning of the state; and
- the establishment of appropriate conditions that will enable the Council of Ministers to control the entirety of the issues related to the national security of the Republic of Poland in terms of analysis, concept and coordination capacity.

The proposed act should cover the matters related to the national security control of the Republic of Poland (today, these issues are governed by the act on the general defence obligation as well as the act on crisis management). At the same time, the existing legislation and organizational structures should be reorganised insofar as they pertain to the same or similar tasks in the sphere of national security.

It is also necessary – within the proposed act on national security control – to clarify the principles pertaining to the control of the state defence in wartime, with particular emphasis on the unambiguous determination of the principles of cooperation of the President and the Council of Ministers in this regard, as well to clarify the competences of the Commander-in-Chief of the Armed Forces in the context of his subordination to the President who exercises the control of the state defence.

Furthermore, it is essential to ensure – within new act on national security control – that security is controlled in a uniform manner at all levels of public administration: national, province, district and commune level. The necessary changes include: the universalization of the organizational structure of the management network (including at local level); the rationalization of the number of planning, organizational and executive structures; the integration – to the extent possible – of the separate crisis planning processes and operational planning processes pertaining to the functioning of the relevant entities in case of any threat or in wartime, and, as a consequence, the integration of the planning documentation, in particular at central level (e.g. the Strategy for National Security of the Republic of Poland, the Political and Strategic Defence Directive of the Republic of Poland or a possibly extended the Political and Strategic Directive National Security of the Republic of Poland[22]).

---

[22] This document would replace the current Political and Strategic Defence Directive of the Republic of Poland.

It should be considered to what extent the integration of planning processes and executive documents within government administration departments, in central authorities, provinces, districts and communes into a single security operational plan (for the given administrative department, province, district and commune) would be practicable. It needs to be taken into account, of course, that the crisis management planning is performed on a bottom-up basis (starting with threats and capabilities that exist within a commune, then within a district, province and finally on a nationwide scale), while defence planning is carried out on a top-down basis, in accordance with the political concept adopted by the state.

It is postulated that the approach based on entrusting the role of coordinators in the process of management of a given area of security on a nationwide (comprehensive) scale to individual ministers be abandoned in favour of having these tasks transferred to a supra-ministerial structure in the form of a Government Centre for National Security.

The recommendations presented above can be implemented within the existing constitutional framework. Should the appropriate conditions arise and a political consensus be reached with regard to a possible amendment of the Constitution, it would be worth considering changes to be introduced with respect to the regulations concerning national security, which would, *inter alia*, involve:

- Eeliminating certain provisions which are too detailed to be retained within the Constitution and to replace them with general constitutional norms;
- Abolishing the separate post of Commander-in-Chief of the Armed Forces in time of war or at least anticipating its status optionally. In case this position retains its constitutional status, a legal possibility should be made for the designation of a functional person who would hold this position in the event of armed conflict;
- Determining in an unambiguous and unconditional manner an authority tasked with the control of the state defence in wartime. Competences in this regard should not be shared with any other entities (the principle of unity of control in wartime). If, however, the principle, relevant to peacetime, of cooperation between the two entities (the President and the Council of Ministers) in the state defence control were to be retained, then appropriate constitutional competences to ensure such cooperation should be conferred upon the Cabinet Council. The composition of the Cabinet Council in wartime should be extended to include the Marshals (Speakers) of the Sejm and the Senate as potential successors of the President.

If the Constitution were to be amended in a manner aimed at transforming the current system of government into a presidential or cabinet system, the following actions would need to be taken:

a) in a presidential model – altering the structure of the National Security Council so that it is transformed from an exclusively advisory entity into a constitutional advisory and coordinating authority, or, alternatively, transforming the Cabinet Council into an authority of this type;

b) in a cabinet model – abandoning the current constitutional position of the National Security Council.

* * *

The main challenge which the national security control subsystem now faces is its complete integration. This integration should pertain, first and foremost, to advisory and staff bodies which support the activities of the decision-making entities. It is also necessary to establish an appropriate control infrastructure as well as to comprehensively regulate the national security control procedures. These components should be guided by the provisions of an act on national security control.

4.3. Preparation of national security operational subsystems

The defence subsystem

Foreign Service (diplomacy) for security. The progressing globalization, the growing international significance of emerging powers, the increasing importance of international economic and financial relations as well as the rapid technological development make it necessary to redefine the tasks lying before diplomatic representations and consular posts.

The structures, potential and principles of operation of the diplomatic and consular services need to be adjusted to new challenges in keeping with the adopted priorities of the Polish foreign policy. Therefore both the role and the methods of work of the diplomatic corps need to be redefined.

The consistent, long-term and efficient implementation of the primary tenets of Polish foreign policy can only be effected by a qualified and apolitical personnel. For this reason, it is essential to:

- Develop and consistently apply in a practical manner uniform principles of recruiting and preparing candidates for work in the diplomatic services;
- Elaborate uniform principles of career advancement in the foreign service, including the continuing education process (culminating with a compulsory examination at the end of each respective stage), and determine career development paths;
- Prepare a remuneration model for foreign service personnel, which encourages skills development;
- Adjust the diplomatic service to the needs of the information technology revolution by introducing new technologies; and
- Ensure the durable protection and defence of the state interests through the continuous operation of impartial, apolitical and competent experts in central institutions (This means, *inter alia*, the exchange of only the political level in ministries should follow the change of government after successive election.).

It is worthwhile to consider the establishment of a separate career path for Polish candidates to the European External Action Service as well as to ensure that the degree of participation of Polish personnel in the Service corresponds with Poland's standing and size – especially in locations which are essential as far as the security of the Republic of Poland is concerned (e.g. in the Eastern Partnership states). It is also important that efforts are made to ensure Polish diplomats' representation in the decision-making structures of international organizations to the maximum possible extent.

The Polish Armed Forces. Irrespective of the possible scenarios regarding Poland's security, it is guaranteed primarily by its own defence potential which ensures the capability of responding to any form of contemporary political and military threats (blackmail, threats of use of force, surprise short-term military actions by surprise, including air strikes (especially missile strikes), special operations, border incidents, subversive incursions without an intention of seizing territories, etc.), in relation to which the capacity of international security organizations to take action is limited.

It is necessary to have the process of the transformation of the Polish Armed Forces expedited, primarily in accordance with the priorities adopted under the decision of the President of the Republic of Poland, dated 8 November, 2011, on determination of the main directions for the development of the Polish Armed Forces and their preparation for the defence of the state for the years

2013-2022. This document points to three priority directions of organizational change in the Polish Armed Forces – the organizational and deployment consolidation of the Polish Armed Forces; the reform of the command and control system; and the streamlining of the training system, including the consolidation of the military education, as well as three most important directions in the technical modernization of the Polish Armed Forces: the development of information systems; the development of air defence systems, including missile defence; and an increased mobility of the Polish Land Forces).

The organizational and deployment consolidation is intended to constrain the dispersion of the armed forces in small garrisons. The effective implementation of this objective is particularly significant with regard to the professional Polish Armed Forces.

There is an urgent need to adjust the armed forces' command and control system at the strategic and political level to the needs of the professional armed forces and the current political, strategic and operational conditions. The system in question was created in the 1990s, at the time when the civilian control of the military had only begun. The number of strategic commands must also be reduced, with the remaining entities being consolidated around the three basic functions: strategic planning (the Polish Armed Forces General Staff), the current general command operations (the General Command) and operational command (the Operational Command). The command authorities responsible for the foregoing should report directly to the minister of national defence. This should, first and foremost, result in an increased potential and quality of the long-term forecasting, planning and programming of the future shape of the armed forces, create proper conditions for the necessary training within the joint operations system and ensure the uniformity of the command system in peacetime, in a crisis and during armed conflicts. The aforesaid issues should be regulated by way of an amended act on the office of the minister of national defence.

The changes which are taking place in the world, and especially their pace, as well as the challenges which the armed forces are facing today (the need for quick and varied response) make it highly desirable to establish units with universal (modular) organizational structures – efficiently commanded and well--equipped units, capable of immediate deployment in any region of operations. It is therefore desirable to ensure a high quality of training, equipment, logistics and support necessary to respond effectively to new operational challenges and to perform by the Polish armed forces their scheduled tasks. The above-mentioned transformation activities are included in the Strategy 2022 on national security system development, which forms one of Poland's nine integrated development strategies.

Photo: Special Forces Command Archive

There is also a need to provide the armed forces with equipment in the form of state-of-the-art computerized combat and support systems, used for the purposes of reconnaissance, cyberspace warfare, command, weapon systems control, precision-guided munitions, remote control of unmanned systems as well as robotic warfare. Achieving this goal requires the decommissioning of outdated military equipment which should be replaced with weaponry and equipment that satisfies the needs of a network-centric operational environment and ensures compatibility with other NATO armed forces (the modernization strategy guided by a "generation leap"). Furthermore, there is an urgent need to attain the capability of the airborne observation of ground objects and the establishment of an efficient surveillance system, coupled with a system of command and target acquisition system. The use of the aforementioned solutions will make it possible to attain the ability to counter surprise attacks, which is crucial from the viewpoint of national defence. This capacity should be additionally reinforced through the maximum mobility of land forces, rapidly deploy able across the Polish territory, depending on the location of a danger. Such mobility should be primarily based on the use of helicopters.

An important objective is the modernization of the air defence system, including the building of a missile defence system aimed to insure more effective national security, as attacks from above are the easiest for the enemy to launch and may reach the Polish territory in a very short period of time. The primary delivery systems today are various types and categories of missiles with differing ranges and payloads – from strategic missiles to the lowest classes of tactical weapons. Consequently, no national defence can be said to be complete without a proper air defence system. Of equal importance is the need to provide the armed forces with modern equipment (such as combat and support helicopters) for the purposes of fighting in the increasingly demanding combat conditions (e.g. asymmetrical warfare).

Fig. 40. Technical modernization priorities for the Polish Armed Forces

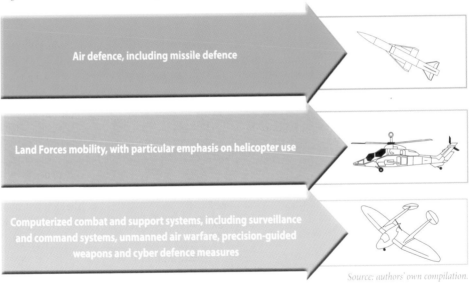

Air defence, including missile defence

Land Forces mobility, with particular emphasis on helicopter use

Computerized combat and support systems, including surveillance and command systems, unmanned air warfare, precision-guided weapons and cyber defence measures

Source: authors' own compilation.

Among the further directions for modernization efforts one needs to point out the need for an increase in the potential and resources of the Polish Navy units through the acquisition of modern weaponry, while concentrating on the protection of the Polish territorial waters, and the capability of performing the necessary minimum of tasks outside the Baltic Sea (the "Baltic plus" option). In the course of modernization the aim should be to furnish the naval forces with modern armaments and equipment, including the national industry potential.

It is also recommended that a national cybernetic defence system be established; such system, encompassing also the resources provided by other government departments – ought to be integrated with similar systems employed by the allied states. In the future, one of the most important long-term transformation tasks should also be the attaining of the capacity to use space technologies for national defence purposes.

As a priority, any new armaments acquired must comply with the criteria related to state security, with an option of being deployable in international operations, while satisfying the NATO interoperability requirements.

Taking into account the scale of modernization needs, it is essential that the level of national defence expenditure in a long-term perspective remains at the present level of 1.95 per cent of GDP for the previous year and that approximately 1/3 of the entire defence budget is allocated to the technological modernization of the Polish Armed Forces.

Technological modernization and organizational change in the armed forces must go in parallel with the professional preparation of soldiers as well as commands, staffs and entire formations for the attainment of specific goals. A modern military training system should, to the maximum extent possible, take into account such preparation of the armed forces which allows them to attain the capabilities necessary on the modern battlefield. The training must be implemented using state-of-the-art methods and technologically advanced equipment which, in particular, allows using real situation simulation scenarios. The professional contents of the training process should be based on adequately updated strategic documents, doctrines, regulations, instructions, manuals, procedures, etc. The experience gained during international security operations must also be applied during the training process.

The military exercises carried out at national level must reflect real conditions created by present-times threats which must be countered and fought back by the armed forces. The training programmes must, to the maximum extent, prepare its participants for the performance of tasks related to state defence. It is also recommended that the exercises encompass the entire defence system, i.e. involve scenarios which test the procedures of cooperation between the armed forces and other services as well as civilian entities at different levels.

For the purposes of rationalizing the costs of training, the acquisition of military equipment and armaments must be accompanied by the purchase of appropriate simulation and training equipment.

September 2012, the Anakonda-12 military exercise.
Photo: Adam Roik/Combat Camera Reporter Team of the Armed Forces Operational Command.

The armed forces should, at the same time, participate in numerous international military exercises, the objective of which is to make them accustomed to cooperation and functioning in a multinational environment (including for the purposes of international security operations) as well as to verification of the efficiency of allied support should a need arise to carry out a joint defence operation. As Poland – from the point of view of NATO – remains a border state, it is recommended that such exercises be carried out within its territory as well, was the case with the 2013 "Steadfast Jazz" allied military exercise.

As far as non-military defence preparations are concerned, there is a need to determine the precise scope of responsibility of individual state entities which participate in the defence planning process at both national and local government levels; the participants of the aforementioned process should be covered by an education and skills development system. Enhancing the capability of administrative and economic structures of the state to operate in crisis situations and to support the national defence efforts is necessary for the survival and the efficient functioning of the state both in case of an external threat and in wartime. The crucial components of non-military defence preparatory efforts include: establishment of a national security control system and the provision of logistical and technical support for such system; meeting the necessary needs of the Polish Armed Forces and the armed forces of Poland's allies; defence training and carrying out defence task performance checks; preparation of enterpreneurs for the fulfilment of defence tasks; and the militarization of selected public administration bodies. The issues referred to above are currently appropriately settled in legal and organizational ways. Nevertheless, due to the dynamically changing nature of the security environment, constant streamlining efforts are necessary in that regard, including the conduct of systematic, joint exercises involving both military and non-military entities.

If the Polish Armed Forces are to be seen as an essential part of the national crisis management system, the efficiency of the procedures related to the provision of aid by military units (e.g. supporting the activities of the Police) aimed at expediting the response to crisis situations needs to be stepped up. Additionally, an increase in the participation of public administration bodies and rescue services in exercises and training programmes at operational level, carried out by the units and institutions of the Polish Armed Forces, will allow the crisis management system efficiency to further improve.

State institutions should also constantly strive for building a favourable image of the armed forces among the society as an attractive and reliable employer as well as for the reinforcement of the military service ethos. This will allow to recruit the best candidates for professional soldiers as well as to increase the efficacy of the National Reserve Forces. The support of the professional army should be provided by the reserve forces, which are rapidly deployable should any threats, both military and non--military, arise in response to the needs of the crisis management process, including actions performed during natural disasters and aimed at the elimination of their consequences, anti-terrorist operations, the protection of property, etc. The underlying concept of the National Reserve Forces should involve the establishment of separate, comprehensive units specializing mainly in providing support to the general public (the so-called "province governors' army").

The military education system must be adjusted to the modern-day needs of the Polish Armed Forces through their organizational consolidation, with an emphasis on technical education and education for prospective commanding officers. Integrating the dispersed potential of military educational facilities and placing a decisive emphasis on the tasks which are of direct importance for the armed forces should result in an increased efficiency of the educational process. It would be advisable to establish two new institutions of higher education on the basis of the existing potential in terms of higher military education; one joint military academy aimed at meeting the needs of the Polish Armed Forces (a military university) and one institution focusing on national security (an academy of national security), which would operate as a supra-ministerial educational institution and which would serve the needs of the entire integrated national security system.

The streamlining of the military medical care system should encompass the adoption of solutions aimed at restoring the medical corps through the establishment of an adequate recruitment, motivation, education and professional development system. There is a need to improve the mechanisms related to the functioning of the healthcare system and the applicable legal regulations, including those regulations which govern the military healthcare service with regard to providing medical support to the Polish Armed Forces in military missions abroad. Activities linked to the technical modernization of the military healthcare service should focus on the acquisition and implementation of modernized medical appliances as well as new equipment and devices enabling the development and streamlining of the battlefield medical evacuation system (including evacuation by air) on tactical, operational and strategic levels. Telemedicine should be one of the top priorities in terms of modernization.

Military intelligence agencies. Preparatory activities involving the Military Intelligence Service and the Military Counterintelligence Service – as components of the defence subsystem – should be closely linked to the process of designing the entire system of intelligence services of the Republic of Poland (see the chapter on the "Protection subsystems").

It is recommended that efforts are made to "reunite" the military special services with the military, i.e. to incorporate them into the armed forces permanently (both in peacetime and wartime), as opposed to the current regulations which provide that they will only be so incorporated at a time of war. Adopting this solution would mean that these services would report exclusively to the minister of national defence, much like all other military structures do. Insofar as military intelligence is concerned, the solution referred to above might entail the ultimate incorporation thereof into the structures of a new General Staff of the Polish Armed Forces, exercising functions traditionally associated with this entity (thus returning to the historical tradition of the Second Department of the General Staff). The purpose of such changes is to have military intelligence services specialized in, and concentrated on, the tasks related to military security (national defence) and distinguished from civilian services in terms of both whom they report to and how they are managed.

Directive 2009/81/EC of the European Parliament of the and Council dated July 13, 2009

Article 2. (...) this Directive shall apply to contracts awarded in the fields of defence and security for:
(a) the supply of military equipment, including any parts, components and/or subassemblies (...);
(b) the supply of sensitive equipment, including any parts, components and/or subassemblies thereof (...)

Defence industry. The national defence industry needs to become more competitive; the achievement of this goal hinges upon a number of activities both on the part of state administration and the defence sector entities.

Insofar as the government administration is concerned, there is a case for implementation of legal solutions which would facilitate the functioning of the defence industry in an open competition environment, on condition that the procurement in a non-competitive mode, covered by the directive 2009/81/EC, may only take place in cases where such conduct is necessitated by the protection of fundamental requirements of state security.

In pursuing this objective it is necessary to take advantage of the available instruments aimed at providing support to the national defence industry, such as: offset instruments, subsidies granted under the Economy Mobilization Plan (EMP), proceeds from the privatization of the Polish defence industry as well as the promotion of the armaments and military equipment (AME) manufactured in Poland. It would be also desirable to improve the government procurement system with regard to AME by the following actions: advance planning with regard to the conclusion of contracts for defence products to enable Polish defence industry entities to obtain the orders in question; conducting pre-emptive R&D activities with regard to those areas which are the most important in light of the long-term needs of the Polish Armed Forces; the initiation of appropriate procedures well in advance; as well as the improved method of financing of orders relating to defence products.

As from defence sector entities, a particularly valuable development would be intensified activities and improved management of Polish defence industry companies, in order to: gain a better understanding of the needs of the prime users with regard to AME; diversify and expand the range of state-of-the-art products as well as improve their delivery schedules, pricing, available warranties etc.; seek for opportunities to rationalize the assortment and production costs; carry an efficient search for opportunities in terms of extending cooperation – in particular with foreign business partners – in the domain of capital resources, technologies, products, industrial cooperation and markets; modify the marketing and commercial strategies allowing exports boost a, and concentrate on product development as the primary guarantee of survival on the market in a long-term perspective.

Poland should therefore develop such structural arrangements which will make an effective contribution towards attaining a high-quality produce by the Polish defence industry according to the expectations of the Polish Armed Forces, and at the same time attaining a level of competitiveness which will allow to cooperate – on an equal footing – with both European and world defence companies.

* * *

The primary preparatory objective of the defence subsystem is to maintain and qualitatively transform the defence potential of the state, particularly to keep the priority status of the capabilities which are necessary to ensure the direct security of the state. The development of the defence potential should at the same time be translated into the further reinforcement of NATO's defence capabilities and the building of such capabilities by the European Union.

The protection subsystems

The judiciary. In order to ensure the full and effective protection of human rights in Poland it is necessary to have a constant and systematic cooperation of all public authorities whose responsibilities lie in the area of human and civil rights and freedoms. In particular, it is advisable to have an ongoing exchange of information concerning the evident violations of human and civil rights and freedoms, the actions taken to remedy any such infractions and the results of such actions.

In order to allow ordinary citizens to have easier access to the justice system, it is necessary to continue the efforts aimed at informatizing the system wherever possible. Informatization, as one of the primary components of the reform of the entire judiciary, may help find a solution to the problem of excessive delays in judicial proceedings. Taking maximum advantage of the possibilities offered by modern information and telecommunications technologies creates an opportunity for increasing the pace of proceedings and the degree of its transparency. An important task should be the practical implementation of changes which will improve information exchanges between individual components of the judiciary system, including, in particular, between the registers maintained within it (criminal register, court register). In order to expedite criminal proceedings, it seems necessary that the option of recording the courtroom proceedings in electronic form be introduced, much as in the case of civil proceedings. This solution would enable an exact record of the proceedings to be accessed at a later stage, ensuring greater transparency in the activities of the court and the reasoning behind the decisions adopted by it in individual cases. Electronic recording of court proceedings constitutes an indispensable component of the process of building trust in the courts among the general public.

It is essential that court proceedings be simplified. In the context of economic freedom it is necessary to increase the degree of trust in state institutions among entrepreneurs by rationalizing the application of preventative measures in criminal proceedings, taking into account the guarantees issued by associations of entrepreneurs with respect to their members, to carry a review of the applicable laws and legal practice with regard to the appointment of judicial experts and the creation of opportunities for educating judges and prosecutors in economics. At the same time, due to the identified cases of incompetence of state officials in the area of applying the law with respect to entrepreneurs, it is necessary to perform a detailed audit of all cases of power abuse or disregard of duties and, as a consequence, to take criminal or disciplinary action against such state officials.

In the context of reforming the Polish Armed Forces it is also worth considering whether the military prosecution service could be restructured by merging it with the civilian prosecution service.

Insofar as the penitentiary system is concerned, it is necessary to correlate the current criminal policy with the investments available for developing the prison system in order to allow the Prison Service to perform their tasks efficiently, both with regard to imprisonment and rehabilitation. Therefore one should seek to take maximum advantage of the opportunities offered by the use of probationary measures[23], including the usage of electronic prisoner monitoring. It is important that individuals who have finished serving their sentences are aided in the task of re-joining society by helping them find work or study. With regard to the above issue an option worth taking under consideration is the introduction of incentives (e.g. tax incentives) for those who decide to employ individuals serving prison sentences.

In order to ensure the proper functioning of the authorities tasked with the protection of human rights it is necessary to establish and streamline the legal regulations in this respect. In addition, it is necessary to ensure appropriate financial resources for this purpose in the state budget. Lack of adequate financing of institutions which form part of the subsystem for the protection of human and civil rights and freedoms may result in neglecting protection of rights of individuals.

One of the most significant problems is also the absence of adequate legal knowledge and awareness on the part of citizens with regard to their rights and the authorities set up to protect them. For this purpose, it is essential, *inter alia*, that actions be taken to disseminate the knowledge on human rights and fundamental freedoms, also in the school curricula, workshops and classes aimed at young people. It is desirable that human rights education and anti-discrimination education be considered part of the lifelong learning process.

---

[23] Probatory measures – measures introduced under the provisions of substantive criminal law and criminal enforcement law which involve putting the offender to the test, giving him or her a chance to improve his or her conduct in non-detention settings, with the enforcement of the sentence being suspended in whole or in part.

Secret services. Among the preparatory objectives with respect to the activities of the secret services, their adequate organization, equipment resources and training are of particular importance. In this regard, one of the challenges regarding transformation is to restrict the excessive number of nationwide secret service organizations. In a model solution there is a case for the existence of 2-4 such services: 1 or 2 services having a general systemic application (internal and external service) and 1-2 sector services (services dealing with the military, economy or anti-corruption practices). Reforming the number of secret services as they exist today, however, is a difficult task (it is easier to establish a new secret service than to dissolve an existing one); the political context, *inter alia*, plays a significant part in this regard. Therefore, while a quantitative reform would be purposeful, it should by no means be considered a top priority. Secret services are a very sensitive component of the national security system and therefore reforms in this regard must be carried out in a cautious and prudent manner. Revolutionary changes are ill-advised and any reforms of this type should be introduced gradually.

At the first stage it would presumably be advisable to improve the system of supervision over the secret services. The direct competences of the Prime Minister should solely be restricted to personnel issues regarding directors of the services as well as the coordination and supervision of the secret services responsible for intelligence and, possibly, for the prevention of corruption at the highest levels of power (if such service were to be retained as a separate entity; however it would seem more advisable to merge the Central Anti-Corruption Bureau with the Internal Security Agency. The coordination and supervision of other services should be exercised by constitutional ministers (the minister of internal affairs and the minister of national defence).

If a Council of Ministers Committee for National Security were to be set up, it should take over the powers of the minister–secret services coordinator, and in addition, the Collegium for Secret Services should also be merged into the Committee. The separate existence of the above entities appears to suggest that the secret services enjoy a privileged status within the state system, which, in the light of their actual (and, in the future, possibly also legal) subordination to the relevant constitutional ministers, finds no grounds.

In order to ensure the optimum management of information at the highest levels of state administration, it would also be advisable to establish an entity (bureau, centre, department, etc.) responsible for preparation of strategic syntheses of the information provided by the secret services and the preparation of integrated evaluations for the purposes of national security control. The task of such an entity would be to gather the information from all state services responsible for the individual spheres of security and its subsequent analysis and evaluation for the supreme authorities of the state. The establishment of the aforementioned institution would make it possible to: ensure the support with regard to the decision-making process, especially when adopting decisions of strategic significance for state security; generate a comprehensive presentation of the situation, available solely to the main decision-makers in the state; prepare relevant plans regard the directions of secret service activity and improve the exchange of information between the most significant components of the state security system. The cell responsible for furnishing syntheses of strategic information should be established within an institution providing administrative support to the proposed Council of Ministers Committee for National Security, or within a new Government Centre for National Security, to be located, in organizational terms, within the Chancellery of the Prime Minister.

Efforts must also be made towards a meaningful standardization of the problems related to the operational and surveillance activities of the individual secret services through the unification of the applied terminology, operational procedures (having regard to the functional specificity of individual services) as well as the rules and scope of their coordination. The rights of the officials of different services, their operational procedures and their professional codes of conduct need to be unified. As a result, it should be possible to efficiently utilize the human resources of the secret services, on condition that the personnel of individual services will be interchangeable.

Given the increasingly transsectoral nature of security threats it is also necessary to establish cooperation platforms for the secret services and other institutions to counteract threats having a particular weight for state security (e.g. cyber crime, terrorism, organised crime activities). These platforms should be maintained in a manner which assumes an evolutionary development of their organizational forms. An example of such an entity is the Anti-Terrorist Centre (an interdisciplinary entity having a status which might be described as supra-systemic from the point of view of the organizational structure of the administration), comprising seconded officers, soldiers and employees of organizations such as the Police, the Border Guard, the Government Protection Bureau, the Intelligence Agency, the Military Intelligence Service, the Military Counterintelligence Service and the Customs Service, having online access to the information resources of their institutions of origin. It is worth pointing out, however, that centres of this kind should be subject to supra-ministerial supervision (due to their supra-ministerial nature) instead of remaining an organizational component of any of the services.

Against this background, it is worth considering the proposal to reduce to a minimum the workload of the secret services attributable to duties related to the legal process (these obligations should be taken over by the Central Bureau of Investigation), concentrating instead on informational and analytical tasks as well as operational and surveillance activities, i.e. tasks and activities aimed at proving the commission of a crime on the balance of probabilities. The obligations of these services with respect to the legal process should be limited solely to highly specialized tasks related, for example, to proceedings in espionage or terrorist cases. This would allow to adopt effective preventative and pre-emptive measures in areas which are particularly sensitive from the viewpoint of the functioning of the state.

The optimization of secret services' work, their consolidation, the systematization of their competences and the attainment of interoperability between such services may be achieved by the proposal to elaborate a new act on secret services which would amend the existing legal regulations in this regard. Also worth considering is preparation of an act on operational (or operational and surveillance) activities for the purposes of unifying and specifying the procedures and competences with respect to the use of operational and surveillance techniques. The drafting and enactment of consolidated legislation on the secret services would also form the basis for improving the efficiency of training and cooperation as well as for facilitating personnel transfers between these services.

Institutions for combating terrorism and political extremism. Both domestic and international institutions responsible for the analysis and exchange of information on terrorist threats continue to evolve, especially at strategic and operational levels. The Polish system of multidimensional and multi-entity countering of terrorism requires the implementation of more robust, statutory coordination mechanisms allowing the Anti-Terrorist Centre to effectively coordinate anti-terrorist efforts, both those which are preventative in nature (staving off terrorist attacks) and those which aim at minimising potential losses. There is a particular need, for adopting legislative regulations governing cooperation between individual entities to replace the current agreements between such entities.

In order to bring about appropriate response to potential threats, it is important to streamline the coordinated exchange of information on terrorist threats between the Police, the Border Guard and the Government Protection Bureau, as well as among the civilian and military secret services and other services (e.g. the Customs Service, tax audit authorities, financial information authorities). Such coordination is necessary for the timely transfer of information concerning criminal acts of a terrorist nature, making it possible to detect, identify, prevent and prosecute such crimes.

Photo: Internal Security
Agency

From the point of view of establishing an integrated and efficient anti-terrorist system of the Republic of Poland, it is essential to develop an algorithm for cooperation and management of activities performed at the scene of a terrorist act as well as the proper implementation of the procedures related to the cooperation of the state services and institutions participating in the anti-terrorist defence system in case of any incidents of a terrorist nature.

Cybersecurity-related institutions. In order to raise the level of cybernetic security, it appears necessary to coordinate activities, in the field of education and legislation in particular. It also appears desirable to introduce organizational changes with regard to the currently operating information and communications technology (ICT) security subsystem. Taking into account the personnel issues with which many state institutions are coping, one of the possible solutions would be to work out procedures of cooperation, information exchange and coordination of activities followed by the entities operating in the field of ICT security, which will allow to better use the human resources available to the given units. The above-mentioned activities can include the following:

- Ensuring that cyclical, comprehensive analyses of the existing level of cyberspace threats carried out. (At present, selected services produce this type of analyses within the scope of their competences.);
- Defining unambiguously the ICT infrastructure having a critical value for the Republic of Poland as well as developing a plan and procedures for its protection;
- Reviewing and, if possible, amending the existing legal acts with regard to their compatibility with the laws of other jurisdictions and/or international organizations for the purposes of facilitating international cooperation in protecting cyberspace and determining precisely the structural rationality, role, scope of responsibility and competences, specific rights as well as rules governing mutual cooperation and information exchange with respect to individual organizations, institutions, organizational units, authorities and services of the Republic of Poland concerning their activities in cyberspace;
- Performing intensive activities aimed at prevention and raising awareness, in the form of training courses and public information campaigns which should concern both state administration entities and – more importantly – ordinary citizens–users of cyberspace on an everyday basis. The public education with regard to these issues is, along with legal and organizational activities and technical measures, one of the most critical pillars of the activities aimed to eliminate the threats which

occur in virtual space. In this context, it is necessary to increase the level of funds available for the development of science and research programmes as well as the creation and implementation of educational programmes for children and young people as a part of the school curricula.

It is also worth considering the introduction of legislative changes which would determine the principles of active defence of cyberspace as well as organizational changes enabling the adoption of pre-emptive measures in the field of ICT security by specialized departments within institutions, organizational units, authorities and services of the Republic of Poland. It would also be legitimate to build mechanisms and systems designed for taking offensive actions in this field, also treated as support for conventional measures – especially since virtual space is becoming an area used for hostile operations not only by hackers or terrorist organizations, but also by state entities.

A review will be needed of the programmes of supplementary training and of the curricula of higher education institutions being under the supervision of the state (including military educational institutions) as well as the scope of the planned research or R&D work, taking into account the needs related to cyber security (with particular emphasis on the safety of state institutions significant from the viewpoint of the security of the state). This would allow to carry out cyclical simulations, trainings and exercises with the involvement of designated companies and institutions as well as the development of national solutions in the field of cryptography and their wider implementation within the national information technology systems.

The primary state entity responsible for the identification, counteraction and neutralization of cybernetic threats is the Government Computer Security Incident Response Team (CERT.GOV.PL), operating within the ICT Security Department of the Internal Security Agency. The overall responsibility for issues related to cyber security should rest upon the Council of Ministers, performing its tasks in this regard through the minister of administration and digitalization, the minister of national defence, the minister of internal affairs, head of the Internal Security Agency and the Head of Military Counterintelligence Service as well as other government administration bodies. If a Council of Ministers Committee for National Security is set up, its scope of competences should encompass a supra-ministerial coordination of the tasks related to cyber security.

The rise of cyber crime calls for equally dynamic countermeasures, implemented in active partnership with the private sector, especially with internet service providers, organizations responsible for internet security and the suppliers of financial services at strategic and operational levels (industry, domestic and international). This partnership is of great importance for the development of IT tools that are useful to law enforcement agencies.

Institutions protecting secret information. The system of protection of confidential information in its current form came into being after the 1989 political transformation. In its current shape it is the result of the act on the protection of confidential information dated 5 August, 2010. This new act was intended to streamline the system of protection of such information, and, in particular, to eliminate loopholes such as the in sufficiently clear definition of its subject matter, the too rigid definition of the method of protecting information, the absence of a sufficiently clear scope of individual responsibility for the protection of secret information as well as the lack of efficient protection possible against nascent threats.

Every organizational unit tasked with the processing of confidential information is under a statutory obligation to implement specific rules of conduct once the emergency state is introduced. Contingent on the situation, actions should be consistent with the guidelines provided by the entity introducing the state of emergency. Heretofore, no final decision has been reached with regard to the tasks carried out by an entrepreneur who holds the industrial security certificate in specific situations (such as martial law). The state services, taking advantage of the laconic wording of the applicable legislation, demand that an entrepreneur (including the one who only holds a third-degree industrial security certificate which merely confirms the ability of such entrepreneur to afford protection to such information, excluding his capability of processing such information within the facilities he uses) prepare a plan for the evacuation of such information. This entails a need to pay the relevant service charge (under a contract with an appropriate security contractor), the amount of which depends on the location where the evacuation is to take place. There are troubles with finding a location to which such materials could be evacuated as the state administration institutions do not accept any such materials for safe-keeping.

It is legitimate to assign the obligations to protect confidential information at times of crisis or war to the appropriate province governor (through the subordinate authorities and organizational entities of government administration and local self-government of the province); such obligations would include, *inter alia*: reinforcing the protection of areas which are particularly vulnerable; reinforcing the internal and external access control (e.g. through detailed checkups of vehicles and individuals in cooperation with the police, city guard and civil defence units) as well as identifying locations to which secret materials are to be evacuated.

The information security of the state and its citizens must be strengthened, as the threats emerge, through a constant enactment of legal regulations and the development of international cooperation within NATO and the EU, with the aim of:

- Preventing cyber crime and ensuring the safe distribution of information (through ICT systems and networks as well as other data carriers), and also through education and compulsory training with regard to the implemented safeguards in order to make sure that the implemented procedures are properly understood and applied;
- Raising the public awareness of threats originating from cyberspace;
- Ensuring that information is monitored at each stage of its life cycle;
- Appropriately classifying and declassifying information according to relevant procedures, especially for the purposes of determining the level and the moment from which the information in question should be afforded a special degree of protection;
- Reinforcing the internal capabilities with respect to ensuring information and IT security with the aim of implementating effective defence measures.

The information security of the state should also be increased by enhancing the quality of safeguards for information and IT resources and by popularizing training programmes and awareness-raising efforts at school education level.

Public order services and guards. The organizational development of the services and guards responsible for the protection of the population, public safety and crisis response remains a constant preparatory objective within the framework of protection subsystems.

It is necessary to precisely determine the responsibilities of individual institutions, services and guards concerning the maintenance of public order, the rules and procedures they follow in performing their tasks and the areas for which they are accountable. There is a need for sharing out competences between the police, the secret services and guards, eliminating any duplication of efforts and forcing the entities in question to engage in actual, as opposed to declaratory, cooperation. The absence of a uniform method of recording, evidencing and comparing the achieved results, in the context of the overlapping competences of individual services, makes it impossible to evaluate their efficacy in an objective and comparable manner. Within the individual areas of law and order there is a need to designate leaders, i.e. institutions specializing in gathering the knowledge (both theoretical and practical) in the given field and coordinating the activities of all components of the defence subsystem, protection subsystems and transsectoral areas. This applies, in particular, to:

- Combating terrorism, including the monitoring of international terrorism, prevention, protection of the critical infrastructure, the training of units earmarked for the active combating of terrorist acts as well as the methods and procedures of preparing the population for possible terrorist attacks. It is also essential to verify the legal regulations aimed at combating terrorism;
- Enhancing mechanisms earmarked for combating organized crime: it is in this context that the ongoing discussion on the organizational and structural changes within the Central Bureau of Investigation of the General Police Headquarters (KGP) should be interpreted. These changes are intended to increase the autonomy of the Bureau through, *inter alia,* separating it from the KGP organizational structures and conferring upon it the status of an organizational entity as well as through providing it with a separate budget – all changes aimed at enhancing the functioning of the Central Bureau of Investigation are most desirable from the point of view of the security of the state and its citizens;
- Combating cybercrime;
- Improving road traffic safety. An appropriate diagnosis of the threats existing in this area should translate into priority directions of the performed activities. It is important that controlling entities responsible for the performance of individual tasks be designated and that effective coordination be ensured. A good example is the initiative adopted by the Ministry of Transport, Construction and Maritime Economy, aimed at establishing a National Road Traffic Safety Programme, based on a number of primary tenets: establishment of an appropriate infrastructure, effective supervision of the conduct of road users; and an extensive educational actions.

Insofar as combating crime and containing its negative consequences are concerned, the institutionalized forms of information exchange between all security entities should be streamlined through the establishment of a nationwide crime database. Furthermore, there is a need for a more extensive dissemination and use of the data obtained through international cooperation as well as the cooperation with Europol, Interpol, within the Schengen Information System (SIS) and through liaison officers. This system should also exercise analytical functions and offer a variety of access levels, depending on the status of the given user. The structure of the system should be built around a database equipped with a search option, modelled after the Information Reporting System/Operational Information System. The system should replace the current National Criminal Information Centre, which in fact contains only the so-called police data. Both the data and the systems used should be standardized in a manner ensuring the compatibility of data contained in separate registers.

In connection with the extensive catalogue of prohibited acts, which encompasses both violent crimes – including crimes against life and health – and crimes which solely affect property, documents, security and communication, as well as other types of crimes, it is necessary to streamline the methods employed for the purposes of combating these crimes, taking into account the multi-dimensional nature of these threats.

It is necessary to introduce solutions which constrain the phenomenon of criminality occurring amongst habitual offenders in penitentiary facilities by imposing a more direct obligation on the Prison Service to cooperate with the Police and other services tasked with the protection of law and order. It should also be whether the Prison Service should be given limited rights to operational and investigative work, subject to any principles which apply to the rights of prison inmates.

Thought should also be given to the idea of establishing a platform for public-private cooperation for combating cyber crime, along with elaborating anew the legal regulations governing the rights and duties of the participants of such platform, designating the sources of financing, determining the rules of domestic and international cooperation (an inter-institutional and cross-border approaches), along with an estimated quantity of the data processed and indicating the technical solutions for such platform.

Legal solutions should be developed and implemented to impose upon investors or proprietors who make construction investments earmarked for organization of mass events, an obligation to install or equip such facilities with devices designed to detect chemical, biological, radiological or radioactive threats. There is also a necessity to elaborate legal solutions which introduce an obligation to install at select train and bus stations a system of monitoring places in which baggage lockers are located as well as systems which enable to analyze high-resolution video feeds for the purposes of detecting abandoned baggage, entries into restricted areas (security zones), dense traffic volume (crowds or gatherings of people), unnatural behaviour of individuals as well as the recognition of vehicle registration plates. The use of state-of-the-art monitoring systems brings about a multitude of new possibilities, such as the detection of biometric parameters, radiological, chemical or biological materials as well as the capability to monitor selected contents in cyberspace. It is important, however, that such sophisticated monitoring systems are not used for the purposes of constant surveillance of all citizens. It is therefore necessary to start a discussion on a legal settlement of possibilities to use modern monitoring systems, including the systems used by private entities, as well as providing for the establishment of adequate control mechanisms to prevent violations of the citizens' rights to freedom and privacy.

It is legitimate to develop rules of informing the society about the threats posed by criminal activities as well as to the preventative actions, including a permanent information programme intended to raise the awareness and shape desirable conduct and behaviour in the event of a threat.

Law and order cannot be guaranteed in the absence of a constant and sturdy cooperation between all entities within the system as well as a wide involvement of the society as a whole, promoted as a patriotic duty. Public authorities should work out a commonly accepted (i.e. transcending any existing divisions) model for the cooperation with society, based on the general dissemination of knowledge at all levels of education and professional activity of all citizens. Within this educational effort, the following components are of particular importance: the general school education (introduction to the curricula the subjects regarding law and order, adjusted to the cognitive abilities of learners and taking into account the dangers which are typical for individual age groups); the incorporation of security issues into the existing compulsory health–and–safety training programmes for all employees and students; the imposition of an obligation upon insurance companies to co-finance the general educational efforts aimed at the society at large in this regard; the promotion of appropriate civic attitudes with respect to abiding by the regulations related to law and order; the striving for the allocation of a specific minimum part of the central and local budgets for the purposes of improving the existing security infrastructure.

In a longer perspective, it is worth considering changes in the structure of the state apparatus responsible for internal affairs, including the elimination of duplications of certain tasks and competences between the minister of internal affairs and the commanders-in-chief of the services. According to one of the presented proposals, the general headquarters of the Police, the Border Guard and the State Fire Service would either be dissolved or transformed into respective departments of the ministry of internal affairs, with the corresponding entities at province level to be reinforced. Under another proposal, the operational tasks performed by the general headquarters would be restricted, with their analytical and information functions to be extended and the standing of the headquarters of the aforesaid services at province level to be reinforced. Both concepts have their advantages as well as drawbacks; it appears that the latter proposal is more in line with the existing situation in Poland, especially if supplemented by moves aimed at depoliticizing the positions of the heads of the Police and other services, for example by having them hold office not coinciding with the term of office of political authorities.

The globalization processes and the resulting absence of territorial barriers to criminal activities have made it necessary to increasingly apply innovative technological solutions in the struggle against crime. It is difficult to imagine a modern, well-organized and secure state that does not take advantage of such technologies.

The constant monitoring of technological development – in the context of activities of the services responsible for law and order – is necessary, since criminals also seek to take advantage of new technologies. Not rarely technological innovations are swiftly and efficiently employed by organized criminal groups, terrorist organizations or even by common criminals and youth offenders. This is proven by the growing threat of cyber terrorism and cyber crime.

An important aspect of the contemporary technological solutions is also the ability to configure them in a variety of ways and to integrate them within increasingly complicated systems, thereby increasing their potential and scope of possible uses. The objective of such systems may be to detect specific events, especially those which pose a threat to citizens, and, consequently, to prevent criminal acts and offences and to aid the process of identifying and tracking down the offenders.

Countering violations of law and order calls for coordinating all aspects of the protection security sector, especially in the field of the prosecution of criminal acts, prevention and, first and foremost, law-making and the protection of human and civil rights. This confirms the integration needs in the field of security. Such coordinating functions could be vested in a Government Centre for National Security.

An important preparatory task regarding the operations of services, guards and other institutions responsible for the protection of the population, public safety and crisis management is technical development. Of late these needs have found an expression, *inter alia*, in the expenses incurred in the years 2007-2011 under the modernization programme for the Police, Border Guard, State Fire Service and Government Protection Bureau. The programme pointed to investment requirements in practically every sphere of activity of the services, from buildings and the infrastructure, through transportation equipment, vehicles and specialist equipment, to the salaries of officers and employees. Both the aforementioned Programme and the spending incurred at an earlier stage have improved the situation in the services, although there remain significant needs in terms of investments. Ensuring the adequate infrastructure and equipment resources as well as the proper conditions of service and work for officers and employees constitutes a guarantee that their tasks will be performed effectively and in a proper manner.

Another component of the system of public order services and formations is the communal/municipal guards. After nearly 20 years of their operation, discussion has begun as to the future of these formations. Certain concepts have been put forward which would extend the scope of competences of the guard, transforming it into a municipal police *sensu stricto*, i.e. a type of government-controlled local police, which would result in the conferral of additional rights, including with regard to their remuneration and pension privileges. In case the status of the municipal guard were to be elevated, it would be necessary to carry out appropriate procedures for the selection, training, supervision and establishment of logistical facilities. On the other hand, there are also proposals for the municipal guard forces to be merged into state police structures, along with the budget funds earmarked for the financing of their functioning.

Rescue and population protection guards. The rules governing the functioning of civil defence and the protection of the population should correspond to the challenges faced by the contemporary state as well as the requirements brought about by Poland's EU membership. In that regard, the key issue is the constant improvements in the field of crisis management, protection of the population and public safety.

Warsaw, October 29, 2009. The "Patrol 09" exercises carried out within the framework of the nationwide exercise programme of the National Contamination Detection and Alert System.
Photo: Grzegorz Jakubowski/PAP

The issues related to civil defence should be regulated in a comprehensive manner in a separate statutory act, given the scope of its tasks. The catalogue of tasks of civil defence derived from the Additional Protocol (Protocol I) to the Geneva conventions on the protection of war victims encompasses a number of tasks related to the civil population, primarily during hostilities, but also in peacetime in the case of natural disasters. It is the state which must decide, however, which tasks are to be performed by civil defence structures and to what extent (e.g. due to the limited economic capacity or human resources) as well as how to solve the issue of filling the positions within the civil defence structures following the announcement of a general or partial mobilization of the Polish Armed Forces.

Necessary changes should have the tasks related to the protection of the population (as well as civil defence) properly placed within the state security system and, in this regard, a clear division of competences of public administration bodies established. All the changes made would result in a harmonization of the applicable laws and the existing regulations adjusted to modern-day threats as well as in streamlined responses to normal and extraordinary situations. For this reason, the primary objectives of statutory regulations should aim at:

- Unifying the terminology related to civil defence and the protection of the population;
- Determining the objectives and organization of the system of protecting the population;
- Determining the principles governing the operation of the system of protecting the population;
- Raising the level of public education with regard to the protection of the population; and
- Determining the rules of participation of citizens in performing the tasks aimed at protecting the population and determining the rules of the planning process within the system of protecting the population (both in peacetime and wartime).

Statutory regulations should also extend to the rules governing the operation of the system of protecting the population (including in wartime), which requires the enactment of regulations on civil defence, as mentioned earlier. In the process, efforts must be made to streamline:

- the cooperation of authorities and entities which perform tasks intended to ensure the safety of the citizens, including rescue operations, in the event of local threats as well as natural disasters, catastrophes and technical failures, through the implementation of qualitatively news legal solutions in this regard;
- The mechanisms for controlling the activities, uniformity of emergency procedures and standardization of equipment;

- The mechanisms for the coordination of rescue operations as well as other tasks related to the protection of the population; the formation of a coherent model for the training of rescue services and providing common training facilities to all entities which participate in the system;
- The functioning of rescue dispatch centres, based on the administrative division of the country and having an identical functionality (this role could be fulfilled by rescue communication centres – which are currently being organized – following their appropriate organizational adjustment to the requirements of the system).

One should mention that the ministry of internal affairs has initiated the work aimed at the systematization of the rules pertaining to the protection of the population and civil defence within the existing legislation. The prepared draft bill on protection of the population supports the proposed concept of covering all the main efforts related to the protection of the population in a single piece of legislation so that the concerned entities are given clear guidelines for action.

The civilization development as well as the new challenges faced by the rescue services and organizations in various types of rescue operations have made it necessary to systematize the existing legal situation in the field of rescue operations and the protection of the population, including the transformation of the National Fire Fighting and Rescue System into a National Rescue System (*Krajowy system ratowniczy*, KSR). In establishing the KSR, efforts must be made to have all rescue entities operate according to uniform rules pertaining, in particular, to: the notification system; the alerting system; the organization and coordination of rescue operations; the procedures applicable to emergency rescue operations; the system of rescue training; communications systems for all rescue entities; the unification of equipment used by rescue entities; the documentation of events; the information exchange and database systems and the criteria of the efficiency of their operation.

The majority of entities should participate in the integrated rescue system under the provisions of applicable laws, except for community rescue and humanitarian organizations, non-governmental organizations and other entities provided for under the response plans. The rescue tasks and activities of the entities participating in the system should be taken on the basis of common rescue procedures and standards with regard to preparedness, equipment and training. This will allow using in a flexible manner the existing rescue potential in the event of any foreseeable threat. It is essential to streamline the mechanisms for granting target subsidies to perform the tasks entrusted to public and non-governmental organizations.

The primary tasks of the national rescue system should be concentrated within the district and take on the form of delegated tasks. At province and national levels, the roles of support or coordination of operations should be played respectively[24].

---

[24] The task of forming a National Rescue System and controlling it should rest upon the district governor. The standards of conduct should be set by the commander-in-chief of the State Fire Service. Other public administration structures should exercise supporting functions (for example the province governor ensures the logistical support and reinforcements, while the mayors and heads of the commune ensure the public base).

In essence, the proposal for the establishment of a National Rescue System would entail the incorporation into that system of all state services pursuant to the statutory obligations and having these services operate under a single command, which should translate into the unification of training standards, procedures, equipment interoperability, common terminology, identical status of officers etc. It also offers an opportunity to link delegated tasks, i.e. legal contracts, to appropriate payments made to specialized non-governmental rescue organizations (e.g. GOPR, TOPR, WOPR), Masurian Rescue Service (*Mazurska Służba Ratownicza*, MSR) and humanitarian organizations (e.g. Polish Red Cross (*Polski Czerwony Krzyż*, PCK), The Polish Scouting and Guiding Association (*Związek Harcerstwa Polskiego*, ZHP), Scouting Association of the Republic of Poland (*Związek Harcerstwa Rzeczypospolitej*, ZHR), Doctors Without Borders), which may provide these organizations with an impulse for further development.

Pursuant to the above-mentioned principles of operation of the system of protecting the population, the primary objectives of the KSR should be: streamlined response of the rescue entities; streamlined activity control mechanisms; streamlined rescue tasks coordination mechanisms; establishment of a consistent model for the training of emergency rescue entities; establishment of a uniform system of requirements with respect to persons participating in rescue operations and rescue service officers; and commissioning of rescue dispatch centres.

In this connection, one should consider extending the draft act on the protection of the population to rescue operations issues in order to create the framework and legal foundations for a modern system of rescue and protection of the population, the creation of a formal and legal synergy between activities of the society and the activities of professional state institutions as well as the establishment of a National Emergency System in order to ensure a functional integration of the area which currently remains dispersed. Non-defence issues contained in the current act on the general defence duty could also be transferred to the proposed act on rescue and protection of the population. This would also entail the transferring from the existing act on crisis management, of some of the regulations which govern control-related issues to the proposed act on national security control.

The Polish EU membership also entails the need to reinforce and streamline the cooperation and coordination mechanisms, especially the mechanisms provided for under Article 222 of the Treaty on the Functioning of the European Union, with particular emphasis on the following areas: the capacity to identify threats and their evaluation; keeping of the means and resources which may be made available to the EU in the event of setting in motion the procedures provided for under the article in question as well the ability to start evaluation (as well as applicable procedures) should the EU's support must be sought.

Border services. Insofar as the subsystem of the protection of state boundaries is concerned, steps should be taken to streamline the integrated EU/Schengen system for border management. Such efforts should result in the designation of main authorities responsible for the exercise of specific state functions and putting in order the competences of individual participants.

Another direction in the process of improving the Integrated Border Management System in Poland would be the scope of the tasks performed and functions exercised by the Border Guard extended to the area of activities currently pursued by the Office for Foreigners. Such solution would optimize the efficiency of the state with respect to combating illegal migration and would constitute a continuation of the Border Guard transformation process, aimed at remodelling the Border Guard into a formation tasked with both border control and migration issues. This is because the issues of migration are directly linked to state security, and for that reason they should be dealt with by a formation of a permanent nature and performing its tasks on an continuous basis.

The significance of migration issues should be expected to rise, also as in consequence of the planned increase in the accessibility of the Polish labour market, which is one of the measures aimed at mitigating the consequences of the expected population decline in Poland. The above-mentioned efforts should be correlated with an amendment of, *inter alia*, the act on foreigners, as well as the development of an action plan and a road map for the implementation of the policy document adopted by the Council of Ministers, entitled "The Polish Migration Policy – Current Position and Proposals for Action". The plan should contain proposals of detailed solutions along with an indication of the entities responsible for their implementation as well as the evaluation of costs and sources of financing.

There is a need to ensure a build-up of cooperation between the Border Guard and the consular services of the Ministry of Foreign Affairs through, *inter alia*, increasing the number of liaison officers operating in Polish diplomatic missions as well as through a more efficient exchange of information. This would allow, *inter alia*, to reduce the number of denials of entry issued by the Border Guard officers on the external border of the European Union.

Taking into account the current potential of the Border Guard, used for the purpose of tasks in marine zones, the role of this formation could be expanded within the marine Search and Rescue (SAR) system, including having the Border Guard take over the overall SAR service duties, as the latter currently reports to the minister of maritime economy. This proposal should be followed by legislative changes, as a result of which the minister of the internal affairs would become responsible for the supervision of SAR activities.

It is also necessary to develop and modernize the systems of communications (digital communications) and databases, to carry out joint purchases (in order to take advantage of the economy of scale) as well as to bring about a broadly-conceived logistical integration within the ministry of the internal affairs; another important requirement is the introduction of a common system of education, e.g. through the establishment of an educational institution (institute or department within the proposed Academy of National Security) which would place an emphasis on the training of management staff for the individual services.

Services for the protection of supreme authorities and public administration bodies. The Government Protection Bureau fulfills a number of policing tasks (protection of individuals and facilities, surveillance of the surroundings which are to be visited by individuals under protection). Attention needs therefore to be given to solutions already applied by other countries, where this type of entity forms a constituent part of the Police (with the status of an office of the general headquarters), while protection tasks are executed by the local police forces under its supervision. Another option is to retain a unit consisting of a few hundred individuals, tasked exclusively with the protection of the top-ranking state persons, with the remaining tasks being entrusted to the Police.

Given the need to ensure the security of the state control system, it is necessary to establish general rules concerning such a dispersal of highest-ranking officials (HEAD status of VIPs) while travelling to different locations that in cases where a number of such persons is present at the same time on board an aircraft (such rules also pertaining to land and sea transport), the level of reasonable risk for the continuity of control of the primary state functions is not exceeded. It is therefore proposed that a separate act is drawn up, containing the primary assumptions of the agreement concluded on 10 February, 2011, by the respective chancelleries of the President of the Republic of Poland, the Prime Minister, the Sejm and the Senate with respect to air transport arrangements for top-ranking officials.

It is important that legal regulations are enacted which provide that the President and the Marshal (Speaker) of the Sejm as well as the President and the Prime Minister ought not to travel on the same flight. The Prime Minister should also refrain from travelling on the same flight with the Deputy Prime Minister (or with all deputy prime ministers in the event that more than one deputy prime minister is appointed). It should also be prohibited for more than half of the members of the Council of Ministers, the National Security Council, the Collegium for Secret Services as well as the highest-ranking military officials to travel on the same flight. It also seems reasonable to prohibit the Marshals of the Sejm and the Senate from travelling together by virtue of their necessity to remain ready to step in for the President should the need arise.

Measures need to be adopted to afford legal protection to the commander of the aircraft against any pressure being exerted by third parties. It is also necessary to implement rules pertaining to making travel arrangements for VIPs using civilian aircraft (introduction of statutory provisions prohibiting the President, the Prime Minister, the Marshal of the Sejm and the Marshal of the Senate from travelling on private aircraft owned by persons or entities that do not have the status of air carriers). VIP passengers should be under an obligation to comply with the basic requirements with regard to flight safety, i.e. requirements as to compliance with deadlines and "on-board discipline", including a mandatory prohibition against accessing the cockpit during take-off and landing. As a result of such legal changes, there should be a specific authority which is legally authorized to enforce the safety rules agreed upon, i.e. the possibility to call upon the provisions of specific legislation in the event that the requirements referred to above are not complied with by VIPs. It is also necessary to enunciate in greater detail the rules and procedures pertaining to air transport arrangements for VIPs in such manner that, among the basic factors which determine the performance of the tasks in question (i.e. political exigencies, economic and financial capabilities, safety requirements), the safety factor is accorded priority regardless of the class of the flight. This rule should be included in a new National Security Strategy.

There is a need to establish a coordination centre for air transport safety with regard to top--ranking state officials, e.g. within the Chancellery of the Prime Minister, the proposed Government Centre for National Security or the Government Protection Bureau. It is necessary to introduce an additional requirement with regard to safety control during the preparatory phase of the operation prior to the decision-making stage and the final approval for its implementation.

The pilot training system needs to be re-examined by placing an emphasis on the compulsory simulation training pertaining to emergency situations during flight. It should be assessed whether it would be legitimate to establish and organize an integrated system for civilian and military aviation operations, especially with regard to pilot training and airfield infrastructure.

New aircraft need to be acquired for the purposes of VIP transportation. At least two airplanes and two helicopters need to be fitted out as airborne state control posts (stations), taking into account the requirements relating to crisis situations (or the outbreak of an armed conflict). A list of the posts of state authority which are critical from the point of view of national security should be included in the Political and Strategic Defence Directive or the Political and Strategic National Security Directive, in the section dedicated to the organization and transformation of the national security control system. A back-up airfield for VIPs in Warsaw also needs to be provided, in the context of the air mobility of the strategic state control system – especially in situations of a crisis (or a war).

It should also be considered whether to establish an integrated, supra-ministerial commission for the investigation of transportation accidents (not limited to aviation accidents).

The dangers which exist in the modern world also call for transformation undertakings aimed at formulating comprehensive solutions regarding the protection of Polish personnel abroad. In the course of protecting the Polish diplomatic missions, consular offices, representations operating with international organizations as well as individuals working with the aforesaid institutions and Polish citizens staying abroad in general, there is a risk of personnel isolation (which means that individuals may for example be abducted, taken hostage or missing). These threats are particularly apparent in the regions covered by the operations of the Polish military contingents. All this makes it necessary to establish an efficient system for personnel recovery.

Due to the constant need for adjusting the forms and modes of operation and protection to new dangers posed by, *inter alia*, the dynamics of asymmetrical conflicts, systemic solutions need to be developed which would allow to coordinate political, diplomatic, military and civilian actions in the process of personnel recovery. Legal regulations should be enacted which would allow to determine rules and procedures for inter-ministerial cooperation in the event of isolation incidents concerning state officials, soldiers and employees participating in military operations as well as in case of Polish citizens being abducted or missing.

It is also necessary to provide back-up to teams responsible for the security of diplomatic missions in areas affected by armed conflicts in which no Polish military contingents are operating, to determine the rules pertaining to cooperation with local services and services of other states and to reinforce the cooperation with foreign services of this kind. The Government Protection Bureau does not have autonomous competences which would allow it to designate the scope of long-term international cooperation within this field.

Other protection subsystems. Having regard to the multi-dimensional nature of the functioning of central and local government institutions as well as private entities within the framework of other protection subsystems, emphasis must be placed on the need to take actions aimed at clarifying the respective competences and improving the coordination of activities so that duplication of efforts is avoided.

Given the number of security service employees (110–150 thousand), the role of the commercial (private) protection sector within the protection subsystems may be taken into consideration. There are two models which are applicable in this case. According to the first of these models, the state should not impose restrictions on its own tasks and competences within the field of security, and even if it allowed a partial privatization of the sector, it should keep strict supervision over it. According to the second model, security remains a service as any other, and the most that the state should do is to supervise the quality of the services rendered.

At this point it needs to be pointed out that private security agencies in other countries are engaged, *inter alia*, in the transportation of prisoners, the protection of court buildings as well as the so-called special purpose areas such as military and nuclear facilities. Therefore the possible benefits from the further privatization of security entities may be tangible on condition that proper supervision and controls over their activities are strict.

There are obviously many types of risks which must be taken into consideration during the law-making process; for example, the private security sector operates on a profit-oriented basis, private security firms do not form a coherent system, being engaged in competitive struggle for their clients, while the degree of their substantive preparation remains insufficient and no regulations exist as to the obligation to ensure the professional development of the employees of security firms. Efficient verification of security service employees also needs to be improved.

* * *

The unwavering preparatory objective with respect to the scope of preparation of protection subsystems within the national security system should be the optimum organizational, technical and training-related development of services, guards and any other institutions responsible for the protection of the population, public safety and crisis management as well as for ensuring that everyone can freely enjoy of his/her rights and freedoms as citizens.

4.4. Preparation of national security support subsystems

The societal subsystems

National heritage protection system. The broadly-defined national heritage has always been – and will always be – a significant part of Polish identity as a nation. While during the period of intermitent subjugation and limited sovereignty of Poland (the 19th and 20th centuries) national heritage formed the cornerstone of Polish resistance against the partitioning/occupying powers and the struggle against them, the modern-day system needs to be based upon new tenets and criteria, encompassing such factors as sovereignty, democratization, relying on strong alliances and organizations in areas which are relevant from the point of view of security (i.e. political, military and economic) as well as the impact of popular culture and globalization. Moreover, the latter influences offer both an opportunity and a challenge with respect to the task of supporting and reinforcing Polish security. There is strong tendency among the Polish society to consider these factors threats and compare them to the efforts aimed at eradicating Poles' national identity, which had been made in the bygone days; such interpretation, however, depreciates the Polish patriotic potential. The modern-day model of patriotism should be based upon historic consciousness, perceiving the developments and accomplishments of Poles as a source of pride; however, it should also be founded on a critical analysis of the deeds and omissions which resulted in many a failure and defeat of the past.

National identity coupled with openness (stemming from the geopolitical position of Poland), seizing the integration opportunities within the great European family (the European Union) and reinforcing the national substance in the fields of culture, education and knowledge should increasingly be the prominent hallmarks of modern patriotism. Apart from traditional tools such as the protection of historic monuments, national memorials, etc., it is also important to effectively and skilfully reach out to the recipients (and especially to the young generation) by using adequate forms of expression.

All this should be supported by adequate financial means and efficient promotional activities both at home and abroad. The broadly-defined Polish culture, the contribution it makes to the European heritage and its proper promotion via modern media should not only imbue the Polish society with a feeling of pride, but also generate the interest therein other societies and nations. Such programme should be developed in an innovative manner.

Education-for-security institutions. The concept of improving the education-for-security subsystem should be directed at altering the structure, organization and programme of the process of education and teaching in this field. It is therefore necessary to adopt a government programme dedicated to education for security and thus increase the efficiency of this dimension of societal education (elaboration of the content and form of this branch of education; integration of the activities pursued by the central and local government administration and by public administration institutions and non-government organizations in this regard).

Efforts must also be made to develop the organization of didactic components. A rational solution would be to establish a supra-ministerial public educational institution – the earlier mentioned Academy of National Security – which would be tasked with the education and skill development in the field of integrated security, including its multi-sectoral aspects. The work of the Academy would encompass the coordination of common, supra-ministerial, specialized operations run for the purposes of providing training for both uniformed and non-uniformed employees of state administration, representatives of parliament as well as employees of local government administration, NGO activists and civilian domestic and international students within the framework of the publicly available educational programme.

Insofar as the streamlining of the education-for-security programme is concerned, the role of NGOs should not be ignored. It is necessary to encourage and intensify cooperation between these entities and the central and local government institutions, for this will allow the sector in question to participate, to a greater extent, in the pursuit of societal objectives related to security – both on individual, societal and national levels.

Ostrów Wielkopolski, 10 January, 2010. Demonstration of rescue operations performed as a part of the Great Orchestra of Christmas Charity (WOŚP) fund-raising event.
Photo: Tomasz Wojtasik/PAP

The diversity of the entities engaged in spreading the education for security makes it necessary to establish a single institution to deal with coordination of the scope of activities and cooperation between such entities. The institution could, for example, take the form of a unit (department, bureau, division) tasked with education for security, operating within the proposed Government Centre for National Security which would itself be set up on the basis of the current Government Centre for Security. The unit would comprise representatives of all ministries which participate in the education-for-security programme, including, first and foremost, the Ministry of Science and Higher Education, the Ministry of National Education, the Ministry of National Defence and the Ministry of the Internal Affairs. The unit would elaborate the general objectives and tasks of education for security analyze the condition of the educational sector and the rules of the system operation, etc. Such a solution would allow the education-for-security programme to operate on an ongoing, universal basis.

Scientific research and development institutions in the sphere of security. Taking into account the evaluation of the current status of scientific research and development operations in the field of security and national defence, a number of areas may be identified that are in need of improvement. There is also an urgent need to guarantee – within the scope of funds earmarked for science – the availability of adequate financial resources for the purposes of scientific research and development in the field of national security.

It is legitimate to retain, within the existing structure of basic research financed by the National Science Centre, a separate thematic panel encompassing the security and defence theory.

It is also essential to work out new solutions regarding the inclusion of applied research "for the benefit of state security and defence", financed by the National Centre for Research and Development, within a single integrated area – national security, comprising defence, protection, societal and economic dimensions.

Extending the scope of issues covered by scientific research and development makes it necessary to establish a body responsible for the coordinated, supra-ministerial policy in this regard. Such body could take the form of a unit included in the structures of the proposed Government Centre for National Security.

Also relevant in this context is the proposal on establishing a supra-ministerial educational institution (an Academy of National Security), the scientific potential of which could encompass the issues of integrated national security within a system covering both basic research and R&D activities.

It is also needed to intensify the cooperation of the scientific community with the industry and to direct their substantive and financial efforts towards projects which would meet the expectations of two or more institutions (ministries) responsible for security.

System for counteracting demographic menaces. Re-examining the heretofore assumptions of pro-family policies and working out mechanisms facilitating and promoting the raising of children would be highly desirable. Among these mechanisms, the following deserve to be mentioned: extension of the maternity leave, financial support (including through a system of tax deduction for multiple–children families), labour market incentives for parents, support for apartment buyers (e.g. in the form of tax deductions, less stringent requirements with regard to loans, reinstatement of support schemes such as "The Family on Its Own" ("*Rodzina na swoim*"), greater availability of nursery and kindergarten care as well as efforts aimed at ensuring appropriate health care level.

In the struggle against unfavourable demographic tendencies it is important to halt or restrict the process of economic migration among Polish citizens. It is therefore of crucial importance that conditions be established which will allow citizens to develop their career domestically, e.g. by enhancing the attractiveness of job opportunities aimed at young and well-educated people, allowing them to fulfil their professional ambitions. Additionally, one of the components of state policy should be to actively encourage those of Polish citizens work abroad to return to Poland.

One of the tools of minimizing the adverse consequences of the demographic decline, but exclusively insofar as to make up for insufficient human resources (not only on the labour market) should be migration policy. If well-educated foreigners consider Poland a place attractive enough to move into and take up employment there, it may be possible to reverse the current tendency. An important issue is to establish an efficient system for integrating migrants with local communitieswith the aim ofavoiding xenophobia, social unrest and resistance like the ones recently seen in some EU states. If one takes into account the statistics which indicate that the largest proportion of migrants originates from Eastern Europe and Asia, then it is those regions at which Poland should aim its activities to promote its labour market. It is also advisable to reinforce the immigration services in order to prevent illegal immigration.

One cannot forget about the Polish diaspora abroad either; encouraging members of the diaspora to return to Poland may be one of the ways of coping with the demographic threats which Poland now faces.

An institution coordinating efforts aiming at diminishing the scope of demographic threats could be the Government Demographic Council. Its powers, however, would need to be extended, for example by conferring statutory competences upon the Council, since its current status positions it solely in the role of a consultative body supporting the Prime Minister. It is then worth tapping into the potential of the Council as it assembles numerous specialists and experts; their knowledge and experience would be used for the purposes of elaborating the concept, providing direction and supervising the actions taken by competent entities.

Health service in the security system. Preparation of the health service for uninterrupted and efficient operations at times of crisis and war should concentrate on improving the existing organizational and planning as well as procedural solutions, particularly at the executive and cooperative levels. Also development of the existing capabilities of the health service should be ensured, taking into account an increase in the potential and capacity to respond to threats which may disrupt the functioning of health care facilities and destabilize the whole system (through a mass influx of patients, insufficiency of available medical staff or deficits in drugs or blood reserves).

It is essential to define clear principles of cooperation and joint action between the Ministry of Health and the Ministry of National Defence with respect to the state security needs, including cooperation in the event of a crisis. There is also a need to elaborate unified and coherent rules pertaining to the adjustment (including financing) of health care institutions with the aim of providing health care to uniformed services.

In order to ensure the security of the state in terms of health care in the event of a threat to state security or in wartime, it is necessary to increase the number of available hospital beds so that there are at least 75 hospital beds available for every 10 000 residents, with 50 per cent of these beds being operating beds, including beds intended to cater for the needs of the Polish Armed Forces, the armed forces of Poland's allies, the authorities and organizational units reporting to the minister of the internal affairs as well as the Internal Security Agency. In the course of planning an increase in the number of hospital beds, attention must be paid to a possible increase in the number of beds in the existing general and specialist hospitals, in health care centres, residential care facilities, sanatoriums and health resorts. In order to attain this objective, it would be advisable to have the management of such institutions submit full information on the possibility of increasing the number of beds, using administrative or social facilities as care units as well as to specify the requirements in this regard. Following an analysis of the dangers, requirements and possibilities, the managers of the aforementioned institutions should take action to implement the relevant measures.

It is necessary to expedite a broader utilization of IT systems based on the examination and analysis of disease symptoms, detecting possible use of biological weapons, using real-time monitoring of behaviours and exercising a support function in the decision-making process. There is also a need to develop an effective system for the detection of smuggling and illegal transfer of biological agents across the borders.

There is a case for reinforcement of military biological monitoring teams. It is also necessary to create such conditions which will allow, in the event of a crisis, the full utilization of the national potential in terms of diagnostic operations, *inter alia*, through the improvement of identification capabilities of laboratory facilities as well as the maintenance of their level of scientific expertise by ensuring the participation of their personnel in both domestic and international exercises. The location of laboratories which are being prepared for rapid diagnostic operations should correspond to the needs

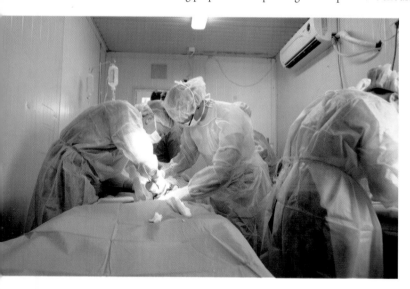

Afghanistan, Ghazni province, 28 December, 2012. Surgery conducted by a team of Polish, Ukrainian and American physicians.
Photo: Waldemar Młynarczyk/Combat Camera Reporter Team of the Armed Forces Operational Command

BIOSAFE 2008 –
international exercises
in biological monitoring,
decontamination and
medical evacuation
procedures.
Photo: Epidemiological
Response Centre of the Polish
Armed Forces (CRESZ)
Archive

The Epidemiological
Response Centre of the
Polish Armed Forces
during the Polish-
American medical rescue
exercises.
Photo: Epidemiological
Response Centre of the Polish
Armed Forces (CRESZ)
Archive

of large urban agglomerations. There is also a need to solve the problem of financing the deposit of reagents used for diagnostic purposes.

It is also necessary to prepare hospital facilities for handling mass casualty events, by performing, *inter alia*, the following actions: establishing hospital crisis management teams, preparing response plans in the event of attacks with weapons of mass destruction, organizing regular training and exercises, and determining the rules of financing such efforts. In addition, there is a need for a systematic rise of the level of knowledge pertaining to biological threats at various levels of public administration as well as among the health service personnel and the personnel of other services which carry out crisis management tasks.

Zakopane, 4 December, 2009. Training dedicated to avalanche safety, organized by TOPR (Tatra Volunteer Search and Rescue) mountain rescuers for representatives of the media.
Photo: Grzegorz Momot/PAP

The media in the national security system. The execution of tasks by individual subsystems (the control subsystem, the operational subsystem and the support subsystem) must take into account the influence of mass media. They are an essential tool for public flow of information. For that reason, the overall concept of making improvements in this regard should focus on developing and deepening cooperation between the representatives of state institutions and the media which are engaged in the protection of national security. It is important that cooperation between the administration and the media not exacerbate the negative consequences of actual or potential threats. Cooperation in this field should revolve around the supply of substantive knowledge on how to behave and where to turn for help should the need arise.

Among the objectives which compose the mission to be fulfilled by the media (and especially the public media), attention must be also paid to issues of national security in the course of the National Broadcasting Council's preparation for the subsequent regulatory strategy. The additional objective should take into account an increased of media participation in raising public awareness with regard to national security, the types of threats which may occur and the methods of preventing them. Of particular importance is the identification of threats to national security as well as the presentation of activities through which ordinary citizens may contribute to an improvement in the level of national security.

There are also proposals for an extension of the university journalist education curriculum through the inclusion of a subject which demonstrates the role of the media within the national security system. Attention must be paid to an appropriate technical training of services which establish contacts with the media so that the information provided by such services is clear and reliable and does not violate the principles relating to security and official secrets.

* * *

The key preparatory objective for the societal subsystems is to streamline the principles, procedures and capabilities in the field of cooperation between the components of the said subsystems and the entities responsible for the protection and security of the state in peacetime, at the time of crisis and in wartime.

The economic subsystems

Financial security institutions. The development and improvement of the capabilities of institutions responsible for the financial security of the Republic of Poland takes on a particular importance at the time of the worldwide financial crisis. In this regard, the issue which takes centre stage is the need for implementation of the macro-prudential supervision of the financial system in order to ensure a better protection of the financial security of the state, including the calling into being of an institution responsible for the restructuring and organized liquidation of banks as well as the inclusion of a representative of the Bank Guarantee Fund in the composition of the Committee for Financial Stability.

It is legitimate to set up a coordinating mechanism for the activities between the institutions responsible for the financial stability and security of the state and the appropriate state protection services, such as the Internal Security Agency or the Central Anti-Corruption Bureau, which would allow to prevent threats in a complementary manner and counter the emergence of mechanisms which border on the illegal from the point of view of criminal provisions relating to financial issues as well as the exploitation of legal loopholes.

It is also necessary to reinforce the fiscal rules and procedures through the introduction of a rule which restricts expenditure increments and budget deficit within the business cycle. It should also make it possible for balance-sheet losses which may occur as a result of the appreciation of the Polish zloty towards foreign currencies held by the National Bank of Poland, to be covered with the profits gained in subsequent years.

It is also important to reinforce the stability of the banking system in Poland, primarily through the continuing growth of the capital base of banks as well as through the diversification of their sources of financing and the lessening of the share of loans, especially in foreign currencies, which are offered by these banks. It is also desirable to expand the control powers of the Polish Financial Supervision Authority so that they cover all financial institutions as well as to embolden the activeness of and intensify steps by the judiciary against entities the actions of which pose a danger to investors or the economy as such.

Energy security entities. The concept of preparing the energy security entities for the efficient performance of their tasks should encompass both regulatory, organizational and investment (financial) steps.

The Polish Energy Policy until 2030 needs to be extended and supplemented with the missing analyses pertaining to the exploitation of shale gas, including the intensification of inter-ministerial coordination and communication within the energy security policy. There are also postulates regarding the preparation of a long-term strategy pertaining to the rules governing the exploitation of geological resources.

Measures need to be adopted which will ensure that the State Treasury retains control over those energy companies which are of key importance from the point of view of state security. Equally important is obligate the province authorities to draw up applicable energy security strategies at the province level which will correspond with the nationwide strategy in this regard, as well as to include in the crisis management plan measures aimed at responding to system-wide malfunctions in the given province.

There is a need to extend the powers of the Geological Service to include the supervision and control of geological resources of the state as well as to enlarge the scope of supervision and control of processes related to the allocation of licences for the exploitation of Polish raw material resources.

Other desirable developments include: the diversification of energy resources supply and the diversification of production structures as well as the build-up of the capacity of liquid fuel storage facilities.

Furthermore, over the next few years, the intensive modernization and development of energy production facilities and transmission networks are to continue in order to enhance the reliability of power supply and the usage of electricity reserves.

Critical infrastructure security institutions. The fundamental objectives of the activities pursued with regard to the protection of critical infrastructure facilities should be as follows:

- Increasing the security level of the critical infrastructure by increasing its resilience (i.e. reducing vulnerability) to threats;
- Integrating (or at least increasing the interoperability and complementarity) with other security programmes (systems), e.g. those operated under the provisions of the Telecommunications Act;
- Integrating the state's critical infrastructure protection systems; and
- Designating a single entity responsible for the planning and programming issues in the field of the critical state infrastructure protection.

The following activities are also recommended:

- Ensuring more favourable conditions for enterprises willing to invest in security measures;
- Introducing a clear division between items of the critical infrastructure at central and regional levels;
- Introducing uniform regulations pertaining to the protection of the critical state infrastructure, i.e. all such regulations should be drawn up in a single piece of legislation;
- Unifying the approach to the issues related to critical infrastructure security (facilities, equipment and areas).

The criteria for qualifying individual items of the critical infrastructure in Poland need to be verified, taking into account the differentiation of the types and levels of such infrastructure as provided for in the EU directives, ensuring the appropriate levels of national defence and security as well as the meeting the needs of the safe functioning of the provinces (the option of designating critical infrastructure at the level of individual districts and large cities may also be considered). One of the foundations of such verification should be the fact that the infrastructure in question has been included in the Defence Response Plan, the Economy Mobilization Plan as well as the Crisis Management Plan at national, province or other level, etc.

Strategic reserves. In accordance with the provisions of Polish law, strategic reserves are created, *inter alia*, in the event of necessity to defend the territory of the state, possible threats to state security, health and public order, natural disasters, efforts to mitigate interruptions in the continuity of supplies necessary to ensure the functioning of the economy and to satisfy the basic needs of citizens as well as to protect the life and health of citizens. The scope of strategic reserves as well as the types of products to be included are determined in the government strategic reserve programme, drawn up by the minister of the economy in cooperation, *inter alia*, with the minister of national defence, the minister of the internal affairs, the minister of health and the minister of transportation, construction and maritime economy.

At present, the solutions applied to the strategic reserve subsystem take into account the changes with respect to threats to state security as well as to the international and macroeconomic environment. The simplification of the reserve system and the unification of procedures have a direct bearing upon expediting the decision-making process as well as improving the efficiency of activities related to the maintenance of the reserves. The critical challenge will be to adopt a government programme for strategic reserves by the Council of Ministers and ensure its financing from the state budget at a level enabling the pursuit of objectives planned in a 5-year perspective.

Environmental protection system. Insofar as the protection of the natural environment is concerned, there is a need for decisive action. Of particular importance is to reinforce the supervision of the installations the failure of which may pose a substantial danger to the environment (the Inspectorate for Environmental Protection) through the extension of the register of monitored facilities. Of similar importance are efforts aimed at increasing the efficiency of the international system for the notification of failures. The recommended course of action would be to draw up a long-term strategy for the exploitation of the national hydrological (water) resources.

There is a need to develop health risk analysis regulations for the procedures relating to: the approval for implementation of investment projects; improvement of the functioning of the state environmental and sanitation monitoring system by providing the appropriate control services with modern equipment and alerting networks; and, finally, joint activities of the Chief Sanitary Inspectorate and the Inspectorate for Environmental Protection in order to improve the quality of drinking water and the joint conducting of educational and training campaigns for the services operating at industrial facilities and for public administration employees, concerning the prevention of technical failures and contamination of the environment. It is also necessary to provide the Fire Service with additional chemical and environmental rescue equipment and to draw up plans regarding the management of risks related to failures.

Responding to industrial accidents requires increasing the societal awareness regarding the threats related to the production, transportation and use of hazardous materials as well as the preparation, in cooperation with local communities, of emergency response plans. This will apply in particular to advance warnings pertaining to nuclear incidents.

Ensuring environmental safety also requires an intensive international cooperation regarding both the consolidation of legal foundations and the development of practical cooperation mechanisms in the event of a danger, including rapid information exchange and cooperation in mutual aid and R&D operations aimed at preventing possible threats. In this context, the activities pursued by Poland should encompass the support for international organizations and agreements pertaining to the global climate policy respecting the development level and structure of the national economies of participating states.

In sum, the important preparatory objective for economic subsystems is to work out adequate strategies and programmes concerning the preparation (i.e. maintenance and improvement) of state economic entities for operations in situations of danger, including undertaking the tasks of operational support for the individual components of the national security system.

* * *

This chapter has presented a model of state structures pursuing state security objectives as well as relations between these structures within the framework of the option of sustainable integration of the national security system. The option provides for such an organization of the national security system which would ensure its internal consistency, balance and integrative nature, thus allowing to combine individual entities and relations between them into a legally and functionally harmonized national security system.

The need now arises to introduce changes into the existing legal regulations at two levels: **the administrative level**, which remains within the competence of individual authorities and institutions, as well as **the legislative level**, relating to system-wide solutions the responsibility for which rests upon parliament. These transformations, involving both structural and institutional changes, should be aimed at establishing a network-based security structure, improving the effectiveness of adopted measures, introducing more economical solutions as well as enhancing the qualitative development of the system. In order to achieve these objectives, it is first and foremost necessary for decision makers to demonstrate the political will and abandon the sectoral thinking approach.

In the event of amending the Constitution, it would be advisable to consider an institution of the changes proposed in this chapter with regard to national security.

It is impossible to state in an arbitrary fashion what should be the method and order of creating an internally consistent legal structure of the national security system. There are a number of autonomous regulations which may be developed, amended and improved without having a bearing upon the remaining legal provisions governing the national security system. However, most pieces of legislation remain functionally linked to one another – from the provisions relating to security in the strict meaning of the word, through provisions which support the attainment of national security objectives and the regulations pertaining to the "hard", physical security of the state and right up to the regulations which concern the broad area of "soft", local and individual security. A recommendable course of action would be to start with the establishment of formal and legal conditions for the **control of national security** in the form of an act regulating this issue.

In a consequence, a reference point for all the remaining special regulations pertaining to other areas within the security system and its functions should be established. This will allow to eliminate the most glaring drawbacks of the current system, making it possible to limit the duplication of tasks and competences of the state authorities, better concretize the responsibilities of officers, simplify the organizational structures within central institutions and systemize the strategic planning functions as well as extend such planning processes to all entities composing the national security system.

At the executive decision-taking level, in order to improve the functionality and internal consistency of the entire system, it is advisable to establish a **Council of Ministers Committee for National Security** as well as to create an administrative structure of this Committee in the form of a Government Centre for National Security, based on the existing Government Centre for Security.

Poland is in need of an integrated, modern and effective national security system; today the system's individual components do not always operate in an optimal manner. The improvement of this system will require efforts by practically all state institutions and authorities in the coming years.

CONCLUSION

The comprehensive approach to national security as presented in this White Book is determined by the nature and pace of change in both the internal and external security environments of the Republic of Poland in the coming years. The authors of this document realize that the presented assessment of the future developments with respect to the security environment is characterized with a relatively high degree of uncertainty, which is typical for any long-term forecasting. In order to mitigate this precariousness, we have presented several variants with respect to the development scenarios in this environment. This has allowed us to design a number of options for strategic action and preparation of the State Bookin the field of security in the coming years.

The present White Book is the first attempt made in Poland to consider the questions of security in a comprehensive manner. Apart from the issues relating to "hard" security encompassing the defence and protection of the state, particular emphasis is placed on new fields, sectors (both societal and economic) and trans-sectoral security areas which have emerged in recent years and which present both challenges for and threats to the security of our state. The issues in question relate to financial, energy, demographic, cybernetic, climatic and environmental security now and in future.

As shown by the analyses, Poland faces the need to tackle a variety of issues of different scale. The current international environment is generally favourable for Poland and its interests, hence the opportunity for a rational and methodical development and conduct of our security policy. This White Book lays substantive foundations for such endeavours. It is also possible to systematically enrich and improve the adopted assumptions, plans and programmes and to verify the traditional approaches – as well to plant new ones – in the course of subsequent periodical strategic reviews, as well as to reinforce the Polish security potential and the standing of our country on the international scene. We should take full advantage of these favourable opportunities in order to be adequately prepared for any "foul weather" in the field of security (which cannot and should not be ruled out on an *a priori* basis).

Si vis pacem, para pacem (if you want peace, prepare for peace) – this paraphrased Roman maxim should guide our efforts aimed at increasing the level of security, the scope of which extends far beyond the traditional military axiom. The present White Book is therefore addressed to state authorities and institutions, civic organizations as well as to the citizens themselves. It should form part of the efforts made within the education–for–security programme as well as form the basis for a debate on this issue, which should be as broad as possible. Security ought not any longer to remain limited to the obligations of the state – it is now also the commitment and responsibility of all citizens.

The publication of the first ever Polish White Book on National Security elevates the process of shaping the Polish strategic culture to a qualitatively new level. The authors hope that its publication will increase the dynamics of the broad debate among citizens concerning Polish national security in the 21st century. The success of this endeavour will be complete if, as a result, reforms are implemented which to reinforce the synergies within the national security system through the integration of the national security control system, the professionalization of operational subsystems (the defence subsystem and the protection subsystems) as well as the preparation of support subsystems (both societal and economic) on a broadest possible scale.

Since we would also like the present White Book to contribute to the ongoing international debate on security issues, especially with the participation of our NATO allies and EU partners, as well as to a broader clarification of the core values which underlie the tenets and contents of the Polish security policy among other actors of international relations, the present document has hereby been published in the English language.

List of tables and figures

List of tables:

Table 1.   World corruption statistics – Poland's ranking
            http://www.transparency.org/cpi2012/results   57

Table 2.   Proceedings initiated, criminal offences established, and crime detection rate in years 2000-2012
            http://statystyka.policja.pl/portal/st/842/47682/Postepowania_wszczete_przestepstwa_
            stwierdzone_i_wykrywalnosc_w_latach_19992011.html   62

Table 3.   Answer to the question: What, and to what extent, may currently and in the near feature constitute
            a real threat to the security of the Republic of Poland?   78

Table 4.   Hierarchy of perceived impact on security.   79

Table 5.   The catalogue of national interests and strategic objectives.   104

List of figures:

Figure 1.   The structure of national security adopted for the purposes of the NSSR.   19

Figure 2.   Strategic cycle of analyses and studies in the field of security   20

Figure 3.   The leading concept of the NSSR   21

Figure 4.   Interactions (feedbacks) among problem area teams during the NSSR.   22

Figure 5.   Historical geo-strategic location of Poland on the East-West line   35

Figure 6.   The universal national security system model   36

Figure 7.   Number of staff and internal structure of the Polish Armed Forces (2012)
             http://www.mon.gov.pl/pliki/File/budzet/budzet_mon2012.pdf   44

Figure 8.   Primary modernization programmes of the Polish Armed Forces
             http://www.mon.gov.pl/pliki/File/budzet/budzet_mon2012.pdf   46

Figure 9.   The Polish defence budget for year 2012 (in millions PLN).   47

Figure 10.   The participation of the Polish military contingents in security operations (since Poland's entry into NATO in
             1999)   50

Figure 11.   Secret services and who they report to   55

Figure 12.   The structure of the General Police Headquarters
             http://www.policja.pl/portal/inf/922/81505/   59

Figure 13.   Degree of personal perception of being under threat from criminal activity
http://www.cbos.pl/SPISKOM.POL/2012/K_062_12.PDF 62

Figure 14.   Tasks and obligations of participants in the event of a crisis situation – terrorist threats
http://rcb.gov.pl/wp-content/uploads/2012/03/KPZK.pdf 65

Figure 15.   The composition of the Government Crisis Management Team 68

Figure 16.   The Schengen system countries in the EU
http://ec.europa.eu/dgs/home-affairs/what-we-do/policies/borders-and-visas/schengen/
index_en.htm#resp_map 69

Figure 17.   Population by gender and age for year 2011 (in thousands, as of 31 December 2011)
http://www.stat.gov.pl/gus/5840_rocznik_demograficzny_plk_html.htm. 75

Figure 18.   Number of births in Poland in 2011 (in thousands, as of 31 December 2011) and in previous years
http://www.stat.gov.pl/cps/rde/xbcr/gus/rs_rocznik_demograficzny_2012.pdf 76

Figure 19.   Answer to the question: Do you think that Poland is a safe country to live in? 77

Figure 20.   Answer to the question: Do you think that Poland is a safe country to live in?
(years 1987-2011). 77

Figure 21.   Answer to the question: In your opinion, what does the security of the country depend on?
Please state the significance for state security of each of the issues mentioned. 80

Figure 22.   Answer to the question: In your opinion, are there currently any threats to the independce of
the Republic of Poland?. 81

Figure 23.   Answer to the question: What is the primary nature of the current threats to the independence
and sovereignty of the Republic of Poland? 82

Figure 24.   Answer to the question: Is the Republic of Poland sufficienty (or insufficiently) prepared to take action
in the event of: 83

Figure 25.   The gross domestic product per capita in selected EU member states and the USA (EU 27=100)
http://epp.eurostat.ec.europa.eu/tgm/table.do?tab=table&init=1&plugin=1&language=
en&pcode=tec00114 89

Figure 26.   Selected macroeconomic indicators for the Republic of Poland in years 2000–2011 (expressed in percentages)
http://www.stat.gov.pl/gus/5840_677_PLK_HTML.htm,
http://www.nbp.pl/home.aspx?f=/dzienne/stopy_archiwum.htm,
http://www.stat.gov.pl/gus/5840_1634_PLK_HTML.htm,
http://www.stat.gov.pl/gus/5840_2844_PLK_HTML.htm,
http://www.stat.gov.pl/gus/5840_2144_PLK_WAI.htm. 90

Figure 27.   The import and export of goods in Poland (in millions EUR) 91

Figure 28. State public debt in years 2005 –2012 (nominal value in billions PLN and expressed as a per centage in relation to the GDP)
http://www.mf.gov.pl/documents/766655/61d2ef0b-ed67-43e6-9e3e-ce7263f5b5af. 93

Figure 29. Areas with long-term potential for the presence of natural gas and crude oil in lower Palaeozoic shale formations (according to P. Poprawa)
http://www.pgi.gov.pl/pl/instytut-geologiczny-surowce-mineralne/2705-nowe-perspektywy-gaz-lupkowy-i-gaz-zamkniety.html 98

Figure 30. Number of terrorist attacks and arrested persons suspected of terrorism in Europe in years 2007-2011
https://www.europol.europa.eu/sites/default/files/publications/europoltsat.pdf. 116

Figure 31. Poland's membership in international organizations and institutions – as of 1 January 2013. 122

Figure 32. Population and demographic forecasts for selected EU states in years 1990 – 2060 (in millions)
http://epp.eurostat.ec.europa.eu/cache/ITY_OFFPUB/KS-CD-10-220/EN/KS-CD-10-220-EN.pdf. 135

Figure 33. Population forecast for years 2010-2035 (in millions)
http://demografia.stat.gov.pl/bazademografia/Prognoza.aspx 135

Figure 34. Degree of innovativeness of selected countries – as of 2012 (on a 0-100 point scale)
http://www.globalinnovationindex.org/gii/main/fullreport/index.html 137

Figure 35. Polish direct investments abroad in years 2002-2011 (in millions EUR)
http://www.nbp.pl/home.aspx?f=/publikacje/pib/pib.html. 140

Figure 36. Universal control system model. 195

Figure 37. Proposed main (central) national security control system. 196

Figure 38. Proposed territorial security control system (province, district, commune) 198

Figure 39. System of national security control positions 200

Figure 40. Technical modernization priorities for the Polish Armed Forces. 205

APPENDICES

Appendix 1

Summary of the main recommendations of the National Security Strategic Review

Operational recommendations

1. Starting point for the identification of national interests and strategic objectives – constitutional interests.
2. Action planning – according to an evolutionary scenario.
3. Main option for the operational strategy – the sustainable internationalization and autonomy of Polish national security.
4. Primary components of strategic planning: 2013 – the National Security Strategy, the Political and Strategic Defence Directive of the Republic of Poland (or an extended Political and Strategic Directive of National Security of the Republic of Poland); 2014 – amended plans for the deployment of the Polish Armed Forces and other operational plans; 2015 – another National Security Strategic Review.

Preparatory recommendations

Actions performed at the legislative level – adoption (or amendment) of the following acts:

1. Act on national security control – objective: to specify the role of state authorities within the integrated national security system in peacetime, in the event of a danger and during armed conflicts, including also at times when extraordinary measures are applied, as well as to ensure the control and coordination functions on a supra-ministerial level.
2. Act on martial law, the competences of the Commander-in-Chief of the Armed Forces and the principles governing his subordination to the constitutional authorities of the Republic of Poland – objective: to specify the role and competences of the Commander-in-Chief of the Armed Forces.
3. Act on emergency rescue and the protection of the population – objective: to ensure a procedural synergy of societal activities and the competent state institutions.
4. Act on secret services – objective: to consolidate the secret services, determine a common code of conduct, to systemize their competences and to ensure the interoperability of the secret services; to establish a centre for the integration of special information.
5. Act on operational activities – objective: to provide a definition of procedures and competences in the application of operational and surveillance techniques.
6. Act on the office of the Minister of National Defence – objective: to reform the Polish Armed Forces command and control system.
7. Act on the establishment of a consolidated military educational facility and a supra-ministerial national security educational facility (Academy of National Security) – objective: to consolidate the higher military educational system.

Actions performed at the government decision-making level:

1. Establishing a Council of Ministers Committee for National Security (a Government Committee for National Security) along with a Government Centre for National Security – based upon the existing Government Centre for Security, an entity performing conceptual and coordinating tasks and providing services to the Committee.
2. Maintaining, in a long-term perspective, a defence budget at the level of 1.95 per cent of the previous year's GDP.
3. The organizational and dislocational consolidation and professionalization of the Polish Armed Forces, including the consistent implementation of modernization priorities (air defence, including missile defence; land forces' mobility, with emphasis on helicopter component; computerized combat and support systems).
4. Ensuring widespread preparation of the state structures and citizens in the field of security, including the adoption of a programme for education, dissemination of knowledge and scientific research pertaining to national security.

Appendix 2

List of main conceptual categories

Basic category

Security – the theory and practice of ensuring the possibility of survival (existence) and the realization of an entity's own interests, including, in particular, by taking advantage of opportunities (favourable circumstances), facing challenges, reducing risks and counteracting (preventing and opposing) all kinds of threats to the given entity and its interests. Contemporary security is integrated (comprehensive, multidimensional) in nature and may – depending on the adopted criteria – be subdivided into various types, fields, sectors, divisions and areas:

a) depending on the type of entity involved, the following types of security may be distinguished: individual (personal) security, group security, national security (including state and territorial security: at the province, district and commune level), international security (regional and global), including interstate security (alliances and coalition arrangements) and transnational security;

b) depending on the subject (content) of security, it is possible to distinguish as many types, fields, sectors, divisions, areas etc. as many potential spheres of activity of the given entity are possible (security issues arise in every sphere of activity):

   i. Within the framework of integrated national security of the Republic of Poland (state security) it is possible to distinguish two constitutional areas thereof: internal and external security, as well as four primary fields of security: defence (national defence, i.e. the military security of a state), protection (civilian, non-military security) as well as societal and economic security (one may, in fact, also speak of "socio-economic security", including societal and economic support of security efforts).

   ii. Within the above fields, one may distinguish – in accordance with the Polish state activity structure, encompassing a number of departments of public administration – national security sectors such as: diplomacy for security, military issues, intelligence and counterintelligence, public security, emergency rescue, societal security (including, *inter alia*, the protection of heritage, education for security, the media in the security system), economic security (including, *inter alia*, energy, financial and infrastructural security);

   iii. Due to the very nature of integrated security there are also security areas which span multiple sectors or fields, such as cyber-security.

Definition subcategories:

Security entity – every consciously existing and intentionally operating entity (whether individual or collective) considered from the point of view of the security thereof. With respect to security analyzed from a political perspective, the main types of security entities are states (nations organized in the form of states), organizational entities of states (e.g. states, federated states, provinces, local government units) as well as international organizations (interstate organizations as well as the increasingly important non-state structures such as multinational corporations or terrorist and criminal organizations).

Interests of a security entity – the aggregated expectations of an entity towards its environment, derived from and shaped by its identity, values, historical heritage, traditions, current needs and future aspirations and goals. One may distinguish between critical interests (pertaining to the continuing existence of the given entity) and desired interests (related to the quality of such existence).

Security environment – the internal and external, military and non-military (civilian) security conditions (the conditions for the realization of the interests of the given entity in the field of security and the attainment of the goals designated by such entity in this regard), characterized by using four basic categories, i.e.: opportunities, challenges, risks and threats.

Security opportunities – circumstances which arise independently of the will of the given entity (phenomena and processes occurring within the security environment) which are favourable to the realization of interests and the attainment of objectives of the entity in question in the field of security.

Security challenges – problematic situations giving rise to decision-making dilemmas faced by the given entity when adopting its course of action with regard to security issues. If security challenges are not properly addressed or responded to, they may, in effect, transform into actual security threats.

Security risks – risks of occurrence of consequences of the actions of the given entity within the sphere of security which are unfavourable to the entity in question.

Security threats – direct or indirect destructive influences affecting the given entity. It is the most classic factor which appears within the security environment; threats can be divided into potential and real threats, subjective and objective threats, external and internal threats, military and non-military threats, threats related to crises and armed conflicts as well as intentional and accidental (fortuitous) threats.

Integrated security – a type of security which is established where links and interactions (both natural and intentionally established) exist between various security entities, types, fields, sectors, divisions, areas etc., resulting in a security becoming integrated into a single, internally consistent whole and ensuring the greater efficiency thereof through the resulting synergy effect.

National security (state security) – a type of security the subject (security entity) of which is the nation, organized in the form of a state.

Areas of national security (state security) – the spheres of activity of the state in the field of security, distinguished from the point of view of the implementation of four main groups of security tasks, i.e. defence (military security, national defence), protection (civilian, non-military safety; protection of the population, infrastructural resources and state structures) as well as societal and economic security, including the societal and economic support of security efforts). In organizational practice, fields of national security are in fact aggregated security sectors.

National security (state security) sectors – components of integrated national security, corresponding (subject to certain corrections where necessary) to the government administration departments operating under relevant statutory provisions or groups of such departments, aggregated due to the similarity of subject matter (proximity in terms of the scope of activities of entities responsible for individual departments).

Trans-sectoral (involving many entities) areas of national security (state security) – components of integrated national security, encompassing the issues typical of various security entities, fields and sectors (e.g. external or internal security or issues related to contemporary multinational, asymmetrical security processes and phenomena, such as, for example, information security (including cybernetic security), prevention of terrorism, non-proliferation of weapons of mass destruction, combating of organized crime). Such areas are frequently identified due to practical needs which are of an urgent nature at the given time and which raise qualitatively novel issues with respect to which there is no obvious recipient within the existing executive structure of the given entity.

External state security – a trans-sectoral area of security the contents of which (objectives, conditions, means and methods) pertain to the external environment of the state (i.e. its surroundings).

Internal state security – a trans-sectoral area of security the contents of which (objectives, conditions, means and methods) pertain to the internal environment of the state.

Information security (including cybernetic security) of the state – a trans-sectoral area of security the contents of which (objectives, conditions, means and methods) pertain to the information environment of the state (including cyberspace).

Miscellaneous conceptual categories:

Strategic objectives of the state in the field of security – operationalized national interests, i.e. the future conditions, phenomena and processes in the field of security (resulting from the disaggregation of individual national interests, made in the context of specific (both current and predicted) strategic security conditions as well as the needs and possibilities (the strategic potential of the state)) which are considered desirable from the point of view of the said national interests. Unlike national interests themselves, which are a relatively permanent category, strategic objectives pertain to specific conditions in the given historical period of existence of the given entity; the objectives in question are attained through the implementation of a security policy.

Strategic activities of the state in the field of security – military and non-military activities of the state and the basic components thereof, aimed at ensuring the possibility of realization of national interests and the attainment of strategic objectives in a dangerous environment.

National security control – the activities of the public authorities and administrative bodies, encompassing the determination of national interests and strategic objectives in the field of security, the preparation of plans of strategic actions leading to the attainment of such objectives, the programming and organization activities aimed at ensuring the adequate preparation of the state in the field of security as well as the coordination and supervision of the implementation of plans and programmes according to the needs which stem from the conditions prevailing within the security environment (opportunities, challenges, risks and threats).

Strategic preparations in the field of security – the activities of all state structures aimed at attaining and maintaining their capabilities which are necessary for the purposes of executing of tasks provided for under strategic action plans. In particular, such preparations encompass planning, budgetary, investment, training and similar activities.

Strategic self-identification – the diagnosis of one's own state as a security entity (the ascertainment of the existing foundations of national security), encompassing an analysis of national identity and the evaluation of the state's strategic potential in its relations with other entities as well as the determination, on the basis of the above, of national interests and strategic objectives in the field of security.

National security (state security) strategy – the concept of maintaining the security of a given state adopted by that state, containing, in particular, the specification of national interests and strategic objectives, the evaluation of future development of the strategic security environment and the rules and methods of attaining strategic objectives in the predicted conditions (the implementation of operational objectives) as well as of the preparation (maintenance and transformation) of a national security system (the implementation of preparatory objectives).

Operational national security (state security) strategy – a division (area) of national security (state security) strategy encompassing the rules and methods of attaining strategic objectives (implementation of operational strategic tasks in the field of national security) in the predicted security conditions (environment) as well as the determination of operational requirements with regard to the national security system.

Preparatory national security (state security) strategy – a division (area) of national security (state security) strategy encompassing the rules and methods pertaining to the preparation (maintenance and transformation) of a national security system (the implementation of preparatory strategic tasks in the field of national security) in accordance with the requirements stemming from the operational strategy.

Sectoral national security (state security) strategy – the concept, adopted by the given state, of executing by the given state sector (department of state administration or a group thereof) of the operational and preparatory strategic tasks in the field of security, entrusted to the given department or departments under the national security strategy. The sectoral strategy encompasses the designation of objectives, the evaluation of conditions, the determination of methods and the allocation of resources within the given sector for the purposes of pursuing objectives in the field of security.

State security strategic potential – human resources (both qualitative and quantitative) and material resources (both natural and man-made) and the level of organizing thereof into a state system, taking into account their positioning and relations with other entities.

National security (state security) system – the entirety of resources, means and forces (entities) earmarked by the state for the performance of tasks in the field of security, organized (into subsystems and components), maintained and prepared in a manner adequate to the purpose of performing such tasks. The system consists of a control system (subsystem) as well as a number of executive subsystems (systems), including operational subsystems (defence and protection subsystems) and support subsystems (societal and economic).

National security (state security) control system – the part of the national security system designed for the purposes of controlling the functioning thereof, encompassing public authorities and heads of organizational units which perform tasks related to national security (including the command authorities of the Polish Armed Forces), along with advisory bodies and administrative (staff) apparatus as well as operating procedures and infrastructure (control and management positions and centres, communication system).

Executive subsystems (including components) of the national security (state security) system – the means and forces earmarked for the performance of statutory tasks in the field of security which remain available to security control authorities; they can be subdivided into:
a) operational subsystems: the **defence subsystem** (the subsystem for state defence capabilities, national defence, military security); **protection subsystems** for the state and the population (civilian, non-military security);
b) support subsystems: **societal and economic.**

Operational requirements for the national security system – the requirements as to the directions for the preparation (maintenance and transformation, improvement and development) of individual subsystems and components of the national security system stemming from the tasks provided for under the operational strategy as well as the plans for the operational functioning of the state and the individual institutions thereof in the field of security.

Appendix 3

List of basic legal acts pertaining to national security

1) The Constitution of the Republic of Poland dated April 2, 1997 (Dz. U. [the Journal of Laws] No. 78, item 483, as amended).

Defence subsystem:

1) Act dated 21 November 1967 on the Universal Duty to Defend the Republic of Poland (Dz.U. [the Journal of Laws] for year 2012, item 461, as amended);

2) Act dated 23 August 2001 on the Organization of Tasks for National Defence Carried out by Entrepreneurs (Dz.U. [the Journal of Laws] No. 122, item 1320, as amended);

3) Act dated 11 September 2003 on Military Service for Professional Soldiers (Dz.U. [the Journal of Laws] for year 2010, No. 90, item 593, as amended);

4) Act dated 10 December 1993 on Retirement Benefits of Professional Soldiers and their Families (Dz.U. [the Journal of Laws] for year 2004, No. 8, item 66, as amended);

5) Act dated 22 June 1995 on Accommodation of the Armed Forces of the Republic of Poland (Dz.U. [the Journal of Laws] for year 2010, No. 206, item 1367, as amended);

6) Act dated 9 October 2009 on Military Discipline (Dz.U. [the Journal of Laws] No. 190, item 1474, as amended);

7) Act dated 25 May 2001 on the Restructuring and Technical Modernization and the Financing of the Armed Forces of the Republic of Poland (Dz.U. [the Journal of Laws] for year 2009, No. 67, item 570, as amended);

8) Act dated 7 October 1999 on Supporting the Restructuring of the Industrial Defence Potential and the Technical Modernization of the Armed Forces of the Republic of Poland (Dz.U. [the Journal of Laws] No. 83, item 932, as amended);

9) Act dated 10 September 1999 on Certain Compensation Agreements Concluded in Connection with Delivery Contracts for the Purposes of Defence and State Security (Dz.U. [the Journal of Laws] No. 80, item 903, as amended);

10) Act dated 17 December 1998 on the Rules of Deployment or Stationing of the Armed Forces of the Republic of Poland Outside the Polish Territory (Dz.U. [the Journal of Laws] No. 162, item 1117, as amended);

11) Act dated 23 September 1999 on the Rules on the Stationing of Foreign Armed Forces within the Territory of the Republic of Poland and their Movements Through this Territory (Dz.U. [the Journal of Laws] No. 93, item 1117, as amended);

12) Act dated 17 November 2006 on Compliance Assessment System for Products for Defence Purposes (Dz.U. [the Journal of Laws] No. 235, item 1700, as amended);

13) Act dated 14 December 1995 on the Office of the Minister of National Defence (Dz.U. [the Journal of Laws] z 1996, No. 10, item 56, as amended);

14) Act dated 30 May 1996 on the Administration of Certain Components of the State Treasury Property and on the Military Property Agency (Dz.U. [the Journal of Laws] for year 2004, No. 163, item 1711, as amended);

15) Act dated 9 June 2006 on the Military Counterintelligence Service and the Military Intelligence Service (Dz.U. [the Journal of Laws] No. 104, item 709, as amended);

16) Act dated 24 August 2001 on the Military Gendarmerie and Military Safety Personnel (Dz.U. [the Journal of Laws] No. 123, item 1353, as amended);

17) Act dated 21 August 1997, – Law on the System of Military Courts (Dz.U. [the Journal of Laws] for year 2012, item 952, as amended);

18) Act dated 27 February 2003 on the Establishment of the Heroes of Westerplatte Naval Academy (Dz.U. [the Journal of Laws] No. 60, item 533, as amended);

19) Act dated 27 February 2003 on the Establishment of the Academy of National Defence (Dz.U. [the Journal of Laws] No. 56, item 496, as amended);

20) Act dated 27 February 2003 on the Establishment of the Jarosław Dąbrowski Military University of Technology (Dz.U. [the Journal of Laws] No. 60, item 534, as amended).

Protective subsystems:

1) Act dated 24 May 2002 on the Internal Security Agency and the Foreign Intelligence Agency (Dz.U. [the Journal of Laws] for year 2010, No. 29, item 154, as amended);

2) Act dated 9 June 2006 on the Central Anti-Corruption Bureau (Dz.U. [the Journal of Laws] for year 2012, item 621, as amended);

3) Act dated 6 April 1990 on the Police (Dz.U. [the Journal of Laws] for year 2011, No. 287, item 1687, as amended);

4) Act dated 12 October 1990 on Border Guard (Dz.U. [the Journal of Laws] for year 2011, No. 116, item 675, as amended);

5) Act dated 12 October 1990 on the Protection of National Borders (Dz.U. [the Journal of Laws] for year 2009, No. 12, item 67, as amended);

6) Act dated 16 March 2001 on the Government Protection Bureau (Dz.U. [the Journal of Laws] for year 2004, No. 163, item 1712, as amended);

7) Act dated 24 August 1991 on the State Fire Service (Dz.U. [the Journal of Laws] for year 2009, No. 12, item 68, as amended);

8) Act dated 9 April 2010 on the Prison Service (Dz.U. [the Journal of Laws] No. 79, item 523, as amended);

9) Act dated 18 February 1994 on Retirement Benefits of the Officers of the Police, the Internal Security Agency, the Intelligence Agency, the Military Counterintelligence Service, the Military Intelligence Service, the Central Anti-Corruption Bureau, the Border Guard, the Government Protection Bureau, the State Fire Service, the Prison Service and their families (Dz.U. [the Journal of Laws] for year 2004, No. 8, item 67, as amended);

10) Act dated 27 August 2009 on the Customs Service (Dz.U. [the Journal of Laws] No. 168, item 1323, as amended);

11) Act dated 21 July 2008 on Civil Service (Dz.U. [the Journal of Laws] No. 227, item 89, as amended);

12) Act dated 27 July 2001 on Foreign Service (Dz.U. [the Journal of Laws] No. 128, item 1403, as amended);

13) Act dated 4 September 1997 on Government Administration Departments (Dz.U. [the Journal of Laws] for year 2007, No. 65, item 437, as amended);

14) Act dated 23 January 2009 on the Province Governor and Government Administration in the Province (Dz.U. [the Journal of Laws] No. 31, item 206, as amended);

15) Act dated 29 August 2002 on Martial Law and the Competences of the Commander-in-Chief of the Armed Forces and the Rules of his Subordination to the Constitutional Authorities of the Republic of Poland (Dz.U. [the Journal of Laws] No. 156, item 1301, as amended);

16) Act dated 18 April 2002 on the State of Natural Disaster (Dz.U. [the Journal of Laws] No. 62, item 558, as amended);

17) Act dated 21 June 2002 on the state of Emergency (Dz.U. [the Journal of Laws] No. 113, item 985, as amended);

18) Act dated 26 April 2007 on Crisis Management (Dz.U. [the Journal of Laws] No. 89, item 590, as amended);

19) Act dated 24 August 1991 on Fire Prevention (Dz.U. [the Journal of Laws] No. 81, item 351, as amended);

20) Act dated 11 August 2001 on the Specific Rules for the Reconstruction, Renovation and Demolition of Buildings Destroyed or Damaged by Natural Disasters (Dz.U. [the Journal of Laws] No. 84, item 906, as amended);

21) Act dated 16 September 2011 on Specific Solutions Related to the Elimination of the Consequences of Flooding (Dz.U. [the Journal of Laws] No. 234, item 1385, as amended);

22) Act dated 8 July 2010 on Specific Rules for the Preparation for Implementing Investments in the Field of Flood Control Structures (Dz.U. [the Journal of Laws] No. 143, item 963, as amended);

23) Act dated 22 June 2001 on the Pursuit of Business Activities in the Field of Manufacture and Trading in Explosives, Weapons, Munitions and Products and Technologies Designed for Military or Police use (Dz.U. [the Journal of Laws] No. 67, item 679, as amended);

24) Act dated 21 May 1999 on Weapons and Munitions (Dz.U. [the Journal of Laws] for year 2012, item 576);

25) Act dated 16 July 2004, – Telecommunications Act (Dz.U. [the Journal of Laws] No. 171, item 1800, as amended);

26) Act dated 17 February 2005 on the Computerization of the Activities of Entities Performing Public Tasks (Dz.U. [the Journal of Laws] No. 64, item 565, as amended);

27) Act dated 5 August 2010 on the Protection of Confidential Information (Dz.U. [the Journal of Laws] No. 182, item 1228);

28) Act dated 22 August 1997 on the Protection of Persons and Property (Dz.U. [the Journal of Laws] for year 2005, No. 145, item 1221, as amended);

29) Act dated 6 June 1997, – the Criminal Code (Dz.U. [the Journal of Laws] No. 88, item 553, as amended);

30) Act dated 6 June 1997, – the Code of Criminal Procedure (Dz.U. [the Journal of Laws] No. 89, item 555, as amended);

31) Act dated 6 June 1997, – the Criminal Enforcement Code (Dz.U. [the Journal of Laws] No. 90, item 557, as amended);

32) Act dated 24 May 2000 on the National Criminal Register (Dz.U. [the Journal of Laws] for year 2012, item 654, as amended);

33) Act dated 6 July 2001 on the Collection, Processing and Transfer of Information Related to Criminal Offences (Dz.U. [the Journal of Laws] for year 2010, No. 29, item 153, as amended);

34) Act dated 23 November 2002 on the Supreme Court (Dz.U. [the Journal of Laws] No. 240, item 2052, as amended);

35) Act dated 20 June 1985 on the Prosecution Service (Dz.U. [the Journal of Laws] for year 2011, No. 270, item 1599, as amended);

36) Act dated 20 June 1997, – the Road Traffic Act (Dz.U. [the Journal of Laws] for year 2012, item 1137, as amended);

37) Act dated 6 September 2001 on Road Transportation (Dz.U. [the Journal of Laws] for year 2012, item 1265, as amended);

38) Act dated 27 October 1994 on Toll Highways and the National Road Fund (Dz.U. [the Journal of Laws] for year 2012, item 931, as amended);

39) Act dated 28 March 2003 on Railway Transportation (Dz.U. [the Journal of Laws] for year 2007, No. 16, item 94, as amended);

40) Act dated 19 August 2011 on the Transportation of Dangerous Goods (Dz.U. [the Journal of Laws] No. 227, item 1367, as amended);

41) Act dated 18 August 2011 on Maritime Safety (Dz.U. [the Journal of Laws] No. 228, item 1368);

42) Act dated 1 December 1961 on Maritime Chambers (Dz.U. [the Journal of Laws] for year 2009, No. 69, item 599, as amended);

43) Act dated 31 August 2012 on the State Commission for the Investigation of Maritime Accidents (Dz.U. [the Journal of Laws] item 1068);

44) Act dated 4 September 2008 on the Protection of Navigation and Sea Ports (Dz.U. [the Journal of Laws] No. 171, item 1055);

45) Act dated 21 March 1991 on the Maritime Areas of the Republic of Poland and Maritime Administration (Dz.U. [the Journal of Laws] for year 2003, No. 153, item 1502, as amended);

46) Act dated 3 July 2002, – the Aviation Act (Dz.U. [the Journal of Laws] for year 2012, item 933, as amended);

47) Act dated 18 July 2001, – the Water Management act (Dz.U. [the Journal of Laws] for year 2012, item 145, as amended);

48) Act dated 8 September 2006 on the State Medical Rescue Service (Dz.U. [the Journal of Laws] No. 191, item 1410);

49) Act dated 14 March 1985 on the State Sanitary Inspectorate (Dz.U. [the Journal of Laws] for year 2011, No. 212, item 1263, as amended);

50) Act dated 29 January 2004 on the Veterinary Inspectorate (Dz.U. [the Journal of Laws] for year 2010, No. 112, item 744, as amended);

51) Act dated 13 June 2003 on the Granting of Protection to Foreigners Within the Territory of the Republic of Poland (Dz.U. [the Journal of Laws] for year 2012, item 680);

52) Act dated 16 November 2000 on the Prevention of Money Laundering and the Financing of Terrorism (Dz.U. [the Journal of Laws] for year 2010, No. 46, item 276);

53) Act dated 7 September 2007 on Serving Custodial Sentences Outside Correctional Facilities Using the Electronic Monitoring System (Dz.U. [the Journal of Laws] for year 2010, No. 142, item 960).

Societal and economic national security support subsystems:

1) Act dated 13 June 2003 on Foreigners (Dz.U. [the Journal of Laws] for year 2011, No. 264, item 1573, as amended);

2) Act dated 24 March 1920 on the Acquisition of Real Property by Foreigners (Dz.U. [the Journal of Laws] for year 2004, No. 167, item 1758, as amended);

3) Act dated 16 April 2004 on the Protection of Nature (Dz.U. [the Journal of Laws] for year 2009, No. 151, item 1220, as amended);

4) Act dated 27 April 2001, – the Environmental Protection Act (Dz.U. [the Journal of Laws] for year 2008, No. 25, item 150, as amended);

5) Act dated 20 July 1991 on the Inspectorate of Environmental Protection (Dz.U. [the Journal of Laws] for year 2007, No. 44, item 287, as amended);

6) Act dated 22 June 2001 on the Implementation of the Convention on the Prohibition of the Development, Production, Stockpiling and Use of Chemical Weapons and on their Destruction (Dz.U. [the Journal of Laws] No. 76, item 812, as amended);

7) Act dated 10 April 1997, – The Energy Act (Dz.U. [the Journal of Laws] for year 2012, item 1059, as amended);

8) Act dated 29 November 2000, – The Nuclear Energy Act (Dz.U. [the Journal of Laws] for year 2012, item 264, as amended);

9) Act dated 27 August 2004 on Publicly Funded Healthcare Benefits (Dz.U. [the Journal of Laws] for year 2008, No. 164, item 1027, as amended);

10) Act dated 30 June 2000, – the Industrial Property Act (Dz.U. [the Journal of Laws] for year 2003, No. 119, item 1117, as amended);

11) Act dated 29 October 2010 on Strategic Reserves (Dz.U. [the Journal of Laws] No. 229, item 1496, as amended);

12) Act dated 30 April 2010 on the National Centre for Research and Development (Dz.U. [the Journal of Laws] No. 96, item 616, as amended);

13) Act dated 30 April 2010 on the Polish Academy of Sciences (Dz.U. [the Journal of Laws] No. 96, item 619, as amended);

14) Act dated 27 August 2009 on Public Finance (Dz.U. [the Journal of Laws] No. 157, item 1240, as amended);

15) Act dated 17 December 2004 on the Liability for Violations of the Public Finance Discipline (Dz.U. [the Journal of Laws] for year 2005, No. 14, item 114, as amended);

16) Act dated 29 August 1997 on the National Bank of Poland (Dz.U. [the Journal of Laws] for year 2005, No. 1, item 2, as amended);

17) Act dated 29 August 1997, – the Banking Act (Dz.U. [the Journal of Laws] for year 2012, item 1376, as amended);

18) Act dated 21 July 2006 on Financial Market Supervision (Dz.U. [the Journal of Laws] for year 2012, item 1149, as amended);

19) Act dated 14 December 1994 on the Bank Guarantee Fund (Dz.U. [the Journal of Laws] for year 2009, No. 84, item 711, as amended);

20) Act dated 28 September 1991 – the Fiscal Control Act (Dz.U. [the Journal of Laws] for year 2011, No. 41, item 214, as amended);

21) Act dated 12 February 2010 on the Recapitalization of Certain Financial Institutions (Dz.U. [the Journal of Laws] No. 40, item 226, as amended);

22) Act dated 28 August 1997 on the Organization and Functioning of Pension Funds (Dz.U. [the Journal of Laws] for year 2010, No. 34, item 189, as amended);

23) Act dated 12 February 2009 on State Treasury Support for Financial Institutions (Dz.U. [the Journal of Laws] No. 39, item 308, as amended);

24) Act dated 29 January 2004, – the Public Procurement Act (Dz.U. [the Journal of Laws] for year 2010, No. 113, item 759, as amended);

25) Act dated 23 December 1988 on Economic Activity (Dz.U. [the Journal of Laws] No. 41, item 324, as amended);

26) Act dated 21 August 1997 on the Restrictions in the Pursuit of Economic Activities by Persons Performing Public Functions (Dz.U. [the Journal of Laws] for year 2006, No. 216, item 1584, as amended);

27) Act dated 27 March 2003 on Spatial Planning and Land Development (Dz.U. [the Journal of Laws] for year 2012, item 647, as amended);

28) Act dated 21 August 1997 on Real Property Management (Dz.U. [the Journal of Laws] for year 2010, No. 102, item 651, as amended);

29) Act dated 17 May 1989, – on Geodesy and Cartography (Dz.U. [the Journal of Laws] for year 2010, No. 193, item 1287, as amended);

30) Act dated 7 July 1994, – the Construction Act (Dz.U. [the Journal of Laws] for year 2010, No. 243, item 1623, as amended);

31) Act dated 23 July 2003 on the Protection and Maintenance of Historic Monuments (Dz.U. [the Journal of Laws] No. 162, item 1568, as amended);

32) Act dated 21 December 2000 on Technical Supervision (Dz.U. [the Journal of Laws] No. 122, item 1321, as amended);

33) Act dated 15 April 2011 on Medical Activities (Dz.U. [the Journal of Laws] No. 112, item 654, as amended);

34) Act dated 20 August 1997 on the National Court Register (Dz.U. [the Journal of Laws] for year 2007, No. 168, item 1186, as amended);

35) Act dated 15 December 2000 on Trade Inspection (Dz.U. [the Journal of Laws] for year 2009, No. 151, item 1219, as amended);

36) Act dated 21 December 2000 on the Trade Quality of Agricultural and Food Products (Dz.U. [the Journal of Laws] for year 2005, No. 187, item 1577, as amended);

37) Act dated 29 August 1997 on the Protection of Personal Data (Dz.U. [the Journal of Laws] for year 2002, No. 101, item 926, as amended);

38) Act dated 20 April 2004 on the Promotion of Employment and Labour Market Institutions (Dz.U. [the Journal of Laws] for year 2008, No. 69, item 415, as amended);

39) Act dated 19 December 1998 on the Institute of National Remembrance – Commission for the Prosecution of Crimes Against the Polish Nation (Dz.U. [the Journal of Laws] for year 2007, No. 63, item 424, as amended);

40) Act dated 12 March 2004 on Social Welfare (Dz.U. [the Journal of Laws] for year 2009, No. 175, item 1362, as amended);

41) Act dated 6 January 2005 on National and Ethnic Minorities and on Regional Language (Dz.U. [the Journal of Laws] No. 17, item 141, as amended);

42) Act dated 2 July 2004 on the Freedom of Economic Activity (Dz.U. [the Journal of Laws] for year 2010, No. 220, item 1447, as amended);

43) Act dated 9 June 2011, – The Mining and Geological Law (Dz.U. [the Journal of Laws] No. 163, item 981, as amended);

44) Act dated 6 July 2001 on the Tripartite Commission for Social and Economic Affairs and the Province Commissions of Social Dialogue (Dz.U. [the Journal of Laws] No. 100, item 1080, as amended);

45) Act dated 26 October 1982 on Upbringing in Sobriety and the Prevention of Alcoholism (Dz.U. [the Journal of Laws] for year 2012, item 1356, as amended);

46) Act dated 30 April 2010 on Research Institutions (Dz.U. [the Journal of Laws] No. 96, item 618, as amended);

47) Act dated 7 September 2007 on the Polish Charter (Dz.U. [the Journal of Laws] No. 180, item 1280, as amended);

48) Act dated 7 September 1991 on the Educational System (Dz.U. [the Journal of Laws] for year 2004, No. 256, item 2572, as amended).

Appendix 4

List of persons involved in the National Security Strategic Review (NSSR)

I. THE NSSR COMMISSION:

Commission Chairman of the NSSR

Prof. Stanisław KOZIEJ — PhD, brig. gen. (ret.), head of the National Security Bureau

Deputy Commission Chairman – Chief of Staff

Zdzisław LACHOWSKI — PhD, deputy head of the National Security Bureau

Deputy Chief of Staff

Kazimierz SIKORSKI — PhD, gen. brig. (ret.), director of the Department of Strategic Analyses of the National Security Bureau

The National Interests and Strategic Objectives Team (T1)

Chairman

Janusz ONYSZKIEWICZ — former minister of national defence, Euro-Atlantic Association

Deputy Chairman

Prof. Stanisław ZAJAS — PhD, National Defence Academy of Warsaw

Members

Prof. Andrzej AJNENKIEL — PhD, Łazarski University in Warsaw

Agnieszka BÓGDAŁ-BRZEZIŃSKA — PhD, Warsaw University

Tadeusz CHABIERA — PhD, Cardinal Stefan Wyszyński University in Warsaw; Euro-Atlantic Association

Robert KŁOSOWICZ — PhD (Doctor Habilitatus), Jagiellonian University in Cracow

Dariusz KOZERAWSKI — Associate Professor, PhD (Doctor Habilitatus), Col., National Defence Academy of Warsaw

Krzysztof KOZŁOWSKI — former minister of internal affairs

Prof. Julian SKRZYP — PhD (Doctor Habilitatus), National Defence Academy of Warsaw; Environment and Humanities University in Siedlce

Mirosław SUŁEK — Associate Professor, PhD, col. (ret.), Warsaw University

Maria WĄGROWSKA — Government Centre for Security (advisor), Euro-Atlantic Association (vice-chairman of the board)

Justyna ZAJĄC — PhD (Doctor Habilitatus), Warsaw University

Prof. Ryszard ZIĘBA — PhD (Doctor Habilitatus), Warsaw University

The Security Environment Evaluation Team (T2)

Chairman

Jerzy M. NOWAK — titular ambassador, PhD (Doctor Habilitatus), Euro-Atlantic Association

Deputy Chairman

Prof. Edward HALIŻAK — PhD (Doctor Habilitatus), Warsaw University

Members

Adam BALCER — MSc, The demosEUROPA Foundation – Centre for European Strategy (director of the programme)

Edward KIREJCZYK — PhD, College of Tourism and Language Studies in Warsaw

Prof. Stanisław PARZYMIES — PhD (Doctor Habilitatus), Warsaw University

Prof. Marek PIETRAŚ — PhD (Doctor Habilitatus), Maria Curie-Skłodowska University in Lublin

Witold SKOMRA — PhD, Government Centre for Security

Andrzej TOWPIK — titular ambassador, PhD

The Strategic Action Concept Team (T3)

Chairman

Paweł ŚWIEBODA — MSc, The demosEUROPA Foundation – Centre for European Strategy (chairman of the board)

Deputy Chairman

Tomasz ALEKSANDROWICZ — PhD, Pultusk Academy of the Humanities; Collegium Civitas in Warsaw

Members

Prof. Bolesław BALCEROWICZ — PhD (Doctor Habilitatus), Warsaw University

Bartosz BOLECHÓW — PhD, University of Wrocław

Jarosław GRYZ — Associate Professor PhD (Doctor Habilitatus), National Defence Academy of Warsaw

Janusz URBANIAK — Col. (ret.), PhD

Prof. Katarzyna ŻUKROWSKA — PhD (Doctor Habilitatus), Warsaw School of Economics

The National Security System Team (T4)

Chairman

Andrzej KARKOSZKA — PhD

Deputy Chairman

Maciej MARSZAŁEK — Associate Professor, PhD Eng. (Doctor Habilitatus), Col., National Defence Academy of Warsaw

Members

Franciszek ADAMCZYK — MSc Eng.

Ryszard DĄBROWA	brig. gen., Main School of Fire Service in Warsaw (rector)
Krzysztof JANIK	PhD, Andrzej Frycz Modrzewski University in Cracow
Mariusz KAŹMIERCZAK	col. (Border Guard), General Headquarters of the Border Guard
Prof. Waldemar KITLER	PhD (Doctor Habilitatus), National Defence Academy of Warsaw
Arkadiusz LETKIEWICZ	inspector, PhD (Doctor Habilitatus), General Police Headquarters
Prof. Jerzy S. OLĘDZKI	PhD (Doctor Habilitatus), Warsaw University
Prof. Jacek PAWŁOWSKI	PhD (Doctor Habilitatus), National Defence Academy of Warsaw
Prof. Andrzej K. RYCHARD	PhD (Doctor Habilitatus), Polish Academy of Sciences
Grzegorz SOBOLEWSKI	Associate Professor, PhD Eng. (Doctor Habilitatus), Col., National Defence Academy of Warsaw

The Advisory Team

Jerzy BAHR	former head of the National Security Bureau
Tadeusz BAŁACHOWICZ	division general (ret.)
Ireneusz BIL	PhD, Aleksander Kwaśniewski's „Amicus Europae" Foundation
Włodzimierz CIMOSZEWICZ	Senator of the Republic of Poland (8th term), the foreign affairs commission of the Senate of the Republic of Poland (commission chairman)
Olgierd DZIEKOŃSKI	secretary of state at the Chancellery of the President of the Republic of Poland
Marek GOLISZEWSKI	Euro-Atlantic Association (chairman of the board); Business Centre Club (chairman of the board)
Henryk GORYSZEWSKI	former head of the National Security Bureau
Piotr GULCZYŃSKI	„Lech Wałęsa Institute" Foundation (chairman of the board)
Andrzej HALICKI	deputy to the Sejm of the Republic of Poland (7th term), commission for constitutional responsibility of the Sejm of the Republic of Poland (chairman)
Grzegorz KOSTRZEWA-ZORBAS	PhD, Vistula University in Warsaw
Prof. Roman KUŹNIAR	PhD (Doctor Habilitatus), Warsaw University
Ryszard ŁUKASIK	fleet admiral (rtd.)
Prof. Wojciech MATERSKI	PhD, second lt. (res.), (Doctor Habilitatus), Polish Academy of Sciences
Tadeusz MAZOWIECKI	former Prime Minister; advisor to the President of the Republic of Poland
Stefan NIESIOŁOWSKI	deputy to the Sejm of the Republic of Poland (7th term), the commission of national defence of the Sejm of the Republic of Poland (commission chairman)
Władysław ORTYL	Senator of the Republic of Poland (8th term), the commission of national defence of the Senate of the Republic of Poland (chairman)
Zbigniew PISARSKI	K. Pułaski Foundation (chairman of the board)
Antoni PODOLSKI	strategic advisor, former director of the Government Centre for Security
Roman POLKO	division general (rtd.), PhD
Jerzy PRUSKI	PhD, advisor to the President of the Republic of Poland, Bank Guarantee Fund (chairman of the board)
Janusz REITER	titular ambassador, „Centre for International Relations" Foundation (chairman of the board)
Prof. Adam Daniel ROTFELD	PhD (Doctor Habilitatus), Warsaw University
Janusz SEPIOŁ	Senator of the Republic of Poland (8th term), the commission for local government and state administration of the Senate of the Republic of Poland (chairman)

Bartłomiej SIENKIEWICZ	Polish Institute of International Affairs
Marek SIWIEC	MSc Eng., European Parliament
Aleksander SMOLAR	Stefan Batory Foundation (chairman of the board)
Anna SZYMAŃSKA-KLICH	MSc, Institute for Strategic Studies Foundation (chairman of the board)
Stanisław WZIĄTEK	deputy to the Sejm of the Republic of Poland (7th term), commission for secret services of the Sejm of the Republic of Poland (chairman)
Marcin ZABOROWSKI	PhD, Polish Institute of International Relations

II. OTHER EXPERTS:

Andrzej BARCIKOWSKI	PhD, National Bank of Poland
Prof. Michał BARTOSZCZE	PhD (Doctor Habilitatus), col. (ret.), Military Institute for Epidemiology and Hygiene in Warsaw
Małgorzata J. CZURYK	PhD, National Defence Academy of Warsaw
Jarosław ĆWIEK-KARPOWICZ	PhD, Polish Institute for International Affairs; the Warsaw University
Andrzej DAWIDCZYK	PhD (Doctor Habilitatus)
Janusz DAWIDZIUK	PhD Eng., Bureau for Forest Management and Geodesy
Mariusz DĄBEK	inspector, Province Police Headquarters in Cracow
Prof. Henryk DOMAŃSKI	PhD (Doctor Habilitatus), Polish Academy of Sciences
Lech DRAB	col., Polish Permanent Representation to the EU in Brussels
Robert GAŁĄZKOWSKI	MD, PhD, Independent Public Healthcare Centre – Medical Air Rescue Service in Warsaw
Prof. Tomasz GOBAN-KLAS	PhD (Doctor Habilitatus), Jagiellonian University in Cracow
Ryszard GROSSET	chief brigadier (ret.), PhD, Helena Chodkowska Management and Law University in Warsaw
Przemysław GUŁA	MD, PhD, Medical Rescue Institute in Cracow
Tomasz HYPKI	MSc Eng., National Aviation Council
Prof. Krystyna IGLICKA	PhD (Doctor Habilitatus), Centre for International Relations Foundation
Alicja JASKIERNIA	PhD (Doctor Habilitatus), Warsaw University
Paweł KĘPKA	junior brygadier, PhD Eng., Main School of Fire Service in Warsaw
Leon KIERES	Senator of the Republic of Poland (7th term), the foreign affairs commission of the Senate of the Republic of Poland (chairman)
Maciej KLIMA	Senator of the Republic of Poland (7th term), commission of national defence of the Senate of the Republic of Poland (chairman)
Tadeusz KOCZKOWSKI	col. (res.), National Association for the Protection of Confidential Information (chairman of the board)
Jerzy KONIECZNY	col. (res.) Associate Professor, PhD (Doctor Habilitatus), Andrzej Frycz Modrzewski University in Cracow
Mariusz KOSIERADZKI	PhD, Warsaw University of Life Sciences
Cezary KOŚCIELNIAK	PhD, Adam Mickiewicz University in Poznań
Ligia KRAJEWSKA	deputy to the Sejm of the Republic of Poland (7th term)
Stanisław LIPIŃSKI	PhD Eng., brigadier (ret.), Main School of Fire Service in Warsaw
Wojciech ŁUCZAK	ALTAIR Sp. z o.o. Aviation Agency (vice-chairman of the board)
Stanisław MAJCHERCZYK	Associate Professor, MD, PhD (Doctor Habilitatus), Academy of Hotel Management and Catering Industry

Grzegorz MAKOWSKI	PhD, Institute of Public Affairs Foundation
Ewa MAŃKIEWICZ-CUDNY	Federation of Scientific and Technical Associations – Main Technical Organization (chairman of the board)
Tomasz MICHALAK	MSc, Department of Customs Policy of the Ministry of Finance (director)
Dariusz MICHALIK	PhD, Ministry of Foreign Affairs
Grzegorz MOZGAWA	division general (res.), Helena Chodkowska Management and Law University in Warsaw
Andrzej MROCZEK	MSc, Centre for Terrorism Studies at the Collegium Civitas in Warsaw
Mariusz NEPELSKI	superintendent, PhD, Police Academy in Szczytno
Andrzej PIECZYWOK	PhD, lt. col., National Defence Academy of Warsaw
Katarzyna PISARSKA	PhD, European Academy of Diplomacy in Warsaw (director); the Warsaw School of Economics
Paweł PONCYLJUSZ	deputy to the Sejm of the Republic of Poland (4th, 5th and 6th term)
Krzysztof PROKOP	PhD, University in Białystok
Jan PYRCAK	gen. (Prision Service, ret.)
Maciej PYZNAR	MSc Eng., Government Centre for Security
Mariusz-Jan RADŁO	PhD, Warsaw School of Economics; SEENDICO Doradcy sp. j. (SEENDICO Advisors)
Mariusz RUSZEL	PhD, Kazimierz Pułaski Foundation
Marcin SAKOWICZ	PhD, Warsaw School of Economics; the National School of Public Administration in Warsaw
Cezary SOCHALA	PhD Eng., lt. col., Ministry of National Defence; the Marshal J. Piłsudski Academy of Protection and Security in Warsaw
Ewa SZAFARCZYK	National Bank of Poland (director of the department)
Joanna SZEWCZYK	senior captain, MSc Eng., Main School of Fire Service in Warsaw
Tomasz SZEWCZYK	MSc, Government Centre for Security
Marek ŚCIĄŻKO	PhD, Coal Chemical Processing Institute in Zabrze (director)
Jacek TOMKIEWICZ	PhD, Kazimierz Pułaski Foundation; Koźmiński University in Warsaw
Agata TYBURSKA	PhD, junior inspector, Police Academy in Szczytno
Prof. Jan WIDACKI	PhD (Doctor Habilitatus), Andrzej Frycz Modrzewski University in Cracow
Andrzej M. WILK	PhD Eng.
Mariusz WITCZAK	Senator of the Republic of Poland (7th term), the commission for local government and state administration of the Senate of the Republic of Poland (chairman)
Przemysław ZALESKI	PhD
Krzysztof ŻMIJEWSKI	Associate Professor, PhD (Doctor Habilitatus), Warsaw University of Technology; Community Council for the National Emissions Reduction Programme

III. COMMISSION STAFF:

Zdzisław LACHOWSKI	PhD, chief of staff
Kazimierz SIKORSKI	PhD, deputy chief of staff

Coordinators:

Andrzej JUSZCZAK	Coordinator, Advisory Team
Łukasz POLINCEUSZ	Team 1
Ewa MAZUR-CIEŚLIK	Team 2
Anita KRZYŻANOWSKA	Team 3
Sławomir KAMIŃSKI	Team 4

Members:

Magdalena ADAMCZUK	Department of Legal and Non-military Affairs
Agnieszka ADAMUSIŃSKA	Armed Forces Supervision Department
Marek AJNENKIEL	Department of Strategic Analyses
Lucjan BEŁZA	Department of Non-Military Security (former director)
Adam BRZOZOWSKI	PhD, col., Department of Strategic Analyses
Paulina CALIŃSKA	Department of Legal and Non-Military Affairs
Marek CIECIERA	Department of Legal and Non-Military Affairs (director)
Maciej CZULICKI	Armed Forces Supervision Department
Michał GRZELAK	Department of Strategic Analyses
Dominik JANKOWSKI	Department of Strategic Analyses
Andrzej JÓŹWIAK	Armed Forces Supervision Department
Czesław JUŹWIK	Armed Forces Supervision Department (deputy director)
Lech KONOPKA	PhD, Armed Forces Supervision Department (director)
Mariusz KOWALSKI	Office of the Chief of the Bureau
Waldemar KOZICKI	col., Armed Forces Supervision Department
Łukasz KULESA	Department of Strategic Analyses (former deputy director)
Witold LEWANDOWSKI	col., Armed Forces Supervision Department
Krzysztof LIEDEL	PhD, Department of Legal and Non-Military Affairs (deputy director)
Joanna MAJ-MARJAŃSKA	Department of Legal and Non-Military Affairs
Mieczysław MALEC	col., Department of Strategic Analyses
Radosław MARCINIAK	Armed Forces Supervision Department
Wiesław MOLEK	Armed Forces Supervision Department
Jarosław PADZIK	Department of Legal and Non-Military Affairs (deputy director)
Paulina PIASECKA	Department of Legal and Non-Military Affairs
Paweł PIETRZAK	Department of Strategic Analyses (deputy director)
Katarzyna PRZYBYŁA	Department of Strategic Analyses
Przemysław SIEJCZUK	Department of Legal and Non-Military Affairs
Karol STEC	Armed Forces Supervision Department
Marek SURMAŃSKI	Department of Legal and Non-Military Affairs
Albert TARAS	Department of Legal and Non-Military Affairs
Janusz TOMASZEWSKI	Department of Strategic Analyses
Paweł TUROWSKI	Department of Legal and Non-Military Affairs
Ryszard ZAKRZEWSKI	Armed Forces Supervision Department

Appendix 5

List of abbreviations

ABW   – Internal Security Agency (*Agencja Bezpieczeństwa Wewnętrznego*)
AME   – armaments and military equipment (*uzbrojenie i sprzęt wojskowy*)
ARM   – Material Reserves Agency (*Agencja Rezerw Materiałowych*)
AW   – Foreign Intelligence Agency (*Agencja Wywiadu*)
BBN   – National Security Bureau (*Biuro Bezpieczeństwa Narodowego*)
BOR   – Government Protection Bureau (*Biuro Ochrony Rządu*)
CAT   – Anti-Terrorist Centre (*Centrum Antyterrorystyczne*)
CBA   – Central Anti-Corruption Bureau (*Centralne Biuro Antykorupcyjne*)
CCS   – carbon capture and storage (*wychwytywanie i składowanie dwutlenku węgla*)
CFE   – Treaty on Conventional Armed Forces in Europe (*Traktat o konwencjonalnych siłach zbrojnych w Europie*)
CI   – critical infrastructure (*infrastruktura krytyczna*)
CSCE   – Conference of Security and Cooperation in Europe (*Konferencja Bezpieczeństwa i Współpracy w Europie*)
CSDP   – Common Security and Defence Policy (*Wspólna Polityka Bezpieczeństwa i Obrony*)
CTBT   – Comprehensive Nuclear-Test-Ban Treaty (*Traktat w sprawie całkowitego zakazu prób jądrowych*)
EEAS   – European External Action Service (*Europejska Służba Działań Zewnętrznych*)
EMP   – Economy Mobilization Plan (*plan mobilizacji gospodarki*)
EPAA   – European Phased Adaptive Approach (*Amerykański system obrony przeciwrakietowej w Europie*)
EU   – European Union (*Unia Europejska*)
FMCT   – Fissile Material Cutoff Treaty (*Traktat o zakazie produkcji materiałów rozszczepialnych*)
GDP   – gross domestic product (*produkt krajowy brutto*)
GOPR   – Mountain Volunteer Search and Rescue (*Górskie Ochotnicze Pogotowie Ratunkowe*)
GSBT   – Commune Teritorial Security Board (*Gminny Sztab Bezpieczeństwa Terytorialnego*)
GZBT   – Commune Teritorial Security Team (*Gminny Zespół Bezpieczeństwa Terytorialnego*)
HNS   – Host Nation Support (*Program wsparcia państwa–gospodarza*)
IKE   – Individual Pension Accounts (*Indywidualne Konta Emerytalne*)
IKZE   – Individual Pension Security Accounts (*Indywidualne Konta Zabezpieczenia Emerytalnego*)
IMINT   – Imagery Intelligence (*źródła obrazowe*)
INF   – Treaty on the Elimination of Intermediate-Range and Shorter-Range Missiles (*Traktat o ograniczeniu systemów rakietowych średniego i krótszego zasięgu*)
ISAF   – International Security Assistance Force (*Międzynarodowe Siły Wsparcia Bezpieczeństwa*)
KGP   – General Police Headquarters (*Komenda Główna Policji*)
KNF   – Financial Supervision Authority (*Komisja Nadzoru Finansowego*)
KOK   – State Defence Committee (*Komitet Obrony Kraju*)
KRMds.BN   – Council of Ministers Committee for National Security (Komitet Rady Ministrów ds. Bezpieczeństwa Narodowego)
KRUS   – Agricultural Social Insurance Fund (*Kasa Rolniczego Ubezpieczenia Społecznego*)
KSR   – National Rescue System (*Krajowy System Ratowniczy*)
KSRG   – National Fire Fighting and Rescue System (*Krajowy System Ratowniczo-Gaśniczy*)
KTO   – wheeled armoured vehicle (*Kołowy Transporter Opancerzony*)
LNG   – liquefaction of natural gas (*technologia skraplania gazu*)
MAC   – Ministry of Administration and Digitization (*Ministerstwo Administracji i Cyfryzacji*)
MASINT   – Measurements and Signatures Intelligence (*źródła pomiarowo-badawcze*)
MEN   – Ministry of National Education (*Ministerstwo Edukacji Narodowej*)
MF   – Ministry of Finance (*Ministerstwo Finansów*)
MG   – Ministry of Economy (*Ministerstwo Gospodarki*)
MKiDN   – Ministry of Culture and National Heritage (*Ministerstwo Kultury i Dziedzictwa Narodowego*)
MNiSW   – Ministry of Science and Higher Education (*Ministerstwo Nauki i Szkolnictwa Wyższego*)
MON   – Ministry of National Defence (*Ministerstwo Obrony Narodowej*)
MPiPS   – Ministry of Labour and Social Policy (*Ministerstwo Pracy i Polityki Społecznej*)

MRiRW	–	Ministry of Agriculture and Rural Development (*Ministerstwo Rolnictwa i Rozwoju Wsi*)
MRR	–	Ministry of Regional Development (*Ministerstwo Rozwoju Regionalnego*)
MS	–	Ministry of Justice (*Ministerstwo Sprawiedliwości*)
MSP	–	Ministry of Treasury (*Ministerstwo Skarbu Państwa*)
MSW	–	Ministry of the Interior (*Ministerstwo Spraw Wewnętrznych*)
MSZ	–	Ministry of Foreign Affairs (*Ministerstwo Spraw Zagranicznych*)
MŚ	–	Ministry of the Environment (*Ministerstwo Środowiska*)
MTBiGM	–	Ministry of Transport, Construction and Maritime Economy (*Ministerstwo Transportu, Budownictwa i Gospodarki Morskiej*)
MZ	–	Ministry of Health (*Ministerstwo Zdrowia*)
NATO	–	North Atlantic Treaty Organization (Organizacja Traktatu Północnoatlantyckiego)
NBP	–	National Bank of Poland (*Narodowy Bank Polski*)
NGOs	–	non-governmental organizations (*organizacje pozarządowe*)
NPT	–	Treaty on the Non-Proliferation of Nuclear Weapons (*Układ o nierozprzestrzenianiu broni jądrowej*)
NSR	–	National Reserve Forces (*Narodowe Siły Rezerwowe*)
NSSR	–	National Security Strategic Review (*Strategiczny Przegląd Bezpieczeństwa Narodowego*)
OCK	–	Civil Defence, National Civil Defence (*Obrona Cywilna Kraju*)
OECD	–	Organisation for Economic Co-operation and Development (*Organizacja Współpracy Gospodarczej i Rozwoju*)
OFE	–	Open Pension Funds (*Otwarte Fundusze Emerytalne*)
OSCE	–	Organization for Security and Co-operation in Europe (*Organizacja Bezpieczeństwa i Współpracy w Europie*)
OSP	–	Voluntary Fire Service (*Ochotnicza Staż Pożarna*)
PAN	–	Polish Academy of Sciences (*Polska Akademia Nauk*)
PCK	–	Polish Red Cross (*Polski Czerwony Krzyż*)
PGI	–	Polish Geological Institute (*Państwowy Instytut Geologiczny*)
PKP	–	Polish State Railways (*Polskie Koleje Państwowe*)
PMCs	–	Polish Military Contingents (*Polskie Kontyngenty Wojskowe*)
PPE	–	Employee Pension Accounts (*Pracownicze Programy Emerytalne*)
PPP	–	Purchasing Power Parity (*parytet siły nabywczej*)
PSBT	–	District Territorial Security Board (Powiatowy Sztab Bezpieczeństwa Terytorialnego)
PSP	–	State Fire Service (*Państwowa Straż Pożarna*)
PZBT	–	Disctrict Territorial Security Team (*Powiatowy Zespół Bezpieczeństwa Terytorialnego*)
R&D	–	research and development (*badania i rozwój*)
RCBN	–	Government Centre for National Security (Rządowe Centrum Bezpieczeństwa Narodowego)
RBN	–	National Security Council (*Rada Bezpieczeństwa Narodowego*)
SAR	–	Search and Rescue (*system ratownictwa morskiego*)
SG	–	Border Guard (*Straż Graniczna*)
SIGINT	–	Signals Intelligence (*źródła sygnałowe*)
SIO	–	Information Reporting System/Operational Information System (*System Meldunku Informacyjnego/System Informacji Operacyjnych*)
SIS	–	Schengen Information System (*System Informacyjny Schengen*)
SKW	–	Military Counterintelligence Service (*Służba Kontrwywiadu Wojskowego*)
SUFO	–	Specialized Armed Security Formations (*Specjalistyczne Uzbrojone Formacje Ochronne*)
SW	–	Prison Service (*Służba Więzienna*)
SWW	–	Military Intelligence Service (*Służba Wywiadu Wojskowego*)
TNW	–	tactical nuclear weapons (*taktyczna broń jądrowa*)
TOPR	–	Tatra Volunteer Search and Rescue (*Tatrzańskie Ochotnicze Pogotowie Ratunkowe*)
UDSC	–	Office for Foreigners (*Urząd do Spraw Cudzoziemców*)
UN	–	United Nations (*Organizacja Narodów Zjednoczonych*)
UOKiK	–	Office of Competition and Consumer Protection (Urząd Ochrony Konkurencji i Konsumentów)
URE	–	Energy Regulatory Office (*Urząd Regulacji Energetyki*)
WOPR	–	Maritime Volunteer Rescue Service (*Wodne Ochotnicze Pogotowie Ratunkowe*)
WSBT	–	Province Territorial Security Board (*Wojewódzki Sztab Bezpieczeństwa Terytorialnego*)
WSO	–	Internal Security Service (*Wewnętrzna Służba Ochrony*)
WZBT	–	Province Territorial Security Team (*Wojewódzki Zespół Bezpieczeństwa Terytorialnego*)
ZHP	–	Polish Scouting and Guiding Association (*Związek Harcerstwa Polskiego*)
ZHR	–	Scouting Association of the Republic of Poland (*Związek Harcerstwa Rzeczypospolitej*)

EDITORIAL TEAM

Chairman:
Stanisław KOZIEJ

Deputy chairmen:
Zdzisław LACHOWSKI, Kazimierz SIKORSKI

Team members:
Magdalena ADAMCZUK, Agnieszka ADAMUSIŃSKA, Marek AJNENKIEL, Monika BIERNAT,
Adam BRZOZOWSKI, Paulina CALIŃSKA, Marek CIECIERA, Maciej CZULICKI,
Mariusz FRYC, Michał GRZELAK, Dominik JANKOWSKI, Andrzej JUSZCZAK,
Czesław JUŹWIK, Sławomir KAMIŃSKI, Lech KONOPKA, Waldemar KOZICKI,
Izabela KRAWCZYK, Anita KRZYŻANOWSKA, Joanna KWAŚNIEWSKA-WRÓBEL,
Witold LEWANDOWSKI, Krzysztof LIEDEL, Joanna MAJ-MARJAŃSKA, Mieczysław MALEC,
Radosław MARCINIAK, Ewa MAZUR-CIEŚLIK, Wiesław MOLEK, Przemysław PACUŁA,
Jarosław PADZIK, Paulina PIASECKA, Paweł PIETRZAK, Łukasz POLINCEUSZ,
Katarzyna PRZYBYŁA, Przemysław SIEJCZUK, Marcin SKOWRON, Kamil SOBCZYK,
Karol STEC, Marek SURMAŃSKI, Paweł ŚWIEŻAK, Albert TARAS, Janusz TOMASZEWSKI,
Paweł TUROWSKI, Dariusz WIŚNIEWSKI, Ryszard ZAKRZEWSKI

Published by
National Security Bureau
Karowa 10 St.
00-315 Warsaw
Poland
e-mail: whitebook@bbn.gov.pl

ISBN 978-83-60846-20-9

The National Security Bureau would like to thank the following entities and persons for
providing photographs for the present White Book on National Security: the Internal Security
Agency; the Government Protection Bureau; the Epidemiological Response Centre of the Polish
Armed Forces, the Special Forces Command; the General Police Headquarters; the General
Headquarters of the Military Gendarmerie; the Customs Service; the Prison Service;
the Independent Public Healthcare Centre – Medical Air Rescue Service; the Border Guard; the
Combat Camera Reporter Team of the Armed Forces Operational Command,
as well as the National Geological Institute for providing the map.

Graphic project, pre-press preparation, printing and binding:
Agencja Reklamowo-Wydawnicza Arkadiusz Grzegorczyk
www.grzeg.com.pl